To Pam, the greatest organiser & party-giver in all of Brighton —

You Are What You Hear

How Music and Territory

Make Us Who We Are

You are the light of this town & Happy travels !!!!

Harry Witchel

YOU ARE WHAT YOU HEAR

HOW MUSIC AND TERRITORY
MAKE US WHO WE ARE

HARRY WITCHEL

Algora Publishing
New York

Library of Congress Cataloging-in-Publication Data —

Witchel, Harry.
    You are what you hear: How music and territory make us who we are. Includes
bibliographical references and index.
    ISBN 978-0-87586-804-2 (trade paper : alk. paper) — ISBN 978-0-87586-805-9 (hard
cover : alk. paper) — ISBN 978-0-87586-806-6 (ebook) 1. Music—Psychological aspects.
2. Human territoriality. I. Title.
    ML3838.W58 2010
    781'.11--dc22
                                    2010027180

Front cover image: © Michael Kloth/Corbis

Printed in the United States

To my father

ACKNOWLEDGEMENTS

It is not possible to complete a project of this size without a phenomenal amount of help from many different contributors, and I can only hope that my gratitude to all those people is equal in sentiment to their tangible contributions. This research project and the book to accompany it took over five years to write up, and there are still aspects of the program that are ongoing. Originally the project started as a series of third-year physiology projects at the University of Bristol, and I am very lucky to have had several sets of quite talented students, most of whom were medical students intercalating in our Honors Physiology program. They contributed their creativity, enthusiasm, and hard work to the making of the data that framed the thinking in this book. My thanks go out to my students Amy Crees, Tim Knowles, Umar Yousuf, Rachel Jennings, Duncan McLauchlan, Lauren Van Lancker, Alice Sai, and Aisha Egala. Special thanks go to Natalie Davies, who in her role as my assistant psychophysiologist was critical in realizing many of the goals that I conceived.

The project morphed into a more entertaining and popular endeavor when it was put before the public. Although I had given numerous public lectures on other topics pertaining to pleasure, I had never thought to present a lecture on music because I knew a lecture with recorded music would be cheesy. It was Elaine Snell, then working with the Dana Centre for the Brain in London's Science Museum, who had the inspiration to have me put together a music talk for the lay public with live musicians; it went exceedingly well right from the start, and the talks that developed from that event have gone from strength to strength, appearing internationally at science festivals and even in formal academic meetings, so I am grateful to Elaine. As a result of her efforts I met two marvelous musicians: clarinetist extraordinaire Karl Dürr-Sørensen and master French horn player and composer Dominic Nunns. Many thanks to the boys for all the fun and music we have shared on our travels. And on behalf of all three of us, I cannot thank enough all the event managers, festival teams and venue directors for bringing our mixture of science and music to your region (or country) and for making the events go as wonderfully smoothly as they have done.

The process of turning this into a book would have been unthinkable without my book team, whose efforts have been intellectually and creatively gratifying over these past five years. No amount of praise could do justice to what has been contributed by Paul Rauwolf, Clare Richardson, Peter Reid, Felix Marx (who did all the research from German language sources), Dylan Trigg, Sonia Afzal, Elena Gualtieri, Martin Trigg-Knight, Nancy Sai, Bruce Humphrey, Clare Nicholls, and Kate Richardson. It would literally have been impossible but for their help. I also thank Martin DeMers and his excellent editorial team at Algora Publishing for making it all come together in this book.

Most importantly, I have been supported by the people in my life, my profession, and my office, who have bravely tolerated me over these last five years as the project took shape. It could not have happened without Milton, Leigh, Pat, Julia, Sylvia, Fred, Cat, Dafna, Giuli, Cath, Mette, Mal, Anna, Joey, and Lawrence. They have shaped my territory.

My final thanks go out to my audiences, who have stimulated me and made me think in a thousand new ways about the pleasures inherent in music.

TABLE OF CONTENTS

PREFACE AND WARNING

This book is a series of interconnected ideas linking music to social territory.

That's what it is. Here is what it isn't. This book is not a summary of the academic literature. Nor is it a reference manual. It makes no attempt to be comprehensive, nor is it organized in a way that is needed for a researcher. In fact, it does not even stick strictly to experimentally derived facts. This book is not an undeviating march in a worthy campaign; it is more like a safari that circles back to where it started. The plan is for the book to be a romp that you can read straight through without ever checking your map, such that by the end you will have a much deeper understanding about an idea that is so intuitive that you might mistake it for a tautology.

The entire idea is this: humans have music to establish and reinforce social territory. That assertion is what my fellow academics would call speculative. This speculative nature is precisely what makes it interesting. On one level the idea is almost obvious; I have heard it mentioned obliquely in the media many times by non-experts,[1] and when I tell people the idea they immediately "get it" and see the connection, even though they may never have thought about music in that way before. After all, it is a scientific fact that many passerine birds use music to stake out territory.[2] But although it seems obvious, scientific treatments of this idea applied to humans are quite rare and have never been developed to the level you will find here.

That is possibly because there is not as much controlled experimental data as one would want as an academic. This field of inquiry is derived from a wide range of diverse academic disciplines (social psychology, physiology, ethology, cultural studies, musi-

---

1 For an example in an academic journal making many of these arguments connecting music, territory and identity at a personal level (albeit in a stream of consciousness form), see Wise JM (2000). Home: Territory and Identity. *Cultural Studies* 14(2): 295–310.

2 Forstmeier W & Balsby TJS (2002). Why mated dusky warblers sing so much: territory guarding and male quality announcement. *Behaviour* 139, 89–111. Catchpole CK (1983). Variation in the song of the great reed warbler Acrocephalus arudinaceus in relation to mate attraction and territorial defence. *Animal Behavior* 31: 1217-1225.

cology, and neuroscience) which would never be put together inside a single experimental program. But music is a broad church. It is endemic in our civilization, *and* in nature, so it invites an interdisciplinary approach.

The word *interdisciplinary* has a problematic reputation in academia. Unlike *multi*-disciplinary research — where one might mix biochemistry with integrative neuroscience to produce an academic paper with a clear conclusion about how a molecule affects the brain — *inter*-disciplinary research commingles academics from much further apart — for example a scientist, a historian, and an artist — giving it the (sometimes undeserved) reputation of being unfocused in its outcomes, as if the final output of the research would be an interpretive dance of how the researchers feel about the topic.

Well, music and dancing go together, and this book is my little interpretive dance. As my brother, who is currently the ballet critic for the *New York Post* would say (in a comic foreign accent), "Daaancing is rouuuund." This book takes a 360 degree perspective. By looking at music from crisscrossing frames of reference, coincidences start to emerge such that, even though some of the "evidence" is observational rather than based on controlled experiments, a picture takes shape, almost like pointillism, that reveals how music reinforces territory.

Territory has had a bit of a rough deal over the past 40 years, and in this book I have revamped it by transmogrifying the term into *social territory*. Robert Ardrey's *The Territorial Imperative* created quite a buzz when it was published in 1966, proposing a biological explanation for Hitler's motive entering World War II (which was then and still remains the most pointless and the most stupid waste of human life there ever was). However, the definition of territory then prevalent — a defended space — meant that over the next two decades, scientists making telemetric measurements of the precise movements of animals found that very few species actually had territories according to that definition.[1] Most animals have "home ranges," and ironically it is we humans — with our locked homes, picket fences and national borders — who create the most conspicuous examples of defended territories in the animal kingdom.

There are comparatively few examples of music being used by humans to defend a space. By contrast, there seem to be many examples where music is used to *define* a space — to say who should be there, what is going on, and what behaviors you should adopt. In many cases, music plainly does have a territorial function, even if we do not sing at each other aggressively as robins do. For territory purists, this discussion may seem more related to social identity than to territory *per se*, but I am keen to show that in many cases music in humans is obviously related to music in birds, and plainly one cannot do social identity research encompassing descriptive interviews with a sage grouse. I have used the term social territory to indicate that a number of these behaviors are shared in humans and in other species.

---

1 When scientists look just at the area the animal frequents, they call it a "home range"; by contrast, a territory is scientifically estimated by the location of defence events. If an animal tolerates others in its locale, many scientists would refuse to call it a territory. Börger L, Dalziel BD and Fryxell JM (2008). Are there general mechanisms of animal home range behaviour? A review and prospects for future research. *Ecology Letters*, 11: 637–650.

Rather than limiting the discussion of territory to behaviors related to physical defense and its precursors, this book looks more broadly at *territoriality*, a term from the study of human nonverbal communication that refers to behaviors that signify ownership, occupancy and belonging — regarding places, objects and other human beings. These latter three categories would include your home, your possessions, and your loved ones. They may seem a fairly broad and indeterminate set of recipient entities, but if you watch people's body language concerning how they spread out and grab things, you can see fairly similar territorial behaviors directed toward a bedroom, a bag, and a boyfriend. The territorial behaviors that I focus on are displays, marking, and gathering, and music has a clear role in all three.

The fact that territorial behavior can be directed toward a person or group completely frees the territoriality I am talking about from the specific confines of a space. The human race is fairly mobile, and as the Beastie Boys say, "Wherever I hang my hat's my home."[1] One theme repeated in this book is that territory is not a place — it is a state of mind that triggers various behaviors of empowerment.

The science behind behaviors is the other theme in this book. Scientists have "problems," which are their favorite questions, riddles, and paradoxes. Unlike normal people, scientists relish their problems — because they live for the process of finding the solution. How do they do this? Delightfully, there is no such thing as *the* scientific method; every scientist does things in a somewhat different fashion, and this book documents that strange and wonderful diversity. The science behind behavior is itself idiosyncratic. Unlike chemistry, where if you follow the recipe, you get the right products, human beings vary moment to moment and they differ from each other. When considering human psychobiology — the study explaining psychology (emotions and behavior) in terms of biology (brains, hormones and electrical signals) — proving A causes B requires some adjustments in how you think about the world, and this book introduces some handy ideas from science to make sense of it all. My thinking is fairly eclectic, so what you'll get is my own special cocktail for "the problem" of music.

There is something special about music, which manifests itself whenever a two-year-old starts jigging about spontaneously to a tune. Music has a power that makes it manifestly different from talking or noise. This book muses upon music. At one point it even attempts to define music, which I freely admit is impossible. As Lord Byron says,

> There's music in the sighing of a reed;
> There's music in the gushing of a rill;
> There's music in all things, if men had ears [...] [2]

A central tenet of this book is that people tend to formulate which music they respond to based on associative memories. If you listen to a particular kind of music during your childhood, then those sounds are going to have special significance for you; likewise, if you are a composer and spend many hours constructing your own sonic

---

1 From their song "High Plains Drifter" (1989). Similar phrases appear in "Any Place I Lay my Hat" by Harold Arlen and Johnny Mercer, performed by Judy Garland and by Barbra Streisand, and in "Wherever I Lay my Hat" by Paul Young.

2 Byron GG (1857). *Don Juan* (canto XV, st. 5). Edited by Widger D, Project Gutenberg EBook #21700.

landscape, you will accord that special prominence. Ultimately, if you have your own definition of music, who am I to say that it isn't true? If you dance around the room to samples of human screams you have recorded from horror movie soundtracks, then I respectfully acknowledge your definition of music and accept that you and I differ in how we respond to your music.

This book considers how *people in general* respond to music. Which people? Well, whenever possible the book explicitly mentions when a scientific study is looking at four-day-old babies, children under five, university undergraduate students, and clinical cohorts. The book also accepts that ethnomusicology has much to say about music in general, and this book examines at many points how different cultures respond to music. However, I am a psychobiologist, not an ethnomusicologist, and when a specific culture is not mentioned, I am almost invariably referring to Western music. Even worse, where not specifically stated, I may be blindly referring to issues that are only relevant to Anglophone Western cultures — again, not out of insensitive chauvinism, but more out of familiarity and my own associative memories. It is my territory.

CHAPTER 1. WHY DO WE LISTEN TO MUSIC?

BECAUSE IT ESTABLISHES SOCIAL TERRITORY.

> I can't listen to that much Wagner. I start getting the urge to conquer Poland.
> — Woody Allen

Territory in Germany was shifting with seismic force by the end of 1989, and erupting from the cracks in the Berlin Wall there was music. German popsters Milli Vanilli finally topped the international charts with "Girl You Know It's True." Then, on Christmas night in Berlin, Leonard Bernstein conducted Beethoven's *Ode to Joy* (the Ninth Symphony) to officially celebrate Germany's reunification. Bernstein wielded the baton over a specially altered score, with the word *joy* ("freude") symbolically transformed into *freedom* ("freiheit").[1] Broadcast internationally, this concert heralded a new message: the German people had triumphed. The Eastern Bloc was finished.

A few days later, another concert was held to mark the New Year, the new decade, and the new Germany. Another icon of popular culture was chosen to lead the festivities: the American actor, David Hasselhoff. Standing above his adoring German fans in freezing temperatures, Hasselhoff mimed his hit "Looking for Freedom." The crowd sang along with the anthemic chorus, "I've been lookin' for freedom, I've been lookin' for so long." To further bedazzle the spectators, the back of Hasselhoff's leather jacket was covered in a synchronized display of flashing electric lights.

This incongruous encounter between Hasselhoff and the end of the Cold War resurfaced in 2004 during an interview with the German media.[2] Hasselhoff felt that his

---

1 Associated Press (1989). Upheaval in the East: Berlin; Near the Wall, Bernstein Leads an Ode to Freedom. *The New York Times*, December 26.
2 He spoke to *Spielfilm* magazine. See: BBC News (2004). Did David Hasselhoff really help end the Cold War? *BBC News Online*, 6 Feb.

role in reunifying the country had been under-appreciated. In a typically forthright way, the actor remarked:

> I find it a bit sad that there is no photo of me hanging on the walls in the Berlin Museum at Check-Point Charlie. After my appearance I hacked away at pieces of the wall that had the black, red and yellow colors of the German flag on it. I kept the big piece for myself and gave the smaller pieces to colleagues at Baywatch.

That quote is not just about Hasselhoff's vanity. Nor is it just bragging about being in Berlin at the big moment. Rather, he has arrived at an insight about the relationship between himself and the place. The insight is about territory. In animals a territory is "a defended space",[1] guarded by fighting, urinating, or some other "display." The flag marked territory. So did the crowd's unity. Even pocketing the souvenirs was a grab at territory. Everything in this episode, from Hasselhoff's act of singing by the Berlin Wall all the way to his later need to display his photo in the museum, is all about this one human need: territory.

In humans territory is often more social than physical, because it sparks a sense of belonging. Social territory defines who belongs "in" and who should be kept "out." This social territory can be a physical place, but being "in" often manifests itself as displays of social connections: songs, fashion items, beliefs, and even hairstyles. For example, in public spaces such as a library a person may display "territorial" behavior to repel others by spreading possessions around. The territory is more about "display" than about ownership, as usually it is surrendered when the person leaves — except for very territorial people who insist on having the same chair in the library week after week.

Being inside one's own territory has many emotional advantages distinct from providing resources. Consider how territory can make car drivers bold and rude, give a winning edge to a sports team, and turn bedrooms into the safest place for sex; in each of these cases, the advantage provided by territory is an empowering mental state rather than a physical resource. Within these examples territory shapes our decisions and changes the meaning of our moment-to-moment existence.

Music contributes to territory so often that we fail to notice the ubiquity of the link: music can soothe babies, pace athletes during exercise and invigorate an army before fighting. Might territory be the reason we have music? Certainly music was one way Hasselhoff marked his territory to arouse emotions that empower — not just in himself, but in everyone watching him. Each facet of his story is territorial, whether he was above the crowd singing or in the corner of the museum symbolically peeing.

***

In 1928, pioneering ornithologist and stay-at-home mother of five, Margaret Morse Nice (1883–1974), became the first ornithologist to accurately survey the territory of wild birds. Nice achieved this by tying bands of colored plastic — taken from celluloid dolls and old baby rattles — to the legs of the song sparrows living within the forty-acre

---

1 This is the 1939 definition of evolutionary biologist and debunker Gladwyn Kingsley Noble; see Noble GK (1939). The role of dominance in the life of birds. *Auk*, 56: 263-273.

floodplain behind her house in Columbus, Ohio.[1] She gave each bird a number-and-letter-code name, and then carefully took notes on each bird's arrivals and departures. Nice also recorded the bird's mate (or mates), the bird's songs, and the extent of its territory. In this way, Nice happily passed the depression years of the 1930s completely immersed in the battles and infidelities of the song sparrows in her backyard. As one of her colleagues wrote, "Occasionally I was invited to her home for dinner ... I found it difficult to concentrate upon the subject at hand, especially when a Nuthatch alighted on my head or a song sparrow hopped across my dinner plate."[2]

A song sparrow may seem peaceful, but Margaret Morse Nice spotted that each male sang most intensely when he was showing off in a male-male competition and when he defended his territory. By patiently keeping records of the birds' movements, she discovered that each male would defend the same territory year after year, gathering all his resources from within the limits of his own zone. More importantly, Nice showed that a female who did not hold a territory of her own would learn to accept the borders of her mate's territory by listening to his song. Margaret Morse Nice's home-based science led biologists to conclude that the reason birds sing is more linked to establishing territory than to attracting a mate,[3] because there are many advantages to having a territory (food, nesting material, caches, and defensive refuges) other than attracting a mate.

For example, David Lack, a British ornithologist who explained speciation by re-visiting Darwin's Finches in the Galapagos,[4] noted that Britain's most popular bird, the robin, also sings to signal the extent of its territory.[5] Lack found that whenever two male robins are put together in an aviary, they fiercely compete for this new territory by singing against each other until one of them gives up — only the winner continues to display in his new terrain by singing. During the autumn season, both males and females will hold territories and sing. As autumn is not breeding season, territory appears to be the only explanation for their musical behavior.[6]

But gathering territory with music occurs in humans as well. Australian Aborigines use music to explicitly define their territory.[7] They believe that some of their traditional songs were composed in the "Dreaming" — the time when the world was first created and ancestral beings traveled the land, creating and naming the landscape in their song.[8] These songs serve not only as mythology, but they also describe the countryside and

1 Dickinson JL (1998). Birds in the Bushes: A Story about Margaret Morse Nice. *The Condor* 100(3): 583.

2 Trautman MB (1977). In Memoriam: Margaret Morse Nice. *Auk* 94, 430-441.

3 The idea of territory was not Nice's invention. She was swayed by the theory of the famous ethologist Niko Tinbergen. Nice's observations of an entire community of birds "in the wild" provided evidence for the theory.

4 Lack D (1947). *Darwin's Finches.* Cambridge: Cambridge University Press (reissued in 1961 by New York: Harper).

5 Lack D (1971). *The Life of the Robin.* London: Collins, p. 219.

6 Lack D (1971). *The Life of the Robin.* London: Collins, p. 223.

7 Maddern E (1988). 'We have survived': Aboriginal music today. *The Musical Times,* 129, 595-597.

8 Maddern E (1988). 'We have survived': Aboriginal music today. *The Musical Times,* 129, 595-597.

the whereabouts of food and water. Each song is thus a "songmap" of a particular area. During initiation, an individual learns the songs that describe his own area of country. Thereafter the young aboriginal uses these songs as a sign of ownership, a title-deed to territory, just as a bird does.[1] The young Aboriginal understands the magical power of the song to mark his own territory.

However, the analogy between human and bird music breaks down because human territory is most often tribal, ethnic, or national. When you control the music, it establishes territory for yourself *and* your social group. When others control the music, it is they who control the territory, and they can quickly repel intruders.

When loitering youths became problematic in the Warrawong Westfield shopping mall in Wollongong, south of Sydney, they were quickly dispersed by being serenaded over the loud speakers with the 1938 recording of "My Heart is Taking Lessons" by crooner Bing Crosby.[2] This idea has since been adapted with great success in railway stations prone to vandalism by troublesome teenagers. Over a six-week period in early 2000, teen-repellent music by Beethoven, Mozart, and Bach was piped into Sydney metropolitan train stations, resulting in an overall seventy per cent drop in vandalism rates, and completely eliminating it at two stations.[3]

When residents were intimidated by local youths hanging around in Cook Park Reserve revving their engines, the Sydney Council of Rockdale resorted to extreme measures. From July 2006, Barry Manilow's "Copacabana," "I Write the Songs" and "Mandy" were blasted onto the land reserve from 9 pm in the evening till midnight for a period of six months. After four weeks the efforts began to pay off. Rockdale Deputy Mayor Bill Saravinovski said, "Barry's our secret weapon,"[4] although classical music, Doris Day's "Que sera, sera" and generally any "music that doesn't appeal to these people" was also used.[5] Unfortunately, the local residents found this music just as annoying as the revving engines, keeping them up late at night. After receiving complaints, Saravinovski caved in only so far as to reduce the volume and diversify the music. "I'm not disputing what the residents are saying. I can't swallow some of the tracks like 'Mandy'," said Saravinovski. "We have tried to reduce the sound and we are reviewing the songs. I don't mind Barry Manilow, but I'm more of an ABBA and Celine Dion fan." In a conflict between groups, music can be used to control territory, and this feature has been adopted in formalized human conflicts such as war.

***

In 1688, an Anglican alliance of Tories and Whigs conspired against the Catholic King James II, who was trying to re-impose Catholicism to Protestant England by force. Their conspiracy paved the way for the Glorious Revolution and the invasion of Eng-

---

1 Storr A (1992). *Music and the Mind*. London: Harper Collins, p. 212.
2 BBC News (1999). Bing keeps troublemakers at bay. *BBC News Online*, 8 July.
3 Cloonan M, Johnson B (2002). Killing me softly with his song: an initial investigation into the use of popular music as a tool of oppression. *Popular Music* 21(1): 27–39.
4 BBC News (2006). Manilow to drive out "hooligans." *BBC News Online*, 17 July.
5 Tijs A (2006). Manilow To Challenge Rockdale Yobbos, 6th June. Accessed 10 May 2010; http://www.undercover.com.au/news/2006/jun06/20060606_barrymanilow.html

land by Dutch forces under William of Orange — who was then crowned William III of England. All the anti-Catholic sentiments that had led to the forced abdication of James II were humorously summarized by the song "Lilliburlero," which satirized the King's Jacobite supporters in Ireland.[1] The song, which made use of an old Irish tune arranged for polite society by Henry Purcell, became so popular amongst both soldiers and civilians that English armies ended up marching to its catchy rhythm for years.[2] Lord Thomas Wharton, who wrote the song, later boasted to have *"sung a deluded Prince out of three kingdoms."*[3] In humans, like in birds, music reinforces territory, which leads to a sense of belonging to a group, a culture, even to an outlook. Clearly, his song had played its part in unifying the English Protestants.

During World War II, 250 years later, Lilliburlero was played on the BBC Home Service program "Into Battle," and soon after it became the regimental march of the Royal Electrical and Mechanical Engineers. Since 1955 it has been the signature for the news on BBC World Service.[4] Despite its genesis in satirizing the enemy, Purcell's Lilliburlero remains a focal point of allegiance to Great Britain. Thus, when music establishes territory, it is for yourself *and your social group*. By doing this music does two extraordinary things: it fosters our solidarity in groups, which we feel as strength and well-being, and it fortifies our will in a crisis, which we feel as determination.

In the 17th century, Ottoman sultans had the music of their elite corps, the Janissaries, performed to display their power. The music motivated their troops and terrorized their enemies. When the Ottomans beleaguered a city, the bands played day and night, demoralizing the defenders locked behind their city walls. European contemporaries report that their musical efforts never failed — the sound of their band made "Heaven and Earth quake."[5] The power of Janissary music made such an impression on Western composers of the late 17th and 18th centuries that music *alla turca* found its way into the compositions of Haydn, Beethoven, and most memorably Mozart's *Rondo alla Turca*.

The Ottomans were not the only empire to use the dual face of music as a means of psychological warfare. American soldiers listen to heavy metal music to psyche themselves up for battle. Their officers, on the other hand, order it to be played to demolish their enemy's courage during sieges. In 1989, in a memorable combination of violence and pop music, former CIA employee and dictator of Panama, General Manuel Noriega,

1   Storr A (1992). *Music and the Mind*. London: Harper Collins, p. 212.

2   Clark JK (2004). "Wharton, Thomas, first marquess of Wharton, first marquess of Malmesbury, and first marquess of Catherlough (1648–1715)," *Oxford Dictionary of National Biography*, Oxford: Oxford University Press. online edn, May 2006.

3   Speck WA (2006). Book reviews: Harris, T. (2005) *Restoration: Charles II and his Kingdoms, 1660-1885*; Harris, T. (2006) Revolution: The great Crisis of the British Monarchy 1685-1720. *The English Historical Review* 494, 1463-1467. See also: BBC Northern Ireland Learning Online edition (2007). William III: Bigot or Hero? Billy Boy's Smash Hit. *BBC online*. Accessed 31 March 2010; http://www.bbc.co.uk/northernireland/learning/william/ backpage.shtml.

4   BBC World Service (2005). What is the BBC World Service signature tune? *BBC World Service*, 10 August. Accessed 31 March 2010; http://www.bbc.co.uk/worldservice/faq/news/story/2005/08/ 050810_wssigtune.shtml

5   Badisches Landesmuseum (State Museum of Baden) (2003), Online Museum: *Karlsruher Tuerkenbeute*. Die Musik der Osmanen. accessed 31 March 2010; http://www. tuerkenbeute.de/kun/kun_han/ OsmanischeMusik_de.php

was blasted out of his refuge and into the arms of American law enforcement officials after a siege fortified with ten days of pop music, loud hits and message songs such as Martha and the Vandellas' "Nowhere to Run" and Linda Ronstadt's "You're No Good."

During the first Iraq war, American soldiers of the 82nd Airborne pumped out AC/DC's "Hell's Bells" and Metallica's "Enter Sandman" in Fallujah, Iraq, hoping to enervate the city's Sunni Muslim gunmen and "break [the] resistance"[1] of captured Iraqi journalists working for Reuters. Sergeant Mark Hadsell, of the US Psychological Operations Company explained that since the captured Iraqis have never heard heavy metal, "They can't take it. If you play it for 24 hours, your brain and body functions start to slide, your train of thought slows down and your will is broken. That's when we come in and talk to them."[2] In stark contrast, playing the very same music to American soldiers only strengthens their determination to fight. Staff Sergeant Gerald explains, "The other day we sounded up our loud speakers and played some music for the marines to give them a morale boost."[3] And what did they play? "Highway to Hell and Back In Black by AC/DC. We do take requests, though."[4]

***

In war there are two faces to the emotions provoked by music — dominance and submission. While your own music gives an aura of victory, that of your enemy carries the poison of fear and helplessness. How can music have these diametrically opposing effects? Territory contains the answer. One consequence of the control of territory is that it changes your level of arousal.

Arousal is the opposite of sleepiness.[5]

Lullabies can lower it, bugles and drums can raise it. Arousal is not intrinsically a good feeling or a bad one. Arousal makes good feelings better, but bad feelings much worse. If you are happy, then being on a breathtaking mountain top will intensify your happiness to euphoria. But if you are already thinking of suicide, being aroused on that same mountain top will beckon you to leap. The sounds making up the music are not the only thing that determines whether you are lifted or knocked down. Depending on who "owns" the music, the same piece of music can stimulate one tribe and depress another. There may be evolutionary reasons why man developed the use of music to control arousal in this way.

The Mekranoti Indians, a hunter-gatherer society living in the Amazonian rainforest of Brazil, use music specifically to wake up their warriors, like musical coffee. This

---

1 BBC News (2003). Sesame Street breaks resistance of Iraqi POWs. *BBC News online*, 20 May.
2 BBC News (2003). Sesame Street breaks resistance of Iraqi POWs. *BBC News online*, 20 May.
3 North A (2003). US psy-ops play it loud. *BBC News Online* 17 March.
4 North A (2003). US psy-ops play it loud. *BBC News Online* 17 March.
5 Sexual arousal is only one small aspect of the scientific definition of arousal. The dictionary definition of arousal concerns "waking, stimulated and inspired." The formal scientific definition concerns movement, hormones, and brain activity. The "opposite of sleepiness" definition is the layperson's definition, because it covers all aspects of arousal while being intuitive.

is arousal in the sense of physically waking up, not just increasing awareness and energy. The Mekranoti sing what anthropologists describe as a "masculine roar" for several hours a day.[1] The fittest of the bunch begin as early as one in the morning, singing lyrics that are aimed at insulting the men who have not made it out of bed yet, falsely declaring:

> Get out of bed! The Kreen Akrore Indians have already attacked and you're still sleeping!

By altering group members' arousal to fit the circumstances and by communicating feelings, music can influence our hearts and even our decisions. The Mekranoti Indians use music to defend their territory. Their songs serve as a deterrent and warning to potential attackers that the Mekranoti are awake and prepared to defend what is theirs. This is especially important in the early morning, which is the best time to attack an enemy tribe. Music prepares the Mekranoti for battle, while it scares off the Kreen Akrore, their enemies. The music safeguards only one army's territory — your gut reaction to approach or withdraw is determined by whether your tribe *owns* the music. The territorial nature of music is the reason why the same piece of music can arouse our comrades to battle lust and our enemies to surrender.

Your own music enhances territory; if territory allays fear, it would mean your own music should allay fear. As a human, listening to your favorite music will decrease the brain activity usually associated with fear;[2] and your favorite music defines what is your territory. Fear is very responsive to territorial behavior. Most people will act much more self-confident and feel safer when they are inside their home. A study conducted in 1978 to investigate the impact of territoriality on the fear of crime in elderly people scored people on the amount of territorial markers they used — such as "keep out" signs, fences and surveillance cameras.[3] The elderly who were classified as *highly territorial* were much less fearful of both property loss and personal assault than their less territorial peers. Territorial behavior reduced the old people's fear of crime — just as music does. So we have good reason for whistling in a dark and eerie cellar.[4] Music has the ability to eliminate your fears and increase your confidence.

Not only can your own music establish safety and comfort but, more importantly, it can reinforce determination. Every teenager who has ever slammed their bedroom door and turned up the music to full volume unconsciously knows this. This is why music was originally the main thrust of MySpace. Founded in 2003, www.myspace.com helps to promote its users' own music. A relatively unknown band or artist sets up a MySpace page replete with their songs, and fans can then choose to become listed as

---

1 Werner D (1984). *Amazon Journey: An Anthropologist's Year Among Brazil's Mekranoti Indians*. New York: Simon & Schuster.

2 Blood AJ, Zatorre RJ (2001). Intensely pleasurable responses to music correlate with activity in brain regions implicated in reward and emotion. *Proceedings of the National Academy of Sciences, USA* 98, 11818–11823.

3 Patterson AH (1978). Territorial behaviour and fear of crime in the elderly. *Environmental Psychology and Nonverbal Behaviour* 2, 131-144.

4 For an image of a child in the dark "gripped with fear, [who] comforts himself by singing under his breath," see Deleuze G, Guattari F (1987). *A Thousand Plateaus: Capitalism and Schizophrenia*, Minneapolis: University of Minnesota Press, p. 311.

friends. Friends can even leave behind a message with their picture, almost like peeing in the corner of the band's web page. The total number of friends a band has on the site corresponds to popularity. Within the music industry, this means power. MySpace has grown into the third most popular website in the United States – more popular than MSN and EBay — with page views in the US of 40 billion per month.[1] When Rupert Murdoch's News Corporation purchased it in 2005, the estimated worth of MySpace was $327 million.[2] It is no coincidence that the very name of the biggest revolution in the promotion and distribution of music — *my space* — is about territory.

The development and growth of MySpace plots a journey from music to social territory. When MySpace was founded in 2003, the prevailing idea was to create a networking site for musicians, with a subsidiary appeal for the general user. Since then, this emphasis on a network of musicians has extended into the domain of creating your own MySpace page, which allows you to modify, customize, and personalize the page to fit your mood and personality. Alongside these personal touches, MySpace now incorporates such additional features such as instant messaging, MySpaceTV, and even MySpace Karaoke. In all of these cases, the musical aspect has arguably become secondary to the social dimension. Now, it is no longer what music you listen to in your bedroom that matters, but how you express your tastes in a virtual territory. The result of this new way to express your territory is that the popularity of MySpace is staggering, going so far as to even overtake pornography on the internet.[3] But when it first started, MySpace was a revolution because it let bands put whatever they wanted up on the web; other sites had banned that because it was essentially advertising. Which is true, it *was* advertising, but its popularity was immense. Web users seeking out a band's advertising makes no sense unless we know what the fans got out of admiring someone else's music.

***

"The Battle of Britpop" began on 14th August, 1995. The battle commenced when Damon Albarn, the lead-singer of the Britpop band Blur, strategically moved the release date of his band's new single to the very same day that his bitter rivals Oasis were to release theirs. Here was a perfect standoff. Blur hailed from the leafy borough of Colchester and got together at London's Goldsmiths College, being the quintessential middle-class art-popsters. Meanwhile, Oasis were from Burnage in Manchester — they had backgrounds in petty-crime and prided themselves on their gritty northern authenticity. The chart duel sparked national headlines as Britain's two biggest bands were to go head-to-head over record sales. Albarn's provocation was not an isolated incident and merely capped a string of petty public taunts. In a televised interview the year before, Liam Gallagher of Oasis had stated he fancied Albarn's girlfriend, in contrast to his

---

1 This refers to US-only page views for December 2008. McCarthy C (2009). ComScore: In U.S., MySpace-Facebook race goes on. *Cnet news*, 13 January.

2 PR Newswire (2007). Internet Entrepreneur & MySpace Founder Brad Greenspan Leads Investment Group Seeking to Take Non-Controlling Stake in Dow Jones Corp. Accessed 20 May 2010; http://www.examiner.com/p-3057-Internet_Entrepreneur__MySpace_Founder_Brad_Greenspan_Leads_Investment_Group_Seeking_to_Take_Non_Controlling_Stake_in_Dow_Jones_Corp_.html

3 Richert M (2008). The internet grows up. *The Guardian* (London) online, 23 October.

---

brother Noel Gallagher who insulted this woman and later said that he hoped Albarn would "catch AIDS and die."[1] A threat to "twat" Gallagher was reported, but Blur's sales figures provided a better retort — Blur's single "Country House" outsold Oasis's "Roll With It" by nearly 60,000 copies.

Although Blur won the battle, Oasis won the war. Oasis's album *What's the Story Morning Glory* sold millions more than Blur's *The Great Escape* in both Britain and America. Years later, Noel said of the Blur-Oasis feud: "Don't dress it up and make it something it's not . . . I worked on building sites and that fundamentally makes my soul a lot more purer than theirs."[2] For Gallagher and Albarn there had been more at stake than personal grudges: they were competing for the allegiance of hordes of young fans. These social groupings defined themselves according to each band's ethos. Blur and Oasis were trumpeting their opposing territories, so that "The Battle of Britpop" was not just about sales: it was about social affiliations and group identity.

Even British Prime Minister Tony Blair managed to get in on the spoils of Oasis's territorial conquest.[3] And Noel Gallagher still votes for the Labor Party: "Another reason to vote Labor is if you f**king don't, and the Conservatives get in, Phil Collins is threatening to come back and live here. And let's face it, none of us want that."[4] But Britpop was not just about reclaiming social territory from conservative voting yuppies — it was also about preserving British cultural territory from Americanization. As one music journalist described it:

> Britain was fast becoming occupied territory. Only there were no tanks rolling through the streets, just ... the unwashed horde of American grunge acts scaling the fortress of the British pop charts. It was time for a change, and music helped — however briefly — to restore national pride at a time when it sorely needed some.[5]

***

The Nazis understood the value of groupthink. When the Germans lost all their weapons — and their national pride — after World War I, the Nazis gained a vast following by mixing music and military discipline. The use of music was official, as stated in one Nazi handbook:

> There should no longer be any larger meetings without musical accompaniment, at least during the entrance of the flags. Whether or not there is music has an important impact on the mood of the meeting, and therefore of the speaker... Lively march music is recommended for the entrance of the flags. If there is not a band, the formations (HJ, SA, SS, NSFK, NSKK) can sing.[6]

---

1 BBC News (2005). Timeline: Blur v Oasis after Britpop. *BBC News online*, 16 August.
2 Lindblad P (2004). Live Forever: Best of Britpop (Film review). *LAS Magazine*, May 27.
3 Harris J (2004). *The Last Party: Britpop, Blair and the Demise of English Rock*. London: Harper Perennial.
4 Everitt M (2005). Noel Gallagher "I'm Voting Labour." *XFM* (London). 12 April.
5 Lindblad P (2004). Live Forever: Best of Britpop (Film review). *LAS Magazine*, May 27.
6 The following paragraphs are our translations from a 1942 handbook on propaganda by Franz J. Huber FJ (1942). ed., Propagandisten-Fibel. Herausgegeben vom Gaupropagandaamt Oberdonau der NSDAP (Wels: Leitner & Co).

In 1937, the Nazis staged a pseudo-military drill with the Reich's 45,000 Labor Servicemen marching and chanting to music, carrying spades instead of guns (Figure 1.1).[1] Being caught up in the swirl of *group coherence* allowed the thousands of individuals to coordinate their actions without hesitation, like a flock of birds turning toward the sunset.

Figure 1.1 – Nazi Labour Servicemen in the Reichsarbeitsdienst (RAD) in parade at the Nazi rally (Reichsparteitag) of 1937.

Nazi propaganda reached its zenith at night. The candle-lit party rallies held each year in Nuremberg brought mysticism, pageantry, and color into the drab lives of twentieth-century Germans. Hitler's entrance was pure theatre. The music stopped — 30,000 people became silent — then the band struck the Badenweiler March, an arresting melody played only when Hitler entered in grand style.[2] The crowd swayed rhythmi-

---

1 Sinclair T (1938). The Nazi party rally at Nuremberg. *The Public Opinion Quarterly* 2: 570-583. A classic example of this can be seen in Leni Riefenstahl's award-winning propaganda film, *Triumph of the Will* (1935). Interestingly, the music of the RAD (based on shellac 78s) is still collected and traded online. Accessed 21 May 2010; http://beemp3.com/download.php?file=7119742&song=Edeltraut%2C+mein+Edeltraut

2 Shirer WL (1941). Berlin Diary — The Journal of a Foreign Correspondent. The American journalist and historian William L. Shirer (1904–1993) provides the most objective glimpse of what these mass events must have been like. Shirer visited the Nuremberg rally in 1934. Six years later Shirer was one of twelve foreign correspondents allowed to travel with the German army during its 1940 offensive at the western front. He obtained one of his greatest stories by using a German sound truck in order to listen to the official surrender of France and was later able to report on the signing of the armistice between France and Nazi-Germany in Compiègne three hours before even Berlin learned about the French defeat. http://www.traces.org/williamshirer.html and http://www.time.com/time/magazine/article/0,9171,851201-2,00.html

---

cally to the music, giving the ritual the air of a cult. As one journalist who witnessed it concluded, "In such an atmosphere no wonder, then, that every word dropped by Hitler seemed like an inspired Word from on high. Man's — or at least the German's — critical faculty is swept away at such moments, and every lie pronounced is accepted as high truth itself."[1] But this is not only true for Germans.

Organizational psychologists, personnel officers and human resources departments have spent a lot of time and money trying to answer the million dollar question: "What makes a great leader?" Only in the last ten years, some academics have finally concluded that the short answer is "followers."[2] Much more numerous than leaders, followers occur not just in genocidal dictatorships and pre-historic tyrannies, but they materialize spontaneously in groups of strangers. In the "Leaderless Group Discussion," a well-established test of *successful* leadership (used for example to rate candidates for officer training in the armed forces), a group of applicants is asked to solve a problem via discussion, and typically aspects of *successful* leadership (and thus of followership) appear within 25 seconds.

There is a reason people become followers. Admittedly, leaders get more than followers, but if everyone tries to be a leader, the results are the worst possible. It becomes a case of too many cooks spoil the broth. Compared with leaders, followers have sometimes been considered as undifferentiated, like a mass of sheep, but more recently experts have suggested that "exemplary," "courageous," and "star" followers are a precondition for successful organizations.[3] Leadership is not the same as dominance;[4] dominance is based on dominant individuals winning the competition among group members for scarce resources, with low ranking individuals essentially forced to do whatever dominant individuals in the group decide. Psychology experiments show that leadership is not only distinct from outright dominance but also incompatible with it; for example, organizations run by dominant managers are more likely to lose their employees,[5] and there is less cooperation among teams of schoolboys when an authoritarian teacher leads them compared to when a laissez-faire teacher does.[6] Followers are seeking good leadership, not domination.

1 Shirer WL (1941). *Berlin Diary—The Journal of a Foreign Correspondent 1934–1941*. New York: Alfred A. Knopf.
2 Collinson D (2006). Rethinking followership: A post-structuralist analysis of follower identities. *The Leadership Quarterly* 17: 179–189.
3 Chaleff I (2003). The courageous follower. 2nd ed. San Francisco: Berrett-Koehler. Seteroff SS (2003). Beyond leadership to followership. Victoria, B.C.: Trafford. Potter EH, Rosenbach WE, & Pittman, TS (2001). Followers for the times: Engaging employees in a winning partnership. In WE Rosenbach, & RL Taylor (Eds.), *Contemporary Issues in Leadership* 5th ed. Boulder, Colorado: Westview Press.
4 Henrich J & Gil-White F (2001). The evolution of prestige: Freely conferred deference as a mechanism for enhancing the benefits of cultural transmission. *Evolution and Human Behavior*, 22: 165-196.
5 Brockner J, Tyler T, & Cooper-Schneider R (1992). The influence of prior commitment to an institution on reactions to perceived injustice: The higher they are, the harder they fall. *Administrative Science Quarterly*, 37, 241-261. Van Vugt M, Jepson SF, Hart CM & De Cremer D (2004). Autocratic leadership in social dilemmas: A threat to group stability. *Journal of Experimental Social Psychology*, 40, 1-13.
6 Lewin K, Lippitt R & White R (1939). Patterns of aggressive behaviour in experimentally created social climates. *Journal of Social Psychology*, 10: 271-299.

The apotheosis of followership is the catchphrase from the film *Wayne's World* (1992), when the two puerile metal-head protagonists kowtow to their idol, Alice Cooper, while shouting, "We're not worthy!" This statement is not a pained or enforced debasement, but a celebration of being able to join in to something bigger than oneself, something literally *awesome*. Apparently not all people are independently trying to maximize their personal territory; most people are "joiners." They have their own small territory in mind, but concurrently assimilate themselves into the larger territory of bigger leaders and their groups.

To provide a rationale for this, evolutionary psychologists have used computer models to show that individuals in groups with effective leadership and followership fare better than individuals who are in a community without followership.[1] Consider an island community that wants to connect themselves to the mainland with either a boat or a bridge; without agreeing to a single course of action, resources would be split initially, at best resulting in half a boat and half a bridge. In the primitive social groups within which man would have evolved, some activities would clearly benefit from group cohesion, such as hunting big game or finding a waterhole that has not dried up.[2]

In order to model how (or whether) individuals would choose to be a leader or a follower, evolutionary psychologists use a game in which the interests of the players are partly conflicting and partly mutual, such as the Game of Leader. In the simplest version with only two players (see figure 1.2), each player can choose whether to lead or to follow.

As shown in the figure, if one player chooses to lead and the other chooses to follow, the leader receives 200 points and the follower receives 100 points. If you imagine that they are hunting big game, this would represent the players hunting together successfully, with the leader receiving the lion's share of the meat. If both players choose to follow, they receive no points, as if the lack of organized cooperation meant that their hunting was unsuccessful. Finally, if both players choose to lead, they have the worst possible outcome: both players lose 100 points, which you might imagine as a fight to establish leadership in which both players are injured and are consequently unable to go hunting. In the laboratory if the two players are anonymous and have to decide in secret simultaneously, nearly 75% will choose to follow, ending up with a zero pay-off,[3] despite the fact that switching from follower to leader has the highest potential gain.

We scorn "fair weather friends" who switch allegiance to a team that wins, because diehard fans remain loyal to their sports team, even if that team loses regularly. This truism illustrates a recurring paradox in social territory: people and animals make loyalty choices that seem blatantly counterproductive from a selfish and rational perspective, but from an evolutionary perspective the behavior (and the tribe that adopts it) will

---

1 Van Vugt M (2006). Evolutionary Origins of Leadership and Followership *Personality and Social Psychology Review*, 10(4): 354-371. One (somewhat controversial) explanation of this kind of evolution is based on group selection; see Sober E & Wilson DS (1998). *Unto Others: The Evolution and Psychology of Unselfish Behaviour*. Cambridge, MA: Harvard University Press.

2 Barrett L, Dunbar R & Lycett J (2002). *Human Evolutionary Psychology*. London: Palgrave.

3 Rapoport A & Guyer MJ (1976). *The 2 x 2 Game*. Ann Arbor, MI: University of Michigan Press.

prosper. In most cases followers remain loyal to their territory, and they do not rethink their choice of team when their leader dies or switches sides. The reason is that followers want more than just their leader. At various points in life, each of us is a follower, and we want a team, a place, a melody. We want it because evolution associated social territory with feelings — more complicated than pleasure, but just as galvanizing — that drive us to reinforce and defend our territory even when it does not seem advantageous in our present situation.

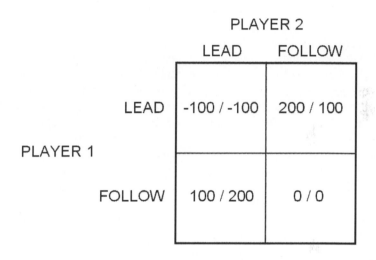

Figure 1.2 - The game of Leader. In this game, each player decides to either lead or follow, and the pay-offs for each player are shown in the figure. In each box, player 1's pay-off is to the left of the slanted line, while player 2's pay-off is to the right. The pay-offs are numerical proxies of reproductive and adaptive benefits and costs.

The argument throughout this book is that behavior has psychobiological momentum; to understand why an animal (such as a human being) has a particular behavior, you have to look back in time to when the behavior evolved. To put it metaphorically: the evolution of behavior is like the rudder of the RMS Titanic: it sometimes changes things too slowly to adapt to circumstances. The meaning of our current behavior may only be appreciated in the necessities of our past: from our infancy, our human kindred, or our fellow vertebrates. However, without any rudder, all behavior would be pointless, and extinction would surely follow. This is why territorial behavior often harks back to the past.

For example, David Lack the ornithologist once placed a stuffed robin near the nest of some live birds, and one hen launched an aggressive attack that lasted forty minutes.[1] At first the hen sang and fluffed her feathers to display her power, but after a short

---

1 Lack D (1939). The behaviour of the Robin. Part I. The life-history, with special reference to aggressive behaviour, sexual behaviour, and territory. Part II. A partial analy-

time she launched into a fully fledged assault, striking the stuffed bird violently. When called to breakfast, Lack picked up what was left of his stuffed bird and walked away. He happened to look back, and he was astonished to see that the hen was still violently pecking at the empty air. The bird delivered four more frenzied attacks, singing louder and louder, failing to notice that her stuffed competitor had vanished. Similarly, Lack's staunch views of natural selection also persisted even after he underwent a religious conversion during adulthood, which he acknowledged led to some intellectual conflict between his theological beliefs and his continuing work as an evolutionary biologist.[1]

***

Almost all territorial mammals — dogs, cats, rhinos[2] — use urine to mark their territory.[3] Why would humans use music instead of scent to mark their territory? Nearly all mammals have scent glands that produce a unique cocktail of chemical pheromones that end up in the urine, and also around the anus, under the chin, and on many other parts of the body, depending upon the animal. Mammals relying on scent marks have a set of proteins accompanying the pheromones in their urine, which bind the volatile pheromones (just like the fixatives in Eau de Toilette) making the scent last up to 24 hours. These proteins can be used by other animals of the same species to identify who made the urine. Human urine completely lacks these proteins — in fact, if these proteins were found in your urine by your doctor, he would probably diagnose you with kidney failure. Unlike dogs, we do not usually use scent to recognize our territories, so we need another way of detecting them. The gibbon uses an alternative to establish its territory: it sings and calls to defend its territory — sometimes a mated pair will sing duets.[4] Could we be like gibbons — using music as an alternative to smell?

To recognize your group's territory, and so achieve a sense of belonging, you must identify what is familiar to you. Just as putting an animal in its own territory alters how the animal behaves, when a human being is in a familiar setting, the situation changes how the body responds. For example, heroin addicts become progressively tolerant to higher and higher doses while in a familiar environment such as their home, but if they then inject in an unfamiliar environment the same dose can be fatal.[5] Familiarity makes

---

sis of aggressive and recognition behaviour. *Proceedings of the Zoological Society of London A* 109: 169–219.

1 After converting to Anglicanism, David Lack published in 1957 *Evolutionary theory and Christian belief: the unresolved conflict*. (London: Methuen). In a testament to his scientific integrity, it was said of him, "David Lack was the only religious man I knew at that period who did not allow his religion to dictate his view of natural selection," from Cain AJ & Provine WB (1991). Genes and ecology in history. In Berry RJ et al. (eds.) Genes in ecology: the 33rd Symposium of the British Ecological Society. Oxford: Blackwell, p. 9.

2 Rachlow JL, Kie JG & Berger J (1999). Territoriality and spatial patterns of white rhinoceros in Matobo National Park, Zimbabwe. *African Journal of Ecology* 37, pp. 295-304.

3 Hurst JL and Beynon RL (2004). Scent wars: the chemobiology of chemical signalling in mice. *BioEssays* 26: 1288-1298.

4 Mitani JC (1987). Territoriality and monogamy among agile gibbons (Hylobates agilis). *Behavioral Ecology and Sociobiology* 20: 265-269.

5 In a Hungarian case report Gerevich et al. found a case of fatal heroin overdose in an unfamiliar environment — a public toilet — where the authors could demonstrate

a huge difference in how resilient and confident you are. You can imagine what familiarity feels like by thinking of what your front door looks like — it should feel familiar. Unfamiliarity would be what you feel when you are walking through a foreign city for the first time.

In 2007, scientists at the University of Lyon showed that the human brain responds to familiar music in the same way it responds to familiar odors.[1] Imagine the following experiment: you lie down inside a huge brain scanner, with your head lying in a doughnut-shaped magnetic coil. The clanging noises of the scanner are all around you and you have to wear earplugs in order not to be disturbed. You then rate a series of smells presented to you as either familiar or unfamiliar by pressing one of two buttons with your right hand. The scanner produces an image of your brain showing the difference between familiar smells and smells you have never encountered before.

The Lyon scientists noted that for familiar smells only areas in the left hemisphere of the brain were activated. When the smell was thought to be unfamiliar, only areas in the right hemisphere were activated, especially the anterior insula, the superior frontal gyrus, and the supramarginal gyrus. It would be impossible to say what these regions do together because each brain region can be ascribed with tens of diverse functions; however, this specific combination of brain activation is like a fingerprint for how the brain responds to familiar and unfamiliar smells.

The Lyon scientists then did an almost identical experiment on the same people, but this time presenting them with familiar and unfamiliar musical excerpts. The distinction made between familiar and unfamiliar items by the participants was much more pronounced for musical excerpts than for smells. The results obtained from comparing the brain scans were astonishing. With few exceptions, not only did both familiar odors and music activate the same brain areas in the left hemisphere, but also exactly the same spots of the right hemisphere were activated for unfamiliar odors and music. The fingerprints were the same. This suggests that, as far as familiarity is concerned, the human brain responds to music in the same way as it responds to odors, only more strongly.

Does this mean that odor and music serve a common purpose for territory, and that, in humans, music plays the more important role? The advantage of smell over a visual sign for signaling territory is that smell is a very pervasive signal: wherever you are on a farm, you can always smell the cows. Sound can also be detected around corners and

conclusively that the same dose and quality of drug had been used safely at the victim's home the previous day: Gerevich J, Bácskai E, Farkas L and Danics Z (2005). A case report: Pavlovian conditioning as a risk factor of heroin "overdose" death. *Harm Reduction Journal*. 2:11. Many studies have used interviews of overdose survivors to demonstrate that the combination of an unfamiliar environment with a tolerated dose of heroin can lead to a deadly combination, e.g., Siegel S (1984). Pavlovian conditioning and heroin overdose: Reports from overdose victims. *Bulletin of the Psychonomic Society*. 22: 428–430 and Gutiérrez-Cebollada J, de la Torre R, Ortuño J, Garcés JM, Camí J (1994). Psychotropic drug consumption and other factors associated with heroin overdose. *Drug and Alcohol Dependence*. 35: 169–174. Darke S, Zador D (1996). Fatal heroin "overdose": a review. *Addiction*. 91: 1765–1772.

1 Plailly J, Tillmann B & Royet JP (2007). The feeling of familiarity of music and odors: the same neural signature? *Cerebral Cortex* 17(11): 2650-8.

through the trees, but sound is a more convincing sign that "trespassers will be prosecuted." Perhaps evolution made use of this property of sound for signaling territory, and our progenitors switched from scent to music. Just imagine what the world would be like today had our ancestors continued to rely on scent marks. Rather than being bombarded by music in department stores, we would be engulfed in a mishmash of smells. Instead of iPods and earphones, commuters would wear breathing masks connected to a circuit board releasing their favorite pheromones.

***

From a psychobiological perspective, music can be used to reinforce social territory. The rest of this book will examine whether this explains the many ways we use music. In particular, the narrative must start with how social territory fits into our lives. Undeniably it creates more than a genuine defense, as illustrated by the young Nazis marching with spades. It cements the cohesion of groups, which allows for the coordination of activity. But it does something more than that, because people enjoy music and seek it out, even when there is no activity to coordinate — in fact, *especially* when there is nothing specific to do: music is central to leisure. But the word leisure makes the activity sound frivolous. When the Mekranoti warriors sing in the early morning, they are in deadly earnest. From an objective standpoint, scaring off an attack that is not happening may seem to us like "doing nothing," or like "imagining being useful," but territory is ultimately a subjective experience, which makes the singing central to their lives.

Territory is not a place — it is a state of mind, which encompasses a varied but important inner experience. This book proposes that the inner experience of territory is the basis of how music can cure. It is also the reason people listen to sad music, and the point of leverage for advertisers and retailers to influence your purchases. Ironically, the feeling you get from reinforcing social territory is one of the most elegant explanations of the Mozart effect, in which listening to the right sort of music can make you excel on IQ tests, if only for fifteen minutes.

The narrative continues by answering why music helps us to get social territory. Music is not just an accident that happens to make us feel good about life, despite the claims of prominent evolutionary theorists.[1] Steven Pinker's *The Language Instinct*, a book about how the brain evolved to have language (originally published in 1994), created a cauldron of foment among psychology of music theorists by claiming that the brain did not evolve to have or take pleasure in music. Instead, he proposed that music was "auditory cheesecake," effectively an accidental phenomenon that happened to be able to tap into the brain's circuitry developed for other purposes such as language — in the same way that eating cheesecake enjoyably satisfies our need to find nutrition even though man did not evolve to eat cheesecake. This proclamation has served as a lightning rod for nearly all other speculation about why we have music, right up to 2010 with the publication of Philip Ball's dissentingly entitled *The Music Instinct*.[2] Here I propose that music can reinforce social territory in a manner analogous to how new species are created: there are both functional adaptations in the music for the territory to be occupied,

---

1 Pinker S (2003). *The Language Instinct*. London: Penguin Science.
2 Ball P (2010). The Music Instinct: How Music Works and Why We Can't Do Without It. London: The Bodley Head.

and variety in music to create arbitrary isolating mechanisms for each social group. In short, the auditory features of the music are important, but so are the past experiences and memories of the listener.

The book will show that the amazing versatility of music as a whole for capturing territory is the reason why young men blare pounding music out of their car stereos and why music makes sex better. Music is recognized for bringing people together, but it has a dark side that can push us apart. Perhaps this will help to explain why music is so powerful, why almost everyone feels an intense attraction to music, and yet we all have conflicting opinions as to what is good music — or even *what is music*. This is not necessarily a bad thing, as life is not meant to be one giant love-in with everyone holding hands in a circle. Music contributes to life as we live it — on our own territory.

CHAPTER 2. WHY DOES MUSIC MAKE SEX BETTER?

THE INNER EXPERIENCE OF TERRITORY

"[I]t appears probable that the progenitors of man, either the males or females or both sexes, before acquiring the power of expressing their mutual love in articulate language, endeavoured to charm each other with musical notes and rhythm."[1]

— Charles Darwin (1809–1882)

Sex and bedrooms. They go together. If your home is your territory, your bedroom is its protected core, and your bed is its innermost sanctum. The bed is where you nest, and it is the safest place you know — a place where you finally end your vigilance and let yourself fall asleep. The bed signifies territory. As long as sex remains an act of intense vulnerability, of being oblivious to much of one's surroundings, most sex will take place in a bed.

This link between territory and sex can be reinforced by music, which is why people play music while in bed having sex. The entire argument of this chapter can be summarized as follows:

Music can reinforce territory, and territory is conducive to sex.

This complex relationship between sex, territory, and music is exemplified by behavior of the New York heavy metal band Manowar. In 1984 Manowar entered the Guinness Book of World Records for the loudest performance on record. Loudness is physically a way to conquer territory, as shown by the Long Range Acoustic Devices of

---

1 Darwin C (1871). *The descent of man, and selection in relation to sex*, Volume II, Chapter 19, London: John Murray, pp. 337. http://darwin-online.org.uk/content/frameset?viewtype=text&itemID=F937.2&pageseq=1

the US military.[1] For Manowar, controlling the space with sound is directly connected to a territorial metaphor; they profess themselves to be "The Kings of Metal." Their 8th album, released in 1996, is called *Louder Than Hell*, and in the words of their bassist Joey DeMaio, "We have a saying that a speaker sounds best just before it blows."[2] According to Manowar there is a direct connection between loudness and sex. DeMaio explained in a German interview, "The reason for [playing so loud] is the vibration is good for the girls. It goes up their legs and hits the spot... [whistles] Orgasm!"[3] While it seems unlikely that scientists will ever verify this claim, for a metal band, Manowar have more than their fair share of female fans. Occasionally a few of their sexiest groupies will mount the stage to disrobe for the musicians and then offer their bodies for brief sexual acts on stage, all while the guitars continue to crash out their ear-splitting mating call.[4]

This is marvelous for the musicians, but not so obviously appealing for the fans. Manowar, which has a self-proclaimed reputation for being outside of mainstream commercial heavy metal, has many fans across the globe. Their supporters are known by the theatrical moniker The Army of the Immortals, and they are ostentatiously loyal, in many cases signing their fan mail in blood. Even though there seems to be a higher percentage of women at Manowar gigs than at many other metal shows, as with all heavy metal, the women are vastly outnumbered by men. If sex and territory go together, most men at a Manowar concert must realize that, statistically speaking, they are fighting a losing battle, and very few of them will obtain a woman at the concert. Why do they still come?

Because territory is intrinsically valuable. If territory were only used for sex, then people would never bother with it on their own. In fact people perform territorial acts often when by themselves. This frequently is why people play music for themselves. Any time you put some music on in order to hear it but not specifically listen to it, such that it is background or ambience, that may be motivated by a need for territory — much like painting the walls of your room a color you find comfortable.

The Manowar example shows that people get sexually attracted when you combine music and territory: deliberately territorial music (e.g., loud and dominant) when mixed with displays of social territory (e.g., a big audience) is especially potent as a sexual catalyst (see Figure 2.1). However, the fans show that not all music is aimed at

---

1 See Cusick SG (2006). Music as torture / Music as weapon. *TRANS Revista transcultural de Música*. Number 10. (Barcelona: Sociedad de Etnomusicología). For the manufacturer of LRADs, see www.atcsd.com

2 Harris C and Wiederhorn J (2007). Metal File: Manowar, A Life Once Lost, Origin & More News That Rules. MTV News, 09 Feb. www.mtv.com/news/articles/1552016/20070208/manowar.jhtml

3 The interview in April 2002 was with Stefan Raab on TV Total, a German late night comedy talk show. It was accessed on 28 April 2010 at http://www.youtube.com/watch?v=Fb-hQoGHKpQ

4 A film of a female groupie on stage at an Athens 4 April 2007 Manowar concert was downloaded (19 Jan 2010) at http://www.youtube.com/watch?v=y9STO5p8Qj0. She is also shown in another clip, http://www.youtube.com/watch?v=VhEmYtljTk U&feature=related. A scantily clad Finnish groupie is seen at http://www.youtube. com/watch?v=Mxtm8_jgb08&feature=related. A set of clips of women on stage with Manowar is on http://www.youtube.com/watch?v=5uQY_GzP2GM

sex, and not all territory leads to (or is geared toward) sex; just as music is valued unto itself, territory has intrinsic value — it is an emotional experience that strengthens you.

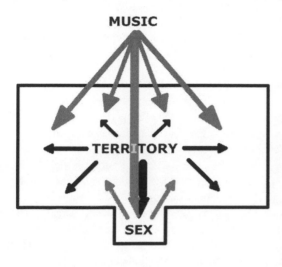

Figure 2.1. How territorial music supercharges the ability of social territory to lead to sex. Although territory can lead to sex (thick black downward arrow), it can lead to many other territorial experiences (i.e., emotions related to territory such as confidence or soothing, other black arrows). Sex is "one corner" of the territorial experience, but not all sex has to begin on your own territory because sex itself is a way to gather more territory (diagonally upward grey arrows). Music leads to many territorial experiences (if it is music "of your territory," set of diagonally downward grey arrows), but music that specifically stresses that it is your territory (loud, showing off, singing "I am the best," grey arrow straight down) leads to the center of territory, and combined with displays of social territory, such as having a big audience, will make the musician very desirable (combined black and grey downward arrow).

Not only is there value to territory that is independent of competing for sex, but in some cases animals act as though territory is more important than sex. A vivid example of this is the Uganda kob (*Adenota kob thomasi*), an antelope-like animal where the males compete directly for territory but not for females. All mating takes place within a male's territory, a court, which is the size and shape of a putting green of short grass, surrounded by another forty such territories (a lek), with the most active and attractive territories being at the center of the lek.[1] Each court is gladiatorially guarded by one pugnacious male, and the territories are hotly contested. They are crucial for a male's reproductive success, as there are only 13 known territorial breeding grounds for a population of 10,000 kob in their habitat of 100 square miles; that works out to about 520 territories for 5,000 males, so on any given day only 1 in 10 males will have a territory. The holder of each court is challenged by other kobs, sometimes with aggressive displays but usually with violence. If a male wins a fight, the ground is his. But when he leaves to graze or drink, which happens twice per day, he loses his ground. Meanwhile, females are drawn on to the lek but are heedless of the powerful buck, as if the grass

---

1 This information about the Uganda Kob concerns those in the Semliki Game Reserve near Fort Portal Uganda. Buechner HK (1961). Territorial behavior in Uganda Kob. *Science* 133: 698-9.

never tasted so sweet as on this lek. While on one such territory the female may mate with the male, but if the female walks over the boundary between one territory and the next, the first male makes no protest and loses interest as the next male becomes the new host for that female.

What makes lekking behavior so interesting is that the animals are doing all their fighting and mate selection based on territory — sex almost seems an afterthought.[1] For example, a group of female kob may be accompanied by a male while foraging, which is convenient and supportive, but does the male no good reproductively. The females will not mate with this companion. No territory, no nookie.

To put status and territory into perspective, 500 years ago most European human males would not have had sex before the age of 25 except if they could afford a prostitute; save for the privileged, celibacy was high, servitude was common, and marriage came late if at all.[2] The modern European right to start a family and the idea that everyone should be able to have a boyfriend or girlfriend if they want one is not how things have always been.[3] Being alpha is a big deal, both for humans and for animals.

What does the male kob think about all of this? "Full speed ahead." To gain territory he charges fervently into battle, even though his chances are slim because the current territory holder nearly always wins. And every time a male returns to his territory after foraging (or after a lion, automobile or elephant makes all the kob abandon the lek), he has to fight his way back onto his territory. While some males only last a day, there have been observations of males holding court as long as seventy-five days. All that fighting seems a lot of work for a patch of grass no bigger than a tennis court. You might be thinking, "Location, location, location," but you would be wrong.

***

Territory is not a place — it is a state of mind. Whether you are talking about a gang on their turf, a priest in his chapel, or a Jane Austen heroine in her family home, there is a psychical aspect that they all share. As a thought experiment, consider how you feel in different places. Are there certain places that make you feel assured, while others make you anxious? In a dark city alley, do you ever find yourself thinking, "I don't belong here"? It is more than the lighting, because in the center of your own territory (in your bed) you can sleep unarmed and naked in the dark, while a dark and lonely alley is not fixed by street lamps. Think of how the outcome of a heated argument depends upon who has the home turf advantage, and why international negotiations to end wars usually take place literally in a neutral territory. The home is not simply a space to be contained in. It is a "center" not in a geometrical sense, but in a psychological one. The home empowers us: we tend to view it as a source of our strength.

1 The theory of territory is that males fight over territory, not over mates. See Nice MM (1941). The role of territory in bird life. *The American midland Naturalist* 26(3): 441-487.

2 Hajnal J (1965). European marriage patterns in perspective. In Glass DV & Eversley DEC (eds), *Population in History*. Chicago: Aldine Publishing.

3 Article 12 of the European Convention on Human Rights (1948) states, "Men and women of marriageable age have the right to marry and to found a family, according to the national laws governing the exercise of this right." This simply means that the state cannot prevent marriage; in the past there have been laws prohibiting marriage based on a variety of issues, including lack of sufficient income.

Although psychological, this empowerment takes on a physical aspect into the material world. While all sportsmen know of the home team advantage, few are aware of how carefully it has been scientifically validated. Scientists, making mathematical analyses, have consistently found that teams playing on their own turf have a small but statistically reliable increased probability of winning.[1] It is not true for all teams (a minority of teams have better luck when playing away). It is not meaningful for any single game (or even for a small series of games). But over the course of a season, it can be measured in virtually every team sport tested, whether professional or amateur.[2]

Scientists have repeatedly tried to ascribe the home advantage to an objective basis, such as familiarity with the field, travel fatigue, or the importance of the game; however, when each of these explanations is carefully tested, they are found to have little or no effect.[3] For English soccer, the team with the home advantage racks up approximately ½ of an extra goal per game, and it does not matter what level or league of play. The home advantage becomes less once a team enters a new league, and then it becomes greater over time as they settle in to the new league; this invalidates the theory that the visiting team underperforms because they are unfamiliar with the playing field or stadium.

The mysterious source of the home advantage seems to have psychological origins. For example, when competing at home, rugby players who took a psychological test one hour before playing scored higher on Vigor and Self-confidence, and lower on Tension, Depression, Anger, Fatigue, Confusion, Cognitive Anxiety, and Somatic Anxiety.[4] The crowds' effects on the home team are not the root of this advantage. In fact, the players' reaction to cheering is not necessarily positive, as was demonstrated by a unique scientific opportunity. When a measles epidemic precipitated a quarantine that excluded fans from eleven basketball games, the performance of the two affected teams improved; in terms of points scored and percentages of successful attempts, both teams performed better in the absence of spectators.[5] So the home advantage is not due to any obvious physical factor such as familiarity with the playing field or cheering.

The mystery of the home advantage seems obvious in animals: territory. When two competitors of comparable size and ability fight, the one on its own territory usually wins. In humans I will call this phenomenon social territory, because not all social territory in humans is tied specifically to a piece of land. This feature of social territory in which the territorial experience transcends the boundaries of space and place was highlighted in 2000 by the international union of Roma, better known as the gypsies. It is not surprising that the gypsies are famed for their music; they need music to reinforce

---

1   Courneya KS & Carron AV (1992). The Home Advantage in Sport Competitions: A Literature Review. *Journal of Sport and Exercise Psychology* 14(1): 13-27.

2   Carron AV, Loughhead TM & Bray SR (2005). The home advantage in sport competitions: Courneya and Carron's (1992) conceptual framework a decade later. *Journal of Sports Sciences* 23(4): 395 – 407.

3   Clarke SR, Norman JM (1995). Home ground advantage of individual clubs in English soccer. *The Statistician* 44(4): 509-521.

4   Terry PC, Walrond N, Carron AV (1998). The influence of game location on athletes' psychological states. *Journal of Science and Medicine in Sport* 1(1): 29-37.

5   Moore JC & Brylinsky JA (1993). Spectator effect on team performance in college basketball. *Journal of Sport Behavior* 16: 77–84.

their *social* territory. Emil Scuka, the founder of the first Roma party of Czechoslovakia, stated,

> The Roma nation is not limited to a territory. It is not a question of a state with precise frontiers, but it is a non-territorial nation that represents at the same time our specific identity.[1]

In humans we seem to prefer the term identity, and a sociologist might categorize much of these effects as part of social identity.[2] The problem with social identity is that sociologists have not developed methods for measuring "identity" in a rabbit or a hummingbird. In humans music very often reinforces this psychological phenomenon whether you call it *identity* or *territory*. Only one other primate besides man has a complicated singing behavior: the gibbon.[3] A mated pair of gibbons will often sing "duets" together in the morning, and the song is plainly to reinforce territory.[4] This book sticks with the term social territory because the term social identity cannot be easily applied to animals' mental states; the phenomenon of social territory is seen in both animals and man, and is most clearly demonstrated by the fact that males with demonstrable territory are sexually attractive, while the same males without territory are not.

***

Paris, September 1827: Hector Berlioz (1803–1869), an impecunious music student at the conservatoire, first lays eyes on the celebrated Irish actress Harriet Smithson (1800–1854). After he watches her play Ophelia in *Hamlet* at the Théâtre de l'Odéon, he falls violently in love with her, and confronting her backstage, he loudly proclaims his love for her.[5] She is scared senseless, but her initial rejection does little to cool his ardor. In addition to barraging her with so many letters that she eventually instructs her maid not to accept them, in the summer of 1828 Berlioz organizes a concert of his own music to win her love. This attempt at sexual display fails singularly, as Smithson is not informed of the concert. Haunted by his obsession for Smithson, for the next year and a half Berlioz composes his most famous work, *Symphonie Fantastique*, which tells his romanticized story of the dreams and suffering of an artist pursuing his beloved. Fantasizing about restoring his status in the wake of his rejected love, the denouement arrives after the artist thought he had killed her, with the reappearance of his beloved in the midst of a witches' Sabbath.

---

1 Berezin M (2003). "Territory, emotion and identity: spatial recalibration in a new Europe." In Berezin M & Schain M (eds.) *Europe with Borders: Remapping Territory, Citizenship and Identity in a Transnational Age*. London: The Johns Hopkins University Press.
2 Tajfel H, Turner J (1979). An Integrative Theory of Intergroup Conflict. In Austin WG, Worchel S (Eds) The Social Psychology of Intergroup Relations. Monterey, CA: Brooks-Cole, pp. 94–109.
3 Indris (another primate) have what are sometimes called songs, but these calls are not really as complicated (or as acquired) as human, gibbon or bird song.
4 Geissman T (2000). Gibbon songs and human music from an evolutionary perspective. In Wallin NL, Merker B, Brown S (eds.). *The origins of music.* (Cambridge, Mass.: MIT Press) pp. 103-123.
5 From Berlioz H (2002). *The Memoirs of Hector Berlioz.* Cairns D (editor & translator). London: Everyman's Library Classics.

This sort of music-making is not the most direct strategy for seducing a woman. The most attractive (and territorial) music would focus on the man being strong in the material world, rather than being weak, day dreaming, and wishing he could kill the indomitable girl. However, even Berlioz's unusual musical narratives can work their charms, albeit in unexpected ways, if they lead to demonstrable territory.

In 1830 Berlioz finally achieves his musical ambition of winning the Prix de Rome, essentially a scholarship connected to a 5-year pension and travel for study in Rome, which has eluded him for the previous five years. He now has status and territory. At about the time of his newfound recognition and financial security, he becomes the prey of a new woman, Camille Moke, an irrepressible and wanton pianist. She notices the virginal Berlioz and asks one of his friends about him,[1] but is told in no uncertain terms that Berlioz is totally obsessed with Smithson and that Moke has no hope. This only strengthens her resolve to make Berlioz fall madly in love with her. She succeeds in less than six months; she and Berlioz are engaged by the end of that year. Unfortunately for Berlioz, the terms of the Prix de Rome require him to study in Rome — without Moke.

After three months in Rome, Berlioz has not received any correspondence from Moke, so he impulsively sets off for Paris to get some news. An unsympathetic letter from Moke's mother finds him while he is still traveling across Italy, and the news is bad. In Berlioz's short absence, Moke has decided to break off their relationship and to marry the scion of the wealthy piano manufacturer, Ignace Pleyel.[2] In a nutshell, as soon as Berlioz abandons his territory in Paris, Moke allies herself with another man in Paris who is rich and has even greater territory than that demonstrated by Berlioz's inchoate fame.

This is not only a loss of face, but a loss of territory — he has lost his fiancée (his one sexual conquest) to another man, and this enflames Berlioz's rage and aggression. True to his Romantic spirit, Berlioz concocts a melodramatic scheme to exact a bloody revenge — a triple murder and suicide. Berlioz's stratagem is to gain entrance to their home disguised as a cleaning girl, and then reveal himself before gunning down Pleyel, his ex-fiancée, and her detested mother.[3] He goes so far as to buy a specially altered maid's dress and a hat with a thick green veil. For the killing, he has brought two pistols, and poison (with which to kill himself should the pistols fail). This is how he imagines what would happen when he gets to Paris:

> I go to my "friend's" house at nine in the evening just when the family has assembled for tea. I say I am the Countess Moke's personal maid with an urgent message. I am shown into the drawing-room, where I deliver a letter. While it is being read I draw my double-barreled pistols, blow out the brains of number one and number two, seize number three by the hair,

---

1 It is sometimes assumed that Moke was Berlioz's first lover, although not his first obsession.

2 Her marriage to Pleyel broke down after a few years because of her "disorderly behaviour and persistent infidelity." She went on to become a recognized pianist in her own right.

3 Moke's mother is an ongoing issue for Berlioz. It is she who most opposed the marriage, and she sent him the letter telling him the engagement was off. Even when the relationship was ongoing, as lovers Berlioz and Moke would uncharitably refer to Moke's mother as *l'hippopotame*.

reveal myself and, disregarding her screams, pay my respects to her in similar fashion, after which, before this cantata for voices and orchestra has had time to attract attention, I present my right temple with the unanswerable argument of the remaining barrel; or should the gun by any chance misfire, I have recourse to my cordials. What a fine scene it would have made. It really is a pity it had to be dropped.

— The Memoirs of Hector Berlioz[1]

His reason returns just before he loses his prize money; he is threatened with having to forfeit the Prix de Rome (the real territory he has won) if he does not stop before crossing the French border. Back in Rome, Berlioz sublimates his fury into his musical work, culminating in composing the overture to *King Lear*, the story of trusting man victimized by evil women — another of Berlioz's plots that parallels his own life.

Two and one half years after winning the *Prix de Rome* and living abroad, Berlioz returns to Paris where he produces a concert of *Symphony Fantastique*; this time he arranges for friends to introduce him properly to Smithson. Smithson has no idea the music has been composed for her when her friends take her to the concert on 9 December 1832. She realizes something might be afoot when during Lélio, the sequel to *Symphony Fantastique*, an actor proclaims, "Oh, if I could only find her, the Juliet, the Ophelia that my heart cries out for!" Smithson has just been through a spell of bad luck professionally, and is now wistful about Berlioz's love for her. What happens next is best described by Berlioz himself: "'God!' she thought: 'Juliet — Ophelia! Am I dreaming? I can no longer doubt. It is of me he speaks. He loves me still.' From that moment, so she has often told me, she felt the room reel about her; she heard no more but sat in a dream, and at the end returned home like a sleepwalker, hardly aware of what was happening."[2] Given her poor treatment of Berlioz, it is incomprehensible to her — not that she is the Muse of this genius, but that he is still in love with her.

With his music gaining a following, it firmly establishes Berlioz's territory, so he is attractive enough to restart his courtship auspiciously, and he ends up marrying the girl of his dreams, literally.[3] It is not just status and success that wins the girl[4] — it is territory, as Berlioz found to his cost after he left Paris and lost Camille Moke.

***

1 From Berlioz H (2002). *The Memoirs of Hector Berlioz*. Cairns D (editor & translator). London: Everyman's Library Classics. Moke's mother had always been opposed to the engagement of her daughter to Berlioz because the marriage would not bring her daughter the requisite rank or wealth.

2 From Berlioz H (2002) *The Memoirs of Hector Berlioz*. Cairns D (editor & translator). London: Everyman's Library Classics.

3 Thus began the relationship that begot their doomed marriage. With her career dwindling, Harriet Smithson slid into alcoholism, and her behaviour became volatile. After five years of marriage, Berlioz left his wife and 5-year-old son to reside with his mistress, the opera singer Marie Récio.

4 To test whether human music results in reproductive success for males, Geoffrey Miller compared the recorded output of prominent jazz, rock, and classical musicians; he found that males produced ten times as much music as females. Furthermore, the output of the males peaked near the age of maximum mating effort. Thus, according to Miller, music-making in humans acts as a male courtship display to attract females.

But it is not just the territory and the audience created by music that effects its sexual benefits. Music in and of itself can reinforce the sense of *belonging* in a relationship, which is why it makes sex better. Just as music can foster a sense of belonging when a person listens to it alone, when two people are listening to music that they both engage with, they will experience a coordinated sense of being part of something bigger, which will make them feel more connected. The music could be gentle or hardcore, but the mutual agreement upon the music will further link the twosome, and if the couples' feelings are synchronized to each other over time by the changes in the music, it will enhance their rapport.[1]

But this sense of belonging extends beyond the momentary rapport and coordination between the two people. Enough people are confident that music is the bedrock of social interaction that there is a dating website that bases its initial testing around your relationship to music. This match-making screening system at www.asoundmatch.com scores potential couples on musical compatibility, which implies that the two people have the *same relationship* to music (i.e., intensity, need, etc.), rather than identical tastes in music. The organizers claim that when comparing musical preference, "Couples who scored closer together had the strongest relationships. Over 85% of the time, couples in healthy, long-term relationships scored within a 10% range of one another."[2] Whether or not this is true, the fact is that enough people believe it to make it a viable business proposition. So the question is: how does music serve in the building of a relationship?

Music reinforces a couple's joint social territory. This explains how music, sex and bedrooms go together. This is true even in a sex club. There is one in Brooklyn, New York, run by one Mistress Wanda, and for $40 per couple, or $90 if you are an unaccompanied man, you can see for yourself.[3] Of course, it comes equipped with bedrooms. People do not usually sleep there, but they still want a bed. This is not just because the bed is a soft place to lie in. The bed represents a territory: for some it will be a refuge, but sometimes sex can be a more territorial act. For example, an Indian portrait of the Mughal Emperor Muhammad Shah (1719–1748) shows the emperor at the moment of penetration of an anonymous beautiful woman, but it is not meant as pornographic; to Indian eyes, his nearby sword, jewels and hookah show that this is "a display of power and virility." [4]

Looking at Western society, Tia DeNora, the doyenne of music in everyday life, described how, as a prelude to intimacy, women like to play soft, sensual music and music that implies sentiment. DeNora writes, "Of the 52 women, I interviewed for the music and daily life study, not one indicated fast-paced or high-volume music as something

Miller G (2000). Evolution of human music through sexual selection. In Wallin NL, Merker B & Brown S (Eds), *The Origins of Music*. Cambridge, MA: MIT Press, 329–360.

1 Gill SP (2007). Entrainment and musicality in the human system interface. *AI & Society* 21(4): 567-605.

2 Lynne. *A sound match.* http://asoundmatch.com/howasmworks.php (accessed Dec 03, 2009).

3 Unaccompanied women can enter for free, as they are considered "sex club gold." See Feuer A (2009). "At a sex club, the outré meet the ordinary." *The New York Times*, 25 February.

4 Dalley J (2010). Two shows that further our love for India. *The Financial Times* newspaper (UK), 12 March.

they associated with intimacy (for example, heavy metal, dance music, aerobic music)."[1] She suggests that the basis for this is that the

> Leisurely pace, whether as a feature of music, speech or action, affords equivocation, interruption, languor, redirection and digression, and so is commensurate with narratives of intimate conduct that feature the liminal and the non-purposive.[2]

The exceptions to DeNora's findings are those people (women included) who like to listen to loud, heavy metal music before and during sex. Perhaps DeNora excluded from her study those women likely to mount the stage with Manowar. Women who live out a narrative with sex on stage prove that sex is not always an intimate act, no matter how liminal.[3] Privacy is optional. DJs have described in detail what music works best to accompany the shenanigans at a sex club, and they proffer both lyrical music and tunes with a pumping beat.[4]

Scientists have proposed that the kinds of men that women find attractive also have a dual nature: a gentle feminine side and a hard masculine side. A research group tested this by asking women to rate a set of men's faces for attractiveness, while the women were allowed to computer-enhance the faces using a slider so that a given face could be made to have a stronger jaw and thicker eyebrows (more masculine) or more rounded and gentle features (more feminine). By repeating the experiment at different times of the month, the results showed that the kind of man a woman finds most attractive alternates to a more masculinized appearance during the days of a woman's highest fertility.[5]

This could explain the seeming paradox of why so many women like Hip-Hop and rap music,[6] despite the fact that it is so hypermasculinized that it often treats women as objects or inferiors. Hip hop evolved in the 1970s in the USA as the new music of the hip hop cultural movement (also including break dancing and graffiti), which in turn had surfaced in New York only a few years earlier, mainly initiated by the Afro-American and Latino inner-city youth. During the last two decades it has been an unqualified success story the world over, and some hip hop artists are amongst the most popular sing-

---

1 DeNora T (2002). The Role of Music in Intimate Culture. *Feminism and Psychology.* 12: 176-178.

2 DeNora T (2002). The Role of Music in Intimate Culture. *Feminism and Psychology.* 12: 176-178.

3 DeNora uses the word "intimacy" in her interviews, and this should not be confused with sexual activity or its prelude; the word intimacy essentially precludes wild sex, sex clubs and sex on stage. DeNora T (2002). The Role of Music in Intimate Culture. *Feminism and Psychology.* 12: 176-178.

4 The terms used are rhythmic and romance. See Kale J (2005). *Sex Between the Beats: The Ultimate Guide to Sex Music.* Venice, California: Blush Books.

5 Johnston VS, Hagel R, Franklin M, Fink B, Grammer K (2001). Male facial attractiveness: evidence for hormone-mediated adaptive design. *Evolution and Human Behavior,* 22(4): 251-267.

6 See North AC, Hargreaves DJ (2007). Lifestyle correlates of musical preference: 1. Relationships, living arrangements, beliefs, and crime. *Psychology of Music,* Vol. 35(1): 58-87. In their survey, among those individuals with a preference, 3.6% of males preferred hip hop compared to 3.0% of women. Compare that to jazz; 4.8% of men preferred jazz but only 2.6% of women did.

---

ers ever. According to Nielsen Soundscan, the rapper Marshall Mathers (better known as Eminem) was the best selling music artist of the last decade;[1] in total he has sold more than 80 million albums, as well as winning nine Grammys and even an Oscar for Best Original Song (2002).

Hip hop has a distinctive slang, and a lot of the songs center on gangland themes such as sex, drugs and hyper-masculinity. As a result, hip hop is associated in the media with scantily clad dancers and a promiscuous, sexualized lifestyle. But these are images of the performers. Among the consumers the correlation of music genres to different lifestyles was recently surveyed among 2,532 music listeners in the UK. Of the 17 specific musical genres listed, hip hop was the most sexually promiscuous; 37% of listeners who preferred hip hop had been with 5 or more sexual partners in the past 5 years, compared to only 1.5% of listeners of country and western music.[2] In trying to explain these differences, some media studies have sought quite direct cause-and-effect relationships between the content of the music and its effects, such as via psychological priming, in which exposure to the stimulus (the music's sexualized lyrics) influences the listener's later thoughts, judgments, and behaviors. The idea is that when you hear songs about sex, sexual thoughts continue to bubble up in the back of your mind. Statistical analyses of hip hop songs have shown that they make an unusually high number of references to impulsive acts (as opposed to mentioning responsibility and consequences as stressed by the Just Say No brigade), and that as time goes on this trend becomes more pronounced.[3] For example, "Whoot! there it is"[4] by 95 South (1993) portrays prostitution as playful banter without acknowledging its overtones of domination and compulsion:

> "Oh girl over there in the blue
> I gotta pocket full of chance so what cha gon' do
> Turn around and let me peek
> And let's play a little bit of hide and seek

1 Montgomery J (2009). Eminem Is The Best-Selling Artist of The Decade: Sales numbers from Nielsen SoundScan reveal Em beat the Beatles in the '00s. *MTV News*, 12 August.

2 This is not necessarily a fair comparison. This data (from North AC, Hargreaves DJ (2007). Lifestyle correlates of musical preference: 1. Relationships, living arrangements, beliefs, and crime. *Psychology of Music*, 35(1): 58-87) does not statistically correct for age. In the UK (as opposed to the US South) Country & Western listeners are likely to be older compared to the rest of the population, and when comparing the number who were widows or widowers, for C&W their cohort had 5.6% whereas for hip hop 0% were widows/widowers. A more fair comparison would be with people who prefer Rock (only 0.5% of whom were widows/widowers): only 6.5% of rock listeners had had 5 or more partners in the past 5 years.

3 Knobloch-Westerwick S, Musto P, Shaw K (2008). Rebellion in the top music charts: Defiant messages in rap/hip-hop and rock music 1993 and 2003. *Journal of Media Psychology: Theories, Methods, and Applications*. 20(1): 15-23.

4 The internet term "w00t" (an interjection of joy at success or triumph, similar to the meaning of "hooray") appeared in the internet lexicon at about the same time as this song appeared, although other explanations for the word woot's etymology have been proposed. Although in the song by 95 South this word is spelled whoot, it has many alternative spellings including w00t, wOOt and woot.

Show me that and I'll give ya this
A twenty dollar bill that's nice and crisp."

Yet the hypermasculinized dominance endemic in hip hop is about more than just sexual dominance, as can be discovered in its lexicon. One of the words that hip hop prizes is *the 'hood*. This glorification of the neighborhood is a bald reference to territory, particularly as it relates to gangs and social loyalties. Hip hop broadens this territorial lingo with ubiquitous references to *homeboys* and *homies* (*home* being the lay word for territory), which identifies men belonging to the neighborhood. On a more subtle note, hip hop mentions specific localities — cities, neighborhoods, and landmarks — much more than commercial rock,[1] because mainstream music producers want music that universalizes experience away from specific locales, so that that the music can be consumed nationally or internationally. By contrast, hip hop is a genre engrossed with its affiliations, and its lyrics both subtly and openly highlight its territoriality. In Western popular music, then, the most overtly sexual music genre is also the most territorial. This is not a coincidence.

Music, territory and sex often go together, even though most women — even heavy metal groupies — would rather not perform sex acts on stage with the band. Sex in bed and sex on stage represent opposite poles of sex's dual nature: can they both relate to being attracted to territory? If so, why would a woman invite a man to have sex in her own bed? Why would people want to have sex in airplanes? Or *al fresco*?

These are not exceptions, but fascinating complications of how sex powerfully elicits the feelings of territory. Although people generally prefer sex on their own territory, in the right mood, people can use sex to gain a strong feeling of territory when it is "borrowed for the occasion." This explains why people would romanticize having sex in strange and dangerous places. If you and your partner have sex in a public place, you snatch the mythology of the place for your territory — like a bower bird gathering its bluest moments. According to one newspaper account in 2001, two smartly-dressed punters amazed the posh Royal Ascot's Ladies Day when they undressed and proceeded to have sex in the middle of the horse track for half an hour, and then took a bow amid applause.[2] In a less self-conscious performance, an unnamed couple "with respectable jobs" stripped and had a steamy sex session on the lawn of Buckingham Palace in broad daylight. Spectators, including soldiers and Japanese tourists filming the event, watched for 30 minutes before police arrested the couple. *The Sun* and other tabloids were indignant that the couple totally disregarded the sign, "Please keep off the grass," which was clearly visible.[3] While drinking initially helps these amorous couples to shed their inhibitions, the couples invariably foray *into* the public space — so there must be some drive not just for sex but for the place itself.

The mile high club is more concerned with place, sex, and danger than with exhibitionism. For example, in a fatal crash of a Piper aircraft on 23 December 1991, the American National Transportation and Safety Board described the probable cause as

---

1 Forman M (2002). *The 'hood comes first: race, space, and place in rap and hip-hop*. Middletown, Connecticut: Wesleyan University Press.

2 Crick A (2009). Passion partners parade privates. *The Sun* newspaper (UK), 30 April.

3 Pyatt J (2009). Who's giving one one on one's lawn. *The Sun* newspaper (UK), 30 April.

"the pilot in command's improper inflight decision to divert her attention to other activities not related to the conduct of the flight" because both fatalities were found partially clothed and the front right seat was in the full aft reclining position.[1]

Sex on commercial flights is also more about place than exhibitionism *per se*. Amanda Holt, a Nortel executive on American Airlines AA110 flight from Dallas to Manchester on 1 October 1999, attempted to live up to Nortel's tag line, "Come Together" when she introduced herself to David Machin, a Hallmark executive, in business class. After they were assigned adjacent seats, they fondled each other, and Holt's blouse and trousers were removed; the court case and ensuing publicity caused them both to lose their jobs and damaged their marriages, yet the airline staff suggested the matter would have been dropped in the air had the couple acquiesced to repeated requests to desist. Determination and persistence are classic signs of territoriality. So is belonging. Ultimately, the mile high club is *a club* — it is something you belong to. Territory is a social construction, reaffirming the connection between you, the other, and a place — in this case, the sky. Sex in forbidden places, once the initial inhibitions are overcome, beckons to reckless consummation, because in many ways completing the orgasm is like graffiti, the social archetype of territorial marking.[2]

* * *

Successfully "marking" territory leads to a confident feeling in humans. Most animal biologists have simply ignored the question of whether marking territory makes an animal more confident. Instead they concentrate on how territorial marks repel intruding animals. But not all scent-marking is motivated by repelling trespassers. In 1999, a team of psychologists and zoologists at the University of Wisconsin found evidence showing that the common marmoset, a New World primate, while resting on its own would suddenly get up, walk a couple of meters, scent-mark, and then rest again.[3] Such marks were deposited by all members of the group and dispersed all over their home range. Interestingly, their marking behavior also became much more pronounced during the rainy season when scent marks were more likely to be washed away. This behavior is not done to repel intruders (who are absent); we can only speculate that it is done because it makes the animal doing it feel good.

Rabbits are also fiercely territorial, and like most other territorial mammals, they scent-mark the area they defend — with time, their territory is reeking with their smell. In the 1970s, wild-life researchers in Australia wanted to know whether the confidence of rabbits is higher if they are surrounded by their own scent.[4] But in rabbits *confidence* is

1 National Safety and Transportation Board (1991). NTSB Identification: MIA92FA051. Aircraft registration: N47506. Stored on microfiche 46312.

2 See Ley D, Cybriwsky R (1974). Urban graffiti as territorial markers. *Annals of the Association of American Geographers* 64(4): 491 and Lindsey DG, Kearns RA (2008). The Writing's on The Wall: Graffiti, Territory and Urban Space in Auckland. *New Zealand Geographer* 50(2): 7–13.

3 Lazaro-Perea C, Snowdon CT & de Fátima Aruda M (1999). Scent-marking behaviour in wild groups of common marmosets (*Callithrix jacchus*). *Behavioural Ecology and Sociobiology* 46, 313-324.

4 Mykytowycz, R, Hesterman, ER, Gambale, S & Dudzinski. 1976. A comparison of the effectiveness of the odors of rabbits *Oryctolagus cuniculus*, in enhancing territorial

difficult to measure. So, the researchers placed two animals in a pen, the floor of which had been impregnated with the smell of one of the rabbits. If a rabbit could detect its own smell, it approached the perceived intruder sooner and was more aggressive. Because the pens did not contain anything that was worth fighting about, such as food or shelter, the scientists concluded that the animals were only competing for space — the territory — and that the presence or absence of their scent often decided which animal was dominant. It would seem that the rabbits felt more confident because they found reassurance in their own territory.

Together, these observations suggest that rabbits, just like common marmosets, feel more confident when they are surrounded by their own scent — because it means they are within their own territory. But it is not really kosher to label an animal emotion as *confident* because we cannot ask for its subjective correlates. What emotion would having *territory* be associated with in humans?

In terms of arousal, territory can provoke seemingly opposite emotions. Where cheering the home team is one side of the coin, its soothing opposite is security. Lullabies are territorial. They exist in virtually every culture tested, and their ability to both focus and relax babies has been tested thoroughly. When babies watch video performances of their mothers singing lullabies, the babies are "mesmerized" by the screen.[1] Given that babies cannot discuss their feelings, the scientists were almost obliged to apply their own lexicon to the babies' reactions, and "mesmerized" is probably as good a word as any because the specific state-of-mind that territory provokes is contradictory. In an army, territory makes you resolved to take the next step forward. In a bed, whether sleeping or having sex, territory makes you feel untroubled in remaining where you are. But if the music stops in the middle of sex, you feel it.

Sex is not a single homogeneous emotion. Neither is territory. Territory makes people feel good; the musical reification of territory is James Brown's "I feel good!" Not *happy*. Definitely not *cheerful*. Good. Territory helps to make everything feel better — that things are as they should be.

There is no single emotion that territory elicits. In fact, it may be easier to describe what territory does *not* do. If you are experiencing territory you will not feel threatened. Or timorous. Territory will not stress you. Nor should you feel overwhelmed, disempowered, unconfident, or that things are just plain wrong. In a word, if you are experiencing territory, you will not feel weak — even upon surrendering to your fate (for example Berlioz's imagined suicide), territory will make you feel empowered. This is the real power of music.

The experience of feeling *empowered* is very different from feeling *happy*. In fact, it is wise to abandon the word *happiness* here because its meaning to different people is so equivocal; rubber fetishists will seek a different constellation of happy feelings from bird watchers. When scientists ask whether happiness is a universal emotion — an emotion that is intrinsic to the human body, visible in every culture in the world, and not learned from your parents — they conclude that it is; but the scientists are not quite right, because happiness isn't even universal between two people in the same family, let

confidence. *Journal of Chemical Ecology* 2: 13-24

1 Trehub SE (2001). Musical predispositions in infancy. *Annals of the New York Academy of Sciences* 930: 1-16.

alone between cultures on opposite sides of the earth. Philosophers make a hash of the word happiness by including whether you are happy with your lot in life.[1] What the scientists really are measuring is momentary *cheerfulness*, because the way those scientists objectively judge "happiness" is whether or not you are smiling.[2]

Technically the only way to judge whether an emotion is universal is to visit a culture where they have never seen a white man. Where they have no television, or radio, or cameras or newspapers. In the 1960s the highlands of Papua New Guinea was inhabited by tribes that had yet to be contaminated by modern culture, so Paul Ekman, the king of facial expression research, went there to determine whether they had the same emotions as white Americans do. He gave them a multiple choice test where they had to match a verbal elicitation of an emotion with photographs of different facial expressions.[3] He could not just ask them, "What do people look like when they are happy?" because that would assume that the tribesmen have a word corresponding to what we think is *happy*. Instead he told them (through a translator) short narratives of emotional experiences (e.g., "Your best friend comes to visit with a gift," "Your child dies" or "You come upon a pig that has been dead a long time"), which then had to be matched with photographs of white Americans with facial expressions of what he proposed are the six universal emotions: happy, sad, fear, anger, surprise and disgust. In virtually every culture, from contemporary Japan to South American primitive tribes, they recognized these emotions.[4] Even stronger evidence that smiling is part of a universal human response is that babies that are born deaf and blind will spontaneously smile — even though they have never seen a smile.[5] So "happiness," in a smiley kind of way, is an intrinsic human emotion.

But *empowered* is not an intrinsic emotion with a specific facial expression. The phenomenological feeling of territory dovetails with feeling *empowered*, which does provoke many psychological changes, but these vary from situation to situation. Although territory is not one single homogeneous emotion, it does have emotional correlates.

Which emotions?

That depends.

The next four chapters explain exactly what it depends on. This chapter showed all the clashing trajectories that social territory can impart to your inner experience.

---

1 Happiness is a rather thorny adjective for scientists because philosophers often define happiness based on having a good life (rather than the momentary pleasure of just having eaten a chocolate bar). Among scientists, the longer-term happiness that is partly based on your assessment of your own life is called "Subjective Well Being." The temporary state of happiness (from music or chocolate bars) is (rather amazingly) referred to by scientists as *happiness*, but to avoid ambiguity I have chosen to call it cheerfulness, which has no connotations of deep philosophical assessment.

2 Ekman P & Friesen WV (1971). Constants across cultures in the face and emotion. *Journal of Personality and Social Psychology*, 17: 124-129.

3 Ekman P & Friesen WV (1971). Constants across cultures in the face and emotion. *Journal of Personality and Social Psychology*, 17: 124-129.

4 Most tribes recognized nearly all of the emotions, but there were exceptions. In Papua New Guinea the Fore tribe could not distinguish fear from surprise.

5 Eibl-Eibesfeldt I (1973). The expressive behavior of the deaf-and-blind born. In von Cranach M & Vine I (Eds.), *Social communication and movement*. London: Academic Press, 163-194.

But which of them will be your actual response to the music? Chapter three shows it depends on your memories and associations. Chapter four shows it depends on the essence of the music. Chapter 5 shows it depends on your personality. And Chapter 6 shows it depends on the context and your mood.

CHAPTER 3. WHY DO SOME PEOPLE LOVE BEETHOVEN AND OTHERS RAP MUSIC?

YOUR RESPONSE TO MUSIC DEPENDS ON YOUR MENTAL ASSOCIATIONS TO IT

> I don't like country music, but I don't mean to denigrate those who do. And for the people who like country music, denigrate means 'put down'.
> — Bob Newhart, television actor and comedian, b. 1929

Pleasurable and unpleasurable music have different effects on the brain, which can be visualized using brain scanning[1] In the last two decades, there have been extraordinary advances in imaging the brain in living people that have allowed scientists to see the brain *at work*.[2] Previous to this, brain scanning could show the shape and size

---

1 Blood AJ, Zatorre RJ, Bermudez P, Evans AC (1999). Emotional responses to pleasant and unpleasant music correlate with activity in paralimbic brain regions. *Nature Neuroscience* 2(4):382-7.

2 The generic term "brain scanning" will be used for PET scanning (Positron Emission Tomography) and fMRI (functional Magnetic Resonance Imaging). Although PET scanning has been around since the 1950s, the revolution in brain science has resulted from the higher resolution data from fMRI that has come about since the early 1990s. Older technologies used for anatomical studies of the brain, such as CAT scans (computer-aided tomography) and MRI scans, could only reveal the structure of the brain but not what parts were active. The effects of music on the brain are often tested with PET scanning because fMRI involves a magnet that makes loud clunking noises — even so, some studies use fMRI with music by carefully timing the observations of the brain to occur when the equipment is quiet. A disadvantage of PET compared to fMRI is that PET is less able to distinguish between nearby regions — PET is said to have a lower resolution. fMRI measures brain activity by determining how much blood is flowing in each part of the brain — theoretically increased brain activity will increase the need for oxygen and nutrients to that region and the nearby blood vessels will expand slightly

of the various parts of the brain; while this was useful for recognizing cancers in the brain, large wounds, and deterioration occurring with Alzheimer's, the overall shape of the brain is not changed at all by a single non-medical event, no matter how emotionally significant the event may seem. However, although emotional experiences are not associated with structural changes in the brain, the mental activity they elicit leads to increased blood flow to the active regions of the brain, to nourish them during their increased need for glucose. In the last 20 years science has learned to measure these small functional changes in the brain, so that for a given stimulus or activity, a map of the brain can be made showing which regions become active. This is very useful for scientists who are interested in the geography of the brain.

However, even for people not interested in the brain's geography, this information can hint at how music leads to pleasure. Functional brain imaging allows scientists to make an argument by analogy about how music does what it does. Each new study of functional brain imaging adds another entry into the global atlas of how each region in the brain behaves — as if we were creating a dictionary for the regions of the brain. When we detect the most active brain regions during pleasurable music, we can then "look up" what they do by finding what other activities result in similar brain scanning results. Depending on which regions of the brain light up during music, we can argue that music elicits at least some similar brain function with these other activities that also activate the same places in the brain. For example, music invariably stimulates a brain region called the primary auditory cortex; other activities known to activate the primary auditory cortex include hearing white noise, listening to speech and hearing a tone — all of which involve hearing sound. Furthermore, if the primary auditory cortex is damaged on both sides of the brain by stroke or is incorrectly formed during embryonic development, the person will be deaf and hear nothing. This is an example of how brain scanning shows that music involves hearing, much like listening to words, white noise or a tone.

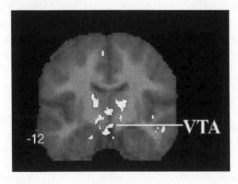

Figure 3.1 - Response to pleasurable music. Black regions indicate regions of specific activity. From Menon V. and Levitin D. (2005). Neuroimage 28:175

But music is more than sound — it is organized sound, deliberately created to elicit responses in listeners, and if we search more deeply, music shares its effects on the brain with other, more provocative, stimuli. For example, scientists at the Montreal Neurological

---

in diameter to allow for increased blood flow. Blood and Zatorre used PET scanning to determine regional blood flow in the brain by injecting a radioactive tracer ([^{15}O] H$_2$O) into the blood; this is quite an achievement, as the half-life of the radioactive oxygen is about 2 minutes, so it has to be manufactured on site with a medical cyclotron and injected immediately into the experimental participant.

Institute found that pleasurable music stimulates a pleasure center in the brain called the VTA (ventral tegmental area), which is often associated with addiction (see Figure 3.1);[1] the VTA is buried quite deep in a primitive part of the brain called the midbrain, and it motivates actions at a very "animal" level. When heroin addicts inject themselves with heroin, the VTA is especially active (see figure 3.2).[2] When coke addicts inject themselves with cocaine, their VTA also gets its jollies.[3] Obviously cocaine and heroin lead to dramatically different experiences: one is a stimulant, the other is a depressant. Presumably, they both share one feature; scientists surmise this has to do with reward, the feeling that "this is a good thing and I want to do more of it."

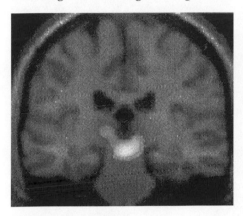

Figure 3.2 - Brain response to heroin. The bright white area indicates a region of specific activity (in this case, the VTA). From Sell LA (1999). Eur J Neurosci 11:1042

Stimulation of the VTA is not limited to illicit drugs. In an extraordinary series of experiments in the Netherlands, scientists researched which areas in the brain respond to ejaculation.[4] The process involved having men come into the scanner laboratory with their partners; the men were not allowed to self-stimulate because the motor areas of the brain are activated whenever an individual makes or plans a movement, which would have resulted in many spurious brain responses that are not intrinsic to ejaculation *per se* — and this would have invalidated the measurements. So, while their heads were inside the

1 Blood AJ, Zatorre RJ (2001). Intensely pleasurable responses to music correlate with activity in brain regions implicated in reward and emotion. *Proceedings of the National Academy of Sciences, USA.* 98(20):11818-11823. In fact, they could not be certain that the VTA *per se* was active because the resolution of PET scanning is not accurate enough. Broadly speaking, they observed the activity in the left dorsomedial midbrain, which would include the VTA, and thus their data is consistent with the VTA being active. They found many elements of the brain's reward system to be activated, and although their resolution was not good enough to specifically demonstrate that the other main reward centre, the Nucleus accumbens, was active, it too was within a region that was indicated by their PET scanning study, the left ventral striatum. A more recent paper that shows the VTA is active during pleasurable music is Menon V, Levitin DJ (2005). The rewards of music listening: response and physiological connectivity of the mesolimbic system. *Neuroimage.* 28(1):175-84.

2 Sell LA, Morris J, Bearn J, Frackowiak RS, Friston KJ, Dolan RJ (1999). Activation of reward circuitry in human opiate addicts. *European Journal of Neuroscience* 11: 1042-1048.

3 Breiter HC, Gollub RL, Weisskoff RM, Kennedy DN et al. (1997). Acute effects of cocaine on human brain activity and emotion. *Neuron* 19: 591-611.

4 Holstege G, Georgiadis JR, Paans AM, Meiners LC, van der Graaf FH, Reinders AA (2003). Brain activation during human male ejaculation. *Journal of Neuroscience* 23: 9185-9193.

brain scanner, the men were manually stimulated by their partners until orgasm was achieved. (As an experimentalist I can imagine the difficulty in recruiting human volunteers for such a study, and I suspect this would have made the study nearly impossible to do anywhere but Holland). The VTA was activated during ejaculation (Figure 3.3).

Figure 3.3 - Male brain during orgasm. The white region (arrow) indicates specific activity. From Holstege G (2003). J Neurosci 23: 9185

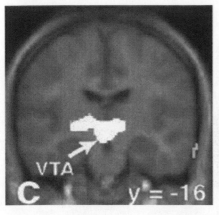

The Netherlands group did not stop with male orgasm. The female orgasm was even more interesting because they compared real orgasms to faked orgasms.[1] The women's partners were not told which was which, and when asked to guess, women readers will not be surprised to learn that the men were no better than random chance at determining what was real and what was not. By contrast, the scanner easily distinguished the two kinds of female orgasm, as the fake orgasms were not accompanied by activity in the VTA. Activity in the VTA is quite revealing about what makes people feel reward, and the VTA is active when people hear and enjoy music. The pleasure pathway in the brain activated by pleasurable music is also important during the action of cocaine and heroin injection, as well as during orgasm.

The problem with trying to measure a *composite* of what pleasure does to the brain when people listen to pleasurable music is that each experimental subject has a different idea of what pleasure is — the pleasure that a fist-pumping metal head feels is nothing like the pleasure that an opera fan feels when they close their eyes and revel in an aria. To maximize their ability to detect any change that was consistent among all the experimental volunteers, scientists at the Montreal Neurological Institute chose to use music that provokes an unambiguous sort of pleasure. Have you ever listened to a piece of music and felt shivers run down your spine or sensed the hair on the back of your neck standing on end? It is a common experience, although when I survey young audiences about half of them have never felt it; the people who do feel it describe the sensation as intensely pleasurable. This strong physiological response is called *chills* or *frisson*, and it causes an increase in heart rate as well as an increase in breathing depth.[2] Although the musical features that causes this (an "unprepared" harmony or sudden

1 Georgiadis JR, Kortekaas R, Kuipers R, Nieuwenburg A, Pruim J, Reinders AA, Holstege G. (2006). Regional cerebral blood flow changes associated with clitorally induced orgasm in healthy women. *European Journal of Neuroscience* 24(11): 3305-16.

2 Blood AJ, Zatorre RJ (2001). Intensely pleasurable responses to music correlate with activity in brain regions implicated in reward and emotion. *Proceedings of the National Academy of Sciences, USA.* 98(20): 11818-11823.

changes in dynamics and texture[1]) are recognized, the precise pieces of music that cause chills are different for every person, so much so that in the study at the Montreal Neurological Institute the "control music" (which did *not* cause chills) used for each subject was the chills music provided by one of the other experimental subjects. This illustrates how the feelings elicited by music result from a complex and personal mixture of the features of the music (e.g., tempo, rhythm) and your individual mental associations to the music (see Figure 3.4), most of which momentarily traverse the mind below the level of conscious thought.

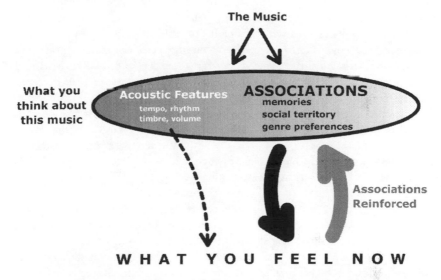

Figure 3.4 - Music influences what you feel via mental associations. Note that the thoughts evoked by the music do not necessarily reach conscious awareness. The acoustic features (e.g., tempo) will also have an effect on your emotions (thin dashed arrow), but this will be substantially less than those feelings evinced by genre preferences, memories and social territory (thick black arrow). Note that associations can be reinforced (thick grey arrow) by your current feelings being added to your associations with this music.

As shown in the diagram, the way you feel about an extract of music you are listening to depends on how you *think* about the music (the oval in the figure). What you "think" refers mostly to unconscious thinking, not deliberative thinking. When you hear music there may be fleeting memories, an image popping into your mind, or an unconscious association with a person you know. Sometimes your associations will include specific memories from the past. Our mental associations are powerful emotional connections that we make between a piece of music and what we experienced when we once heard it; these feelings are often highly personal and idiosyncratic — for every set of lovers, the words "they're playing our song" refers to a different song.

1 Sloboda JA (1991). Musical structure and emotional response: Some empirical findings. *Psychology of Music*, 19,110-120

A filmed example of using mental associations to music in order to elicit emotions is in *A Clockwork Orange*: the violent antihero Alex is scientifically "re-educated" to avoid violence. He is repeatedly forced to watch filmed scenes of violence while being administered a drug that makes him feel wretched, such that thereafter whenever he sees ultraviolence, he would re-experience the sick feeling of the drug. This kind of training by association was first made famous by Pavlov on dogs,[1] although such a deliberate use of Pavlovian punishment in humans would be considered unethical. In the story, as an unanticipated effect of the treatment, the music accompanying the violent films (Beethoven's Ninth Symphony) also provokes the distressing feelings originally caused by the drug; this reaction to Beethoven's Ninth allows Alex's enemies to torture him using this music. The film ends with the doctors reversing the training by performing brain surgery that allows Alex to tolerate (and even enjoy) violence and Beethoven once again. In *A Clockwork Orange*, the mental associations Alex has to Beethoven are considered so emotionally powerful that they are metaphorically compared to brain surgery.

When listening to a song, your brain will also interpret (at an unconscious level) the actual sounds — not just whether it is loud or slow, but whether it is a sonorous French horn or a spooky xylophone (Figure 3.4, dashed line).[2] However, the mental associations you have with a piece of music will usually dominate your emotional response, trumping whatever feelings might be suggested by the acoustic features. I find this situation arises in my lecture demonstrations whenever we play Henry Mancini's theme from The Pink Panther. If you listen to that music with fresh ears, it is quite furtive and ominous, which is what you would expect. The Pink Panther movie is about a jewelry heist, and you can hear sneakiness in the theme tune. The way it does that is by sharing many features with suspenseful music from horror films: it is slow and staccato, yet there is a lot of extreme variation, such as when the melody suddenly becomes louder, speeds up, gets higher in pitch and even turns into vibrato. Nevertheless, when I lecture to audiences with live musicians playing this melody, no one finds the music apprehensive. Mostly people just giggle, probably because they remember that cartoon of a spindly pink panther doing a dance that looks like the hula hula.

***

1 The precise nature of the training could be disputed. Pavlov, whose work concerns classical conditioning, simply associates a new stimulus or cue for an extant cue that leads to an emotional or physiological response (i.e., the drug is the extant cue, the new cue is violence, the natural response to the drug is nausea, and now the violent stimulus leads to the nausea). Later work by behaviorists using what is now described as instrumental conditioning involves changing behavior (or shaping new behaviors) by rewarding or punishing behaviors. In the case of Clockwork Orange, although the ultimate result was behavior change, the direct result was that the new stimulus led passively to a feeling, i.e. classical conditioning.

2 As opposed to associations determining your taste in music, Dan Levitin speculates that the physiology of the ear plays a role in musical preference: "Pitch can also play into preference. Some people can't stand the thumping low beats of modern hip-hop, others can't stand what they describe as the high-pitched whininess of violins. Part of this may be a matter of physiology; literally, different ears may transmit different parts of the frequency spectrum, causing some sounds to appear pleasant and others aversive." Levitin D (2006). *This is your brain on music: The science of a human obsession.* New York: Dutton.

In 1976 Beethoven's fifth symphony was transmogrified into a 3-minute disco monster hit called "A Fifth of Beethoven"; this danceable classic, which reached number one on the Billboard Hot 100, was played over and over in discotheques as well as appearing in the film *Saturday Night Fever*.[1] One can assume that the majority of listeners were familiar with the original classical piece as well as the funked-up version. However, if we do a thought experiment of what would have happened at a New York disco in 1977 if the DJ had played the classically instrumented version of Beethoven's Fifth Symphony instead of the discofied adaptation, we could guess that there would have been rebellion and chaos amongst the dancers.

Similarly, the choice of instrumentation could define musical territory in Northern Ireland during the troubles. In musicology circles there is a recorded example of a guitarist who tried to contribute to a music evening at a Gaelic Athletics Association, but he was frozen out; he persevered, whereupon he was asked to leave immediately because the guitar was not an Irish instrument. Eventually he did leave, but apparently not fast enough. The next day he was attacked by masked men, and his left hand was mutilated with an axe.[2] This gruesome tale illustrates more than that the guitar is unaccepted in Irish music sessions; when music is used to define what is supposed to happen in a territory, there are rules about the instruments used and the sounds they should make. Liking music seems to be related to territory, and territory appears to be very quickly expressed by particular sounds.

However, liking or disliking a piece of music depends on some attributes of the sounds that are essential to any sounds, not just to music. For example, weapons creating extreme loudness can cause nosebleeds, as well as pain, headaches and confusion. The US armed forces "soften the enemy" using Long Range Acoustic Devices (LRADs), which are capable of projecting a meter-wide "strip of sound" that is intelligible at 1,000 meters at sea, with a maximum loudness of 151 decibels; these LRADs can be used directionally to project deterrent tones at the enemy that confuse them and cause them to move (and become vulnerable), as if they were hit by a smoke bomb. Although deterrent tones are provided by the manufacturer, young US soldiers have their own MP3 players and are allowed to select music with which to attack the enemy.[3] Loudness is scientifically observed to be one of the most important determinants in how people respond to music.[4]

---

1 The song was performed by Walter Murphy and his Big Apple Band, and it reached the number one single spot on 9 October 1976. The song later was used in the sound track to the movie Saturday Night Fever, and it was voted into the top 100 on Billboard's Greatest Songs of All Time.

2 Stokes M (1994). Introduction. In Stokes, M. (ed.) *Ethnicity, Identity and Music: The Musical construction of Place*. Oxford: Berg Publishers.

3 See Cusick SG (2006). Music as torture / Music as weapon. *TRANS Revista transcultural de Música*. Number 10. Barcelona: Sociedad de Etnomusicología. For the manufacturer of LRADs, see www.LRADX.com

4 Gregory AH (1998). Tracking the emotional response to operatic arias. In Yi SW (ed.), *Proceedings of the Fifth International Conference of Music Perception and Cognition*. Seoul, Korea: Western Music Research Institute, College of Music, Seoul National University.

The tempo of a piece of music is the next most important feature of whether it is liked, although this begs the question of whether it has a steady rhythm at all.[1] The rhythm of the piece is often referred to as its pulse, with the other meaning of the word *pulse* (the listener's heart rate) suggesting that heart rate and tempo should be related. Although now discredited, during the 1970s it was proclaimed that the perfect tempo for dance music was 120 beats per minute, which was twice the resting human heart rate.[2]

The color and texture of a sound, its timbre, can also determine whether the sound is enjoyable or aversive. For example, many people find the noise created by scraping chalk down a blackboard to be abhorrent, although the cause of this remains contested by scientists;[3] in fact most of the emotional effects of timbre remain poorly understood.[4] The timbre of the human voice and its singing are the most pivotal features determining how people feel about music because the voice naturally calls attention to itself.[5] In Western music often the most popular form of music *on average* is really just popular music that irritates the least number of people; the least common denominator of taste is music that does *not* call attention to itself, so-called "easy listening."[6]

This idea bore fruit in 1922. Shortly before retiring from the US Army, its Chief Signal Officer Major General George Squier decided to create Wired Radio, a pioneering communications service that "piped in" programs of recorded music to businesses and subscribers. His simple conviction, that music makes people feel better, was aligned with a simple quest: to break the silence of workplaces and businesses. In 1934, the year of his death, Squier combined "music" with the made-up name of a company he admired,

---

1 Often when discussing "essential" preferences for certain kinds of music, I refer to the literature on children's preferences because they have less sophisticated tastes and have had less time to learn idiosyncratic preferences. For an example of a preference for fast tempos, see LeBlanc A, Cote R (1983). Effects of Tempo and Performing Medium on Children's Music Preference. *Journal of Research in Music Education* 31: 57-66.

2 Musical tempo does not usually match the heart rate of dancers. The tempo of dance music has been seen to change over the decades, particularly becoming faster since the 1960s. In addition, comparatively few individuals have a resting heart rate as low as 60 bpm; furthermore, dancers are not "at rest," and with few exceptions, most songs and dance styles will not raise the dancers' heart rates as high as 120 bpm.

3 Compare these two opposing articles: Halpern L, Blake R, & Hillenbrand J (1986). Psychoacoustics of a chilling sound. *Perception and Psychophysics*. Psychonomic Society. pp. 77–80. Cox TJ (2008), Scraping sounds and disgusting noises. *Applied Acoustics*, 69(12): 1195-1204.

4 In the last 20 years William Sethares's research on timbre has overturned much of traditional music theory that has been accepted as consensus since Helmholtz in Victorian times; Sethares has shown convincingly that consonance and dissonance are a function of timbre and overtone, rather than just of pitch. He has demonstrated that with specific overtone series that octaves can be dissonant while traditionally dissonant intervals (e.g. the 7th) can be consonant. Sethares W (1992). "Relating Tuning and Timbre." *Experimental Musical Instruments* IX (2).

5 Gregory AH (1998). Tracking the emotional response to operatic arias. In Yi SW (ed.), *Proceedings of the Fifth International Conference of Music Perception and Cognition*. Seoul, Korea: Western Music Research Institute, College of Music, Seoul National University.

6 LeBlanc A (1979). Generic Style Music Preferences of Fifth-Grade Students. *Journal of Research in Music Education* 27: 255-270.

"Kodak," to re-brand his brainchild — and the legendary Muzak was born. In its forma-
tive years Muzak gained a reputation as a provider of so-called elevator music, used to
ease the fears of early skyscraper users. Since then is has developed into a multinational
brand, used by organizations and businesses across the world to both pacify and alleviate the boredom of their patrons, being in equal parts recognizable, soothing and hated.[1]

People are extremely fast and accurate at interpreting and responding to music. It
is possible to demonstrate that listeners can respond to the tiniest fragment of a piece
of music and this response occurs in a fraction of a second. I have done this with work-
shops, where I have run exercises that presented tiny snippets of five very different recordings of music (varying from a William Orbit dance classic to Tchaikovsky's *Dance of
the Sugar Plum Fairies*). If you ask people to rate whether they like each piece or not, they
will have no opinion if the music is only 250 milliseconds long (one quarter of a second),
but if the music lasts just half a second, people will not only be able to form opinions,
but these opinions will be nearly identical to the opinions they will have if they listen to
enough of the piece to recognize it.

The ear's fast recognition and response makes sense evolutionarily. Timbre is the
key to survival.[2] Timbre is what lets you recognize your mother's voice from a stranger's.
It also lets you know if she is going to help you or scold you. The timbre of a sound is the
first part of a sound to be recognized, and to be judged. For a baby that instantaneous
judgment is effectively territorial; the voice of any member of the family means all is
safe, but the noise of potential predator means danger. Besides volume, people will be
more influenced by timbre than any other intrinsic feature of the music. Consider the
following thought experiment: you are trained to make music by smashing glass bottles
on rocks. Each bottle makes the correct pitch as you break it, and you can use a music
tape editor to align the sounds so you produce a perfect, consonant tune. Yet, most
people would find such glass-breaking music irritating, despite the pleasant melody.
The instrumentation shapes the initial emotional response to the music, while melodies
often need time for features like the major or minor mode to unfold; just as the timbral
quality of natural sound rapidly identifies whose territory it is (e.g., a mother's voice),
the instrumentation of a musical piece is often the most territorial aspect of music because it is so rapidly recognizable. But this still leaves unanswered how people choose a
musical territory in the first place: how can teenagers choose their musical tastes based
on their peer group, when they choose their peer group based on their musical tastes?

***

---

1 For example, comedienne Lily Tomlin once said, "I worry that the person who thought
  up Muzak may be thinking up something else." There is an international organization
  "PipeDown" (The Campaign for Freedom Against Piped Music) that organizes legal
  "but witty" protests against piped music.
2 Timbre is not only important in distinguishing individuals, but also in recognizing
  sounds in nature. There is an entire interpretive practice called timbral listening, in
  which perceiving the texture and color of music and sound is valued equally to detecting pitch and harmony, i.e., the timbre of the sounds is as important as the notes. This
  is most relevant when considering some non-western music such as the throat singing of Tuva. See Süzükei V (2006). Listening The Tuvan Way. In Levin T (ed.), *Where
  Rivers and Mountains Sing: Sound, Music and Nomadism in Tuva and Beyond*. Bloomington: Indiana University Press.

The composer and virtuoso pianist Frédéric Chopin (1810–1849) had a personality that wallowed in resignation. He fell in love while on a trip to Germany with Maria Wodzińska, the daughter of a family friend.[1] A year later he made another trip from Paris to Germany and asked for Maria's hand in marriage. Maria agreed, but Maria's mother insisted on delaying the announcement until Maria's father (then in Poland) could bless the engagement. Back in Paris, Chopin waited. Weeks, months, finally over a year passed, when Maria's mother notified him that the relationship was to be stopped. Chopin collected Maria's letters to him in an envelope, wrapped it with a red ribbon, and labeled the packet, "Moja bieda": my sorrow. As Chopin himself said, "I wish I could throw off the thoughts which poison my happiness. And yet I take a kind of pleasure in indulging them."

Many people have favorite kinds of emotions (or emotional combinations) they like to feel, and that theme will be recapitulated throughout this book.[2] For the purpose of understanding why people like a particular song, it is sufficient to accept that every person will prefer a particular mix of emotions; later this book will answer the question *why*. These favorite emotions will often manifest in the preference for a particular music genre. Take the genre *Doom Metal* as an example: it is exaggeratedly depressive, often slow and minimalist, but can be ugly and heavy or sometimes melodic and sorrowful.[3] The archetype doom metal album is Candlemass's sardonically entitled *Epicus Doomicus Metallicus* (1986).[4] According to one webzine article by an aficionado, "Doom metal is made for those beings that are overly sensitive and depressed, and aren't doing anything about it"; the writer then provides a tongue-in-cheek introduction to the topic:

> I was initially going to write an introduction describing how I first en-countered doom metal many moons ago, and how the music has affected my life and so on; but I won't, because none of you would care. No, not a single one of you cold-hearted people would give a damn. So I'll just go sit alone in my corner, thinking about life and the state of this bleak world and listen-ing to some doom metal — and you can write this damn article yourselves if you want.[5]

The ironic and "twisted" tone of these comments cloaks their candor — being de-pressed is somewhat looked down upon, especially in extreme metal circles; these con-current emotions of melancholy and sarcasm are a powerful amalgam and are very much in keeping with the feelings of doom metal music. Likewise, Chopin's understated ego was very much in keeping with his piano playing, which was described as being so quiet

---

1 Szulc T (1998). *Chopin in Paris: the Life and Times of the Romantic Composer.* New York: Scribner.
2 See the chapters on sad music, aggressive music and violent music.
3 See Kahn-Harris K (2002). "I hate this fucking country": Dealing with the global and the local in the Israeli extreme metal scene. In Young R (ed.) *Music, Popular Cul-ture, Identities.* Amsterdam: Rodopi BV, pp. 133-152. See also Azevedo P (2006). Doom Metal: The Gentle Art of Making Misery. *Chronicles of Chaos* webzine. Accessed on 22 March 2010; www.chroniclesofchaos.com
4 Some would say that Black Sabbath is the progenitor of doom metal; however, the genre did not formally exist back in the 1960s.
5 See Azevedo P (2006). Doom Metal: The Gentle Art of Making Misery. *Chronicles of Chaos* webzine. accessed on 22 March 2010; www.chroniclesofchaos.com

---

that it was difficult to hear in the otherwise silent concert halls. Is this link between quietness and sad resignation idiosyncratic to Chopin (and sometimes Doom Metal), or is it a universal for human listeners? As shown with the loud LRAD weapons, loudness can contribute to whether a piece of music is liked or aversive, but is there something about quietness, or any acoustic features of music, that universally expresses a particular emotion, such as sadness?

To test this, in 2008 scientists went to Cameroon to expose members of an isolated tribe to Western music for the first time. The Mafa ethnic group live in the Extreme North in the Mandara mountain range, in settlements that lack electricity. They are culturally isolated because of the pervasiveness of malaria and other diseases, and many of the Mafa live traditionally and have never heard Western music.[1] After listening to Western piano music and being asked to choose whether the music was happy, sad or scary, the Mafa scored significantly above chance for all three emotions, showing that there is a universal understanding of emotions evinced by the Western music in their experiments. However, this is less impressive than it sounds: keeping in mind that 33% should have recognized the sad music by random chance, the Mafa were able to identify the sad music "correctly" less than 50% of the time, while Westerners doing the same experiment recognized the right emotion over 90% of the time.

So these universal sounds of sadness in Western music may be statistically significant, but there are other cues in the music that confound the detection of sadness for the Mafa. Can we identify the central elements in this universal language of sad music? The question is especially complex, given that sadness is not a homogeneous emotion but manifests itself many ways, ranging from restless torment to listless depression. Nevertheless, stereotypical sad music will have many recognizable acoustic features; it will be slow, quiet, and mostly low in pitch — much like a depressed person's voice. Much has been made of the fact that sad music tends to be legato (the opposite of staccato), having long notes with no breaks between them, like the sound of a motorcycle advancing through its gears. Sad music will be monotonous, not in the sense of boring, but in the way the sounds do not vary much; it will be consistent in volume, and the music will stick near the same pitch, not moving around very quickly. One way Samuel Barber's *Adagio for Strings* expresses sadness, particularly the sluggish sorrow of loss and finality, is to have individual chords that start very quietly and get fuller over time. However, in Western music theory, the apotheosis of sadness is playing in the minor key. But is the sadness of the minor key in some way essential to music — and is it recognized innately?

As the study of the Mafa in Cameroon shows, scientists and their methods have become increasingly sophisticated in order to determine whether music can communicate emotions in a consistent way. The first big, well-controlled study for that question was based on selecting adjectives on a questionnaire. In the 1930s the pioneering music psychologist and feminist, Dr Kate Hevner (1898–1984) was the first academic to conduct systematically controlled experiments to measure emotional responses to complete pieces of music, and her test for measuring music appreciation became a standard

---

1 Fritz T, Jentschke S, Gosselin N, Sammler D, Peretz I, Turner R, Friederici A & Koelsch S (2009). Universal Recognition of Three Basic Emotions in Music. *Current Biology*, 19(7): 573-576.

for many years. Without being able to record her music, the real challenge was simply rendering the music in the days before MIDI and computer controlled music synthesizers; the pieces had to be played live by a specially trained pianist who had to *avoid* any musical elements of emotional expression.

To systematically measure the emotional impact of the minor key, Hevner measured responses of over two hundred college sophomores to excerpts of live music played by her trained pianist; these excerpts were identical to one another except for the major or minor mode.[1] She then asked the students to select adjectives from a long list to describe what they had just heard — from "sad" to "happy," "serene" to "agitated," "clownish" to "grotesque" (Figure 3.5).

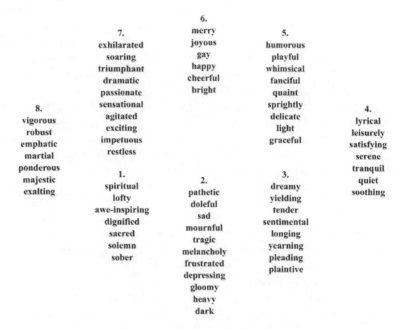

Figure 3.5 - Kate Hevner's "Adjective Circle," (1936). This was used to measure and categorize the subjective emotional responses of experimental subjects to music. It foreshadows emotional descriptions based on one axis of high to low arousal (from group 8 to group 4) and from negative to positive valence (from group 2 to group 6).

Hevner's result was that even when people were from different backgrounds and social classes, most *do* think music is sadder when it is played in a minor key.[2]

1 Hevner K (1936). Experimental studies of the elements of expression in music. *American Journal of Psychology*, 48: 246-268.
2 Sad music was strongly associated with the minor key, but the word most strongly associated with the minor key in Hevner's original study was "pathetic." Hevner K (1936). Experimental studies of the elements of expression in music. *American Journal of Psychology*, 48: 246-268.

In Hevner's study she measured the relationship between different notes (i.e., composition) and the listener's response, but other studies have tested how simply the performance can communicate emotions; musicians can play the same notes but change *how* they play the notes. In one example guitarists were asked to play 4 different versions of *Greensleeves*: sad, happy, angry and fearful; these recordings were then rated by listeners who did not know the desired emotion.[1] The result was that the listeners were successful at decoding the various performances' emotional goals, and that sadness was definitely slower and more legato than other performances. Thus, there are musical features that can communicate specific emotions, and Hevner showed that the minor mode is one of them, but is it innate?

The primacy of the fast timbral responses belies the idea that the emotional differences between minor and major are innate. Kate Hevner's study said they were, but all her subjects were university students in Minnesota. Are we *born* thinking that music in the minor key is sad? The answer is "No," according to Simone Dalla Bella, whose 2001 experiment employed the inexperienced and unbiased minds of young children. Dalla Bella and his colleagues gathered an assortment of three- to eight-year-olds and played them excerpts of music that had been made to sound happy or sad by adjusting the mode, swapping from major to minor key. They found that while six- to eight-year-olds could use the mode to discriminate between happy and sad songs, the five-year-olds' judgments were not affected by whether the piece was in a major or a minor key. Children are not born with this understanding; they must *learn* it. In fact, many of the emotional cues in music that we seem to "just know" are actually learned unconsciously by listening to music in context — nobody needs to be told that that stage diving is more appropriate at a punk gig than at a Mozart recital.

The difference between major and minor, like stage diving, is an example of a learned association; by contrast, it is innate to associate high pitched screeching with being helpless or thwarted. People learn implicitly by generalizing: you understand that stage diving can happen with any punk band, not just *The Sex Pistols*. This ability to generalize explains how most of the associations we learn about music are not rigidly attached to specific songs; the associations are more general and act like language. These generic associations are what make up the acoustic features of sad music — slow tempo, monotonous, and low pitches. These do not seem arbitrarily chosen. They resemble the acoustic features of the sad voice. The broader question of whether the acoustic features of all emotions in music are analogous with those of the voice has been pursued vigorously by academics. Patrik Juslin, a music psychologist in Uppsala, has written a 45 page review of the topic, with one table presenting an overview of 41 different academic studies that related to this question.[2] In a nutshell, the voice and music seem to express emotions in similar ways.

---

1 Juslin PN (2000). Cue Utilization in Communication of Emotion in Music Performance: Relating Performance to Perception. *Journal of Experimental Psychology* 26(6): 1797-1813.

2 Juslin PN & Laukka P (2003). Communication of Emotions in Vocal Expression and Music Performance: Different Channels, Same Code? *Psychological Bulletin* 129(5): 770–814.

This implies that the way sad music moves us is based on the evolutionarily con-
served acoustic features that the voice uses to express sadness. However, not all acoustic features in music are created equal: some you are born with, some you have to learn.
The innate acoustic features are the ones you can control as a performer: tempo, volume,
timbre. We might call those *vocal* (or universal) features, whereas the ones you have
to learn are harmony, tonality or melodic progression — *musical* acoustic features.[1] Not
only do musical features like the minor key take children longer to learn, but they take
longer to recognize when you hear them. We typically respond in a split second to vocal
features, especially timbre; our instantaneous response to a piece of music is based on
the *mixture* of instruments and voices for a piece of music — whether an opera or Swiss
yodeling — that coalesces into a timbral signature.

***

Every piece of music seems to have an emotional signature that is so intuitive that
it can create overpowering feelings, as if the acoustic features could control your emotions. For example, the musical ingredients of the infamous *Jaws* theme-tune, composed
by the multi-Oscar-winner John Williams, were deliberately contrived to produce fear.
In 1975, Steven Spielberg climbed to stardom after unleashing *Jaws* on an unsuspect-
ing public. The opening scene was of such visceral power that the US population took
the film's poster tagline "Don't Go In the Water" quite literally. This opening scene,
which began as a point-of-view shot of an underwater creature moving swiftly to the
surface followed by a skinny-dipper being ravaged by a shark, was accompanied by a
custom-made score containing all the musical features necessary to build up menace
and suspense.

And it worked: On July 11ᵗʰ 1975 the *New York Times* ran the headline "Impact of 'Jaws'
has Anglers and Bathers on the Lookout."[2] *Time* magazine added "formerly bold swim-
mers now huddle in groups a few yards offshore." The film is also said to have caused a
shark-fishing craze along the East Coast of the US, which dramatically reduced nearly
all shark species over the next three decades.[3] Spielberg has stated that Williams' ter-
rifying score is largely to account for the commercial success of *Jaws*.[4] The score consists
of a slowly alternating pattern of two notes (E and F) followed by suspense-induc-

---

1 The words that have been formally used in the music literature are 'segmental' for
   vocal/universal acoustic features such as timbre and tempo and "suprasegmental" for
   musical features such as harmony and melody; for the purposes of this book I have
   used the more intuitive terms listed. For the formal academic argument, see Scherer
   KR, Zentner MR (2001). "Emotional effects of music: production rules" in Juslin PN,
   Sloboda J (eds.) *Music and Emotion: Theory and Research*, Oxford: Oxford University Press.
2 New York Times (1975). "Impact of 'Jaws' Has Anglers and Bathers on Lookout," *New
   York Times*, 11 July.
3 Bistori A (1976). Anglers To Hunt Sharks; Shark Fishing Off the Jersey Coast Shark
   Fishing To Begin Soon. *New York Times*, 23 May.
4 Internet Movie Data Base (1975). Trivia for Jaws. IMDB.com. In Spielberg biog. – also
   in DVD re-release, interview material, 2005. In fact, when John Williams first played
   the infamous theme for his inexperienced director, Steven Spielberg laughed and
   said, "That's funny, John, really. But what did you really have in mind for the theme of
   'Jaws'?"

ing pregnant pauses, a pattern which repeats and speeds up to mirror the audience's mounting trepidation.

The tempo of a piece can have a significant impact on the emotion it induces. The following chart shows how some musical features (e.g., tempo and articulation) correspond to different emotions (see figure 3.6).[1]

The chart suggests that part of the reason that the *Jaws* theme is menacing is because its tempo starts out 'slow'. However, the emotional impression from a musical extract invariably results from the combination of several acoustic features. For example, a slow song could be sad, but it could also be stately, menacing, or bored, depending on the pitch and the articulation of the piece; as with most scary music, the slow tempo of *Jaws* varies, occasionally racing to an eye-popping attack of horns. Another reason that the *Jaws* theme is foreboding is that the notes are *staccato* — brief and disconnected, like the sound of hammering a nail.

Despite all these menacing acoustic features, the music from *Jaws* no longer makes people hide under their blankets. I myself have given numerous public lectures in which live musicians play the *Jaws* theme on a bass clarinet and French horn, but no one in the audience panics. This fugue of fright, that made millions into landlubbers in the 1970s, has *never* inspired fear in any of my audiences — but it does cause smiles and a few snickers every time. The emotion elicited by *Jaws* is amusement.

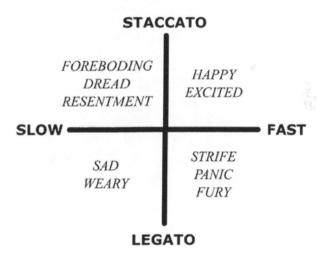

Figure 3.6: How the emotion of a piece of music relates to tempo and articulation.

The following chart (Figure 3.7), which is a more sophisticated version of one shown earlier, illustrates how your emotional response to music depends more on your mental associations than on its acoustic features.

---

1 This is based loosely on Patrik Juslin's work of the early noughties, see: Juslin P (2001). Communicating emotion in musical performance: a review and theoretical framework. In Juslin PN & Sloboda JN (eds). *Music and Emotion: theory and research.* Oxford: Oxford University Press, 309-337.

The mental associations you have with a piece of music may be to a specific memory (your first kiss), or to a specific idea (a National anthem), but mostly your associations will be more general feelings based on your genre preferences. If your territorial associations to a piece of music are very strong, they will swamp out any emotions hinted at by the acoustic features of the music.

What is interesting is how the entire system feeds back on itself (the grey curved arrow in the figure). While associations influence how you feel, how you feel will influence your associations — you might remember Abba songs from a long time ago, but when you dance to them now at a wedding, that new experience also adds to your associations to the song. The way people feel about the theme from Jaws has been influenced by associations to that music that they have gathered over time; the Jaws theme is musically a very menacing piece, but people laugh at it now because they associate that music with a movie about a rubber shark that scared people in the 1970s.

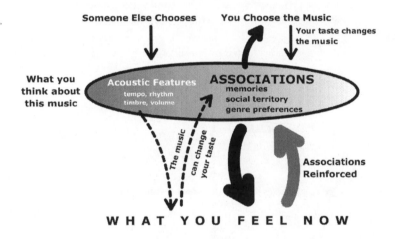

Figure 3.7 - How associations and acoustic features influence what you feel about the music you are listening to. Although associations (including genre preferences) play a larger role than many acoustic features, repeatedly playing music when you feel good can add the sounds of that music to your social territory.

This feedback between feelings and associations complicates our responses to music. Even if you were omniscient and knew all the mental associations that a person might have to a piece of music, it would be difficult to make predictions about what songs that person would like because there are several (often conflicting) influences on how music affects the mind. This is the reason that two different people in the same family can have opposite responses to the same piece of music, and even how the same individual can have different responses to a single piece of music on different days. The emotions you feel toward a piece of music can even change as you listen to it, as I found with "Shuckin' the Corn," a very fast piece of banjo music from the film *Deliverance*. If I play a ten-second excerpt of this song to a lecture-audience, almost everyone will smile — the short excerpt is always found to be amusing, and at the end of it I always shout at my audience "Yeeeeeeeeeeee-Haw!" But when I run experiments and play the entire three minutes of the song, people become really irritated by the end of it. What was once amusing has become increasingly annoying. Presumably the initial amused response is based on just remembering (and feeling superior to) rednecks ("Squeal like a pig!"), but after three minutes we respond by feeling that there has been a territory evoked by the banjo music that is not our own.

By contrast, if you hear a piece of music for the first time, and you have no strong associations with it, your emotions may be most influenced by its acoustic features. Those acoustic features may get associated with how you feel at the time, which, if you *willingly connect* to the experience, can be insidious and may in the long term influence what you think about that kind of music, even changing what genres you like.

I once conducted an experiment where Nokia, who commissioned the study, asked us to measure people's heart rate in response to a selection of songs in order to find "the most exhilarating pop song ever."[1] I had to listen to the songs along with the volunteers, so I had to listen to all the songs over and over again. One track, "Love Machine," was by the UK pop group *Girls Aloud*, a girl-band I dislike almost by default. But I *owned* the experience, because it was *my* experiment, and I was listening to it by choice, so the song battered its way into my head, and I found myself occasionally humming it even after the study ended. I'd been hit by what, in the music industry, is popularly referred to as a *grower*. My response had changed while repeating the same experience of listening to the music even though the song itself hadn't changed.

***

Fania Fénelon, a Parisian cabaret singer and pianist, was sent to Auschwitz in 1944[2] only to be saved from a lonely and degrading death by her extraordinary musical talent; the camp commandant recruited an orchestra from among his women prisoners, allowing them to exist in exchange for making music. As members of the Women's Orchestra, Fénelon and her friends were conscripted to play beautiful, "abominably incongruous" classical music for the amusement of the Nazi guards and, agonizingly, to set the step as their comrades were marched into the gas chambers. She developed an aversion for her beloved *Madame Butterfly* after she was forced to sing it time after time for her captors, the dreaded SS officers — "I reflected that when I got back I wouldn't be able to listen to a single bar of Puccini's work."[3] It was not the particulars of the music itself, nothing intrinsically happy or sad about the melody or rhythm that she hated, but rather it was the events it came to symbolize, its associations. These powerful emotional connections are often highly personal and idiosyncratic — only Fania Fénelon thinks of the Nazis

---

1 Kirby T (2006). If you're happy and you know it, listen to Lily. If not, it's the Verve. *The Independent* newspaper (London, UK), 11 December.
2 She was in the women's camp at Birkenau, which was part of the large Auschwitz complex.
3 Fénelon F, Routier M (1980). *Playing for Time*. English translation of *Sursis pour l'Orchestre* by Landry J. London: Sphere Books.

when she hears Puccini. Even when arbitrary, the mental associations that we make between any song and our memories of past experiences with that song have the power to dredge up intense love or hatred.

The fact that our mental associations can dominate our emotional response to music explains why there are such massive differences in opinion between people, and even in one person over time. People can have a large number of mental associations to a song, and some of them may not even be based on their experiences with the music itself. Consider the sudden unpopularity of James Blunt. At the end of 2005 his number one single "You're Beautiful" suddenly became the UK's favorite wedding song,[1] and by January of 2006 he won "Best International Newcomer" at the NRJ Music Awards, as well as being voted "Best Pop Act" and "Best Male" at the Brit Awards. But then he was denigrated at the NME awards with "Worst Album" later the same year. Essex FM even banned his best-known single from the airwaves, yet nothing in Blunt's music had changed — he had not suddenly gone from writing his heartfelt ballads to writing head-thumpers.[2] What had happened?

In the strange case of James Blunt, his privileged social context played against him. Far from being the "earthy" itinerant songster — the image his clothing portrays — James Hillier Blount was an ex-pupil of the exclusive Harrow School and a former officer in the British Army.[3] When people had originally purchased Blunt's albums, they were buying into the romantic image of a love-sick working class boy who has suffered real hardship serving his country in the front line of the armed forces. When his social background was revealed, the fans felt cheated. Newspaper editors recognized feelings of class animosity and exploited this by publishing articles denouncing his right to success.[4] By the end of the year no one would own up to buying Blunt's album (begging the question of the whereabouts of the 2 million who had done just that!) A stage name, once seen at the top of singles charts everywhere, had become cockney rhyming-slang for the most censored word in the English language in just a matter of months.[5] In a 2006 survey that asked 2,059 people to list the most annoying things about living in the UK, James Blunt was found to be more irritating than traffic wardens, noisy neighbors and real estate agents.

Blunt's heart-rending melodies did not go platinum ten times over just because they were pretty. His best-selling image was that of an ordinary soldier and folksy musician who found success through hard work. People liked Blunt's music because they liked what he *represented*. It took a while before the press realized that he had come from a very well-placed military family and had lived a life of incredible privilege; the fact that his stage name was not his real name, which was posh (Blount), made it seem like he was pretending to be something he wasn't. When people stopped liking *him*, they stopped

---

1 The Sun (2005). *The Sun* (London) newspaper, 5 November.

2 Yahoo music news (2006). English radio station bans James Blunt songs. *Yahoo music news*, 29 May.

3 Hardy P (2006). Me and My Motors, the *Times Online*, 12th February. BBC News (2006). Blunt Words of a Sensitive Soldier, *BBC news online*, 16 February.

4 He was called, "The poshest chap in pop" in The Sun online (2008). Posh Blunt's topless babes. *The Sun* newspaper, 22 July.

5 Online Dictionary of Cockney Rhyming Slang. accessed March 31 2010; http://www.cockneyrhymingslang.co.uk/slang/J /

liking his music. Our *associations* to a piece of music, which dictate our emotional response to it, can be related to our feelings about the artist, independent of our experiences while listening to the music.

UK's Most Annoying Things:

1. Cold callers
2. Caravans
3. Queue-jumpers
4. *James Blunt*
5. Traffic wardens
(Source: Survey by Lactofree)[1]

[1]BBC News (2006) Singer Blunt "irritates public." BBC News, 31 July.

But our emotional responses to music are not based *solely* on our direct associations with the artist. Plainly not everyone who ultimately bought one of the ten million of James Blunt's first album *Back to Bedlam* had previously read one of the ingratiating reviews such as on mp3.com.[1] So those buyers probably did not have any associations with the artist. Perhaps some of them were introduced to Blunt's music by a friend (or by a favorite radio station), and they may have received some pre-existing associations that way, but obviously some people just listened to the music and they liked the sounds they heard. But this begs the question of how a person knows which sounds to like; if people based their preferences on associations, they would have to be carefully introduced to each new song, and if it was based on the acoustic features of the music, people would listen to the same songs forever. How can people like a song they have never heard before, and why would they want to?

***

Koi carp have acute hearing but obviously do not make music. As such, they provide the most vivid example of the process of learning what kind of music to respond to. In the late 1990s Ava Chase, then at Harvard University in Boston, set out to do an experiment showing that her koi carp could be taught to distinguish between classical music and the blues.[2] Chase trained her three pet store koi carp (Cyprinus carpio) named Beauty, Oro, and Pepi,[3] by playing music to them in the apparatus below (see figure 3.8, the underwater speaker is labeled "S"). Using a behavioral technique called *conditioning*[4]

---

1 Monger JC (2005) James blunt. Accessed 31 March 2010; http://www.mp3.com/albums/658343/summary.html

2 Chase AR (2001). Music discriminations by carp (Cyprinus carpio). *Animal Learning & Behavior* 29(4): 336–353.

3 Although originally ordinary Koi carp, Chase did not just go to a shop, buy some fish, and do the experiments. These carp were 7–11 years of age, and she had been doing experiments with them for 5 years prior to this study.

4 The process is technically operant conditioning, which is more recently called instrumental conditioning. Operant conditioning is distinguished from classical conditioning (the famous experiment on Pavlov's dogs) because classical conditioning is

similar to the Pavlovian training mentioned with *Clockwork Orange*, she initially trained her fish to distinguish John Lee Hooker's *Blues Before Sunrise* (vocal and guitar blues) from a collection of Bach's oboe concertos.

The way the training worked is that the fish were rewarded with a food pellet (released from dispenser D and presented to the fish in the nozzle N) if they pressed the button (B in the figure), but only if they pressed the button during John Lee Hooker; they got nothing if it was Bach or silence. Over time, all three fish became incredibly accurate, and they were at least three times more likely to press the button when it was John Lee Hooker. To prove that the training really worked, Chase changed the rules so that only Bach was rewarded, and after 30 training sessions the fish learned the new rule and preferentially pressed the button to Bach.

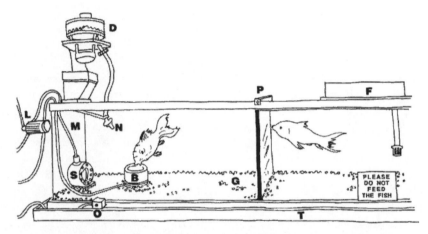

Figure 3.8 - The experimental tank used to train fish to distinguish the blues from classical music. Original image from "Reliable Operant Apparatus for Fish: Audio Stimulus Generator, Response Button, and Pellet-Dispensing Nipple," by AR Chase and W Hill, 1999, Behavior Research Methods, Instruments, & Computers, 31, p. 471. Copyright 1999 by the Psychonomic Society. Reprinted with permission.

The fish may have been able to differentiate the guitar from the oboe, just because of the timbres of the two instruments, so Chase removed most of these acoustic features (especially the timbral cues) by exchanging all the music for versions played on a MIDI keyboard;[1] these are the electric keyboards where with a push of a button you can change the sound the instrument plays from "piano" to "flute." When the music was switched between different synthesized "instrumental" sounds, the fish could still distinguish John Lee Hooker from Bach. Chase then used other classical and blues pieces

---

essentially a passive process, whereas in operant conditioning the animals take action and are rewarded for it.

1   In fact, Chase noted that when she used some Vivaldi guitar concertos the fish had particular trouble, as if they had been identifying the blues based on the presence of the guitar.

that the fish had never heard before, and they still could tell classical from the blues — although Pepi stopped responding completely after Paganini's 24th Caprice for solo violin was played on a MIDI keyboard, so he was excused from the rest of the study. This series of experiments proves that the subtleties of musical genre can be learned by association, even by a fish. Being able to recognizing genre shows that the fish can generalize some aspect of the music. But what is it that fish can generalize?

When we hear a piece of music, there are numerous associations that come into our minds about its genre, many of which are barely related to how the piece sounds. The comedian Dudley Moore achieved a comic effect by subverting the contextual associations we have with the classical music genre. Introduced to the audience in a formal fashion while wearing a tuxedo and sitting at the grand piano with the repose of a maestro, Moore would begin to play what sounded like a Beethoven piano sonata. Expecting a classical melody to match the familiar somber tones and intonations, Moore instead wove in the *Colonel Bogey March*, the famous whistling tune from *The Bridge on the River Kwai*.[1] The audience was presented with the sight and sounds of a pompous concert pianist, playing in the style of the famous German composer, but with a melody pattern that couldn't help but recall that after World War II, veterans had set the tune to a vulgar verse about Adolf Hitler.

The joke is based on thwarting our expectations, but precisely which expectations does Moore manage to subvert, given that we are hearing this jumble of music for the very first time — when we have no memories of it? When listening to a song do we make moment to moment predictions of where the piece is going to go, like a GPS road navigation system?[2] If this were the case, then surely we would make multiple predictions every moment, which means we would have predicted hundreds of possible cadences as the piece progressed. The brain wouldn't do that. It hardly seems helpful. The only way to explain how we respond to a new piece of music is if we recognize something about the music as it goes along.

Tension and resolution are the most frequent emotions (or cognitive states) that occur in response to music. This fulfilling and thwarting of expectations is music's most abundant and deliberate *modus operandi*, happening on a second-by-second basis as well as more generally for the totality of the piece.[3] In many ways music *plays* with the listener's expectations, as if it were a game, consistent with the double-meaning that one *plays* musical instruments. The simplest children's game where tension and resolution comprise the entirety of the appeal is *peek-a-boo*, although see-saw and swinging on a

1   A film of the performance can be seen on http://www.youtube.com/watch?v=GazlqD4mLvw (as of 26 March 2010).

2   GPS is the abbreviation for global positioning system, which is a navigation system based on detecting signals from man-made satellites in stationary positions orbiting the earth.

3   Musicologist David Huron devotes an entire book to demonstrating the importance of expectation in music, which has been very well received among academics, although it is a bit detailed for the novice. Much of his argument focuses on explaining how your brain can find a musical phrase "unexpected" or surprising even if you have heard it before. See Huron D (2007). *Sweet Anticipation: Music and the Psychology of Expectation*. Cambridge, Mass.: MIT Press.

swing have similar structures.[1] Among adult activities, tension and resolution are central in narrative art forms (e.g., drama, novels), and they also constitute the enjoyment of orgasm.

The instantaneous nature of our detecting tension and resolution becomes clear if we do a little thought experiment. Imagine if you will that it's just you and me, and we're in a café having a conversation. As we talk, in the background there is some music playing on the stereo, a bit of Mozart. Only unbeknownst to us, the owners of the café are evil scientists, and what they have done is they have doctored the recording of Mozart so that one note at the end of a phrase is definitely wrong — it has one duff note on it. The note they have changed is still played on the right instrument, at the right loudness, and it is as musical as any other sound in the excerpt, but it is definitely the wrong note, in the wrong key. As you and I are having this conversation, and the music is playing quietly in the background, would you notice the bum note, and how would you respond to it?

I can almost assure you, if you could hear the music, and you are familiar with Western classical music, that when the music system played the duff note, our conversation would stop instantly and we would look to the speaker, even though we had not been consciously thinking about the music up to that point. I think the most interesting thing about this is that it does not require formal musical training; all trained musicians will verbally be able to describe exactly what happened to the music, but even people who have no musical training at all will respond in exactly the right way. You don't actually have to be musically literate to know when the music leaves out the tonic, or to know when the music has hit the wrong note. Given that we could do this without consciously attending to the music, perhaps the word *expectations* is not the perfect terminology.

The elements of music have a way of fitting together, and when something incongruent appears, it arouses a strong emotion — and if that incongruity appears suddenly, it is funny, which is the basis of most humor. A musical example is Joseph Haydn's notorious *Surprise Symphony* of 1791 (Symphony No. 94 in G major). When the playful composer wished to rouse his phlegmatic English audience whom he took to be somnolent, he punctuated the tranquil opening to the second movement of his symphony with a very loud and abrupt G-note accompanied by drums. "A terrible and unexpected crash on the drum is heard, which convulses the whole audience like an electric shock" recounted an eyewitness to the first performances. "The entire audience was completely staggered, especially the ladies."[2] As if nothing had happened, Haydn then returns the piece to the quiet strains it began with, and the shock is never repeated.

When you start listening to a song, you rapidly choose a paradigm about what that piece of music is supposed to sound like, and if it breaks with the pattern, then your

---

1 Where being high in the air is tension and being near the ground is resolution. For a description of peek-a-boo that includes tension and resolution, see Parrott WG, Gleitman H (1989). Infants' Expectations in Play: The Joy of Peek-a-boo. *Cognition and Emotion* 3(4): 291-311.

2 Firnhaber JC (1932). A Correction, Contributing to Musical History. Der Freimüthige, December 3rd, 1825, in Unger M, 'The First Performance of Haydn's 'Surprise' Symphony' *The Musical Times* 73(1071): p. 413. London: Musical Times Publications Ltd.

emotions will say so. This is the reason most people are shocked when music is atonal. These expectations about music, which are central concepts in your social territory, are highly context-dependent. For example, you might reflect, "I don't think that oboe fits in that punk song." Similarly, you may have a strange territorial displacement when you first hear a familiar rock song like Eric Clapton's *Layla* (originally made famous played on the electric guitar) re-orchestrated onto acoustic "unplugged" instruments. Whether music comes from your own social territory usually determines if you will feel positive associations to the music, but if you have willingly entered someone else's territory, their music may appeal to you as well, such as when you hear Indian music in a curry restaurant. If you visit an exotic country the sound of that language may intrigue you or fade into the background, but the same language would probably make you feel quite uneasy if it was at a party in your own home.

One idea prevalent throughout the science of music is that music is processed in a similar way to language. Language is extraordinary because it is exceptionally complicated; from a child's simple vocabulary of 2,000 words, one can formulate a near infinite number of grammatical sentences that "make sense," even though the sentences may deviate dramatically from your previous associations or experiences. For example, you can instantly make sense of the sentence, *the green cat played the plastic piano cleverly*, yet you have never heard a sentence like it before. It is extraordinary that even a five-year-old child, and not a particularly bright one, can learn language at this level, yet even some of the most complicated computer programs designed to do this, called *chat-bots* [1] (from *robots* that *chat*) still cannot simulate a quite simple conversation unless there are enormous restrictions placed upon what can be said.

One extremely important observation about how we learn language is that when children learn their native tongue, they learn the rules of grammar *implicitly* rather than *explicitly*. That is, a child does not have to learn what a noun is in order to be able to place nouns into sentences in the correct order, e.g., "the cat is black" is correct while "black the is cat" is not a sentence. Although the implicit learning of language may seem obvious, nearly all the traditional methods for teaching foreign languages to adults rely upon explicit learning of grammar. Consider the following statements:

> The piano was played
>
> The conductor was played
>
> The violin was in the played

Any eight-year-old who can speak English could tell you which of these are wrong. But she probably couldn't explain why — and certainly couldn't tell you that the second represents a semantic error and the third a syntactic error. Children acquire these abstract rules without ever having to learn them explicitly — the eight year old was never taught them, and doesn't even know she knows them. But the wrong word in the wrong place is instantly recognizable to her, in the same way that a bum note in the middle of a Mozart sonata is. When we learn about music we don't just memorize the specifics of each and every piece we hear, but we also become familiar with its underly-

---

1 As of this date, some beguiling chatbots that try to learn English conversation can be found at http://talk.jabberwacky.com and http://www.abenteuermedien.de/jabberwock.

ing grammar. With no formal musical training, or even conscious awareness that we are listening to the music, a wrong note in the wrong place will grate, alerting our perception systems that something is amiss.

This is because when we become accustomed to a particular genre, we learn its grammar — its structure, instrumentation and timbres. Once learned, we become sensitive to incongruities in the music in the same way that we can identify that there's something awry in the sentences above. The Koi carp learned to distinguish Bach from the blues by generalizing the grammar of these two genres, and Dudley Moore's comic pianist routine is funny because it juxtaposes our clothing generalizations for classical music onto our mental associations with cheery movie music. Grammar is how we can immediately like new music, because the grammar allows us to generalize and make associations based on familiar music.

In conclusion, the evaluation we arrive at for a new piece of music synthesizes associations at three very different levels (see Figure 3.9). The mixture of innate cues (attributes such as loudness, tempo) and learned cues (e.g., a "barbershop quartet," major/minor key) triggers implicit memories in the listener that allow him/her to "make sense" of the mixture of auditory cues, of which there may be many. If the music is too far from the listener's territory, the music may be rejected or disliked; by contrast, if the music is very near the listener's territory (comprising favorite emotions and expectations), the music may be embraced upon listening to it for the first time.

Note that the listener's territory and their favorite emotions influence one another, rather than being independent (curved arrow labeled "2"); for example, if a listener likes feeling sad then they may develop a genre preference for doom metal, and if the listener likes to feel intense emotions (see chapter five), they may prefer loud music (punk, thrash metal, or rap). The fact that the popular music industry focuses on teenagers may explain why the territory of pop music is centered on love songs, when folk and popular music of past centuries often concerned narrative events (e.g., ballads) or more prosaic emotions.

Similarly there is a relationship in both directions between the listener's favorite emotions and their auditory expectations (curved arrow 3). If the music makes a sudden "unexpected" change in dynamics or harmonics, it may lead to chills, which may be one of the favorite emotions of the listener. On the other hand, if the listener's favorite emotion is being immersed in detail, discovering the unexpected, and never being bored, the listener may develop a taste for aleatoric music, which will always confound the listener's explicit expectations.

Finally, there is a relationship in both directions between the listener's territory and their auditory expectations (curved arrow 1), such that certain kinds of deviations from the established territory may lead to revitalized interest while other transgressions away from territorial expectations (e.g., tonal classical music) can lead to irritation of otherwise well-liked music. This is why *Unplugged* (1992), an entire record album of Eric Clapton's songs rearranged onto acoustic instruments, had sales that made it number 1 on the Billboard Album charts in the USA, as well as winning 6 Grammy awards including Album of the Year. By contrast, a piece of Mozart with a bum note in the wrong key would be upsetting to someone familiar with Western musical styles.[1] The over-familiarity with elementary rhythmic rules may lead to the development of more "sophisticated" tastes that value the interference with simple expectations (see chapter four for a discussion of sophistication); this taste for sophistication may explain why some genres and social territories embrace syncopated rhythms. This is an example of one of the main ways people can evolve their genre preferences based on territory.

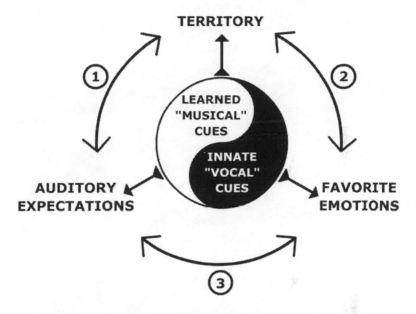

Figure 3.9 - How music leads to a listener's response based on territory, expectations and emotions. The sounds of the music (central circle) are cues that lead to three different sets of mental associations: territory (whether you own it), expectations (whether the sounds are coherent with its genre), and your favourite emotions. These divergent types of associations can influence each other (curved arrows).

---

1 Zentner MR, Kagan J (1996). Perception of music by infants. *Nature* 383(6595): 29.

CHAPTER 4. IS MUSICAL TASTE 100% NURTURE, OR IS THERE A ROLE FOR NATURE?

THE RESPONSE TO MUSIC DEPENDS ON THE ESSENCE OF MUSIC.

All the good music has already been written by people with wigs and stuff.
— Frank Zappa (1940–1993)

Can you tell the difference between music and noise? Here is a little thought experiment: Imagine what you would *feel* if I played you a series of sound recordings, each lasting about ten seconds. These recordings would include either industrial noises, random sounds from nature, music from primitive cultures in the Amazon basin, or trendy new music from your own culture (and territory) that you haven't heard yet. Would you be able to say which is music and which isn't? Would you feel better when listening to music from your own culture?

You would almost certainly feel different when listening to music from your own territory, but you might hesitate before saying what is and isn't music. At its most fundamental level, music is sound that coordinates emotions; however, industrial noise can also elicit emotions, as can speech, so there must be other requirements before a sound achieves musicality. Given that musicality is not limited to music itself, one way of looking at how musicality coordinates emotions is in the context of speech. The need for social cohesion is greatest in the emotional interaction between mother and infant. Human mothers need to coordinate their babies' emotions through sound, simply because human babies (unlike many other infant primates) are not carried on the mother's body all the time.[1] This could explain the development of baby-talk, which is officially known as "infant directed speech" or *motherese*. For example:

---

1 A fully developed argument for why mothers had to sing to their babies (ultimately leading to the conclusion that speech developed from music, rather than vice versa)

WHO's a ↑good ↓giiiiiiirl? Yeah, WHO's a good giiiiiiirl?

Speech itself has its own musical elements, with pitch, tempo, and rhythm playing a part in our understanding; all those musical elements of speech — which are commonly described as voice tone and inflection — are referred to in linguistics as *prosody*. Prosody is not an adjunct to speech, but an integral part of what is being communicated. Babies are interested in and sensitive to rhythm, melody and tempo in speech long before they understand words.[1] One group of psychologists in California ran a series of experiments using filtered speech to compare the importance of words to voice tone.[2] They used many different languages, but filtered out the words electronically so that all that was left was a muffled voice with its speech patterns, tones and tempo.[3] Two kinds of filtered voices were played: normal adult voices, and baby talk. The result for normal adult speech sounded like low, continuous murmurs, whereas the motherese sounded more like highly distinctive musical glissandi. The babies' level of interest in the speech was judged simply by whether they looked at the speaker when the voice was played. The result: babies prefer baby-talk. It did not matter which language the mothers were speaking; the babies always were more interested by the baby-talk.

The reason is because baby-talk is musical; this musical aspect makes it is possible for a baby to relate and respond to it. Baby-talk is higher and more variable in pitch, with shorter phrases, repetition, longer pauses and highly enunciated vowels (see figure 4.1):

In virtually all cultures, whatever their adult language, baby-talk that has low pitch sounds with falling contours (e.g., "There, there") is meant to soothe a distressed infant. By contrast, rising pitch contours are meant to engage their attention and elicit a response. Warnings and sounds meant to discourage the baby, although rare, have been found to be nearly identical to those made by non-human primates: brief and staccato calls with steep, high-pitched contours. These elements of prosody are added to speech unconsciously not only by mothers and fathers but by nearly all care-givers attempting to communicate with infants. The fact that the musical elements of speech, which are evolutionarily important for babies, can communicate emotion so clearly may explain the affective power of pure music.

If we automatically switch to baby-talk when speaking to babies so that they can benefit from our emotions and our language, what happens when we talk to a dog? A group in Australia has analyzed how mothers talk to their cats and dogs, and compared

---

can be found in Mithen SJ (2005). *The Singing Neanderthals: the Origins of Music, Language, Mind and Body*. London: Weidenfeld & Nicolson.

1 Fernald A (1993). Approval and disapproval — infant responsiveness to vocal affect in familiar and unfamiliar languages. *Child Development* 64(3): 657-674.

2 One study showed that the infants definitely preferred filtered speech that originated as baby-talk: Fernald A & Kuhl P (1987). Acoustic Determinants of Infant Preference for Motherese Speech. *Infant Behavior and Development* 10: 279-293. Another study showed that the acoustic elements preferred by babies were used in a global range of different languages: Fernald A, Taeshner T, Dunn J, Papousek M, de Boysson-Bardies B & Fukui I (1989) A Cross Language Study of Prosodic Modifications and Mothers' and Fathers' Speech to Preverbal Infants. *The Journal of Child Language* 16: 477-501.

3 The filtering was a simple low pass filter.

---

that to how the same women spoke to their infants or to adults.[1] The mothers were asked to have a 15 minute *naturalistic* conversation with their pet, as well as with their baby, and with an adult. They were also given the task of playing with and naming a toy *shark*, a toy *shoe* and a toy *sheep* because mothers hyper-articulate their vowels when talking to babies. Again, the scientists distilled the emotions from these monologues by electronically filtering out the words from the recordings, such that the only parts of voice remaining were the muffled speech patterns, tones and tempo. The pitch when talking to their pets was similar to talking to an infant, and the emotional content of the pet-talk was similar to the baby-talk. However, unlike the baby-talk, the vowels for the pets were not over-enunciated; the vowels and pauses for pets were comparable to how one would speak to an adult.

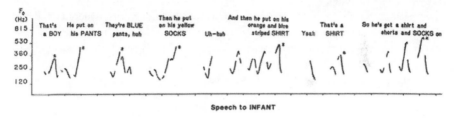

Speech to INFANT

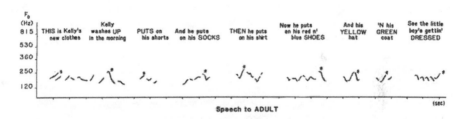

Speech to ADULT

Figure 4.1 - Examples of main pitch contours in the speech of one mother describing the picture book to her infant and to an adult; her adjustments in prosody were automatic, and her only instructions were to read the book aloud to the infant or adult. (Words in uppercase letters are those occurring on pitch peaks, which are marked with an asterisk in each utterance.) Reprinted with permission from Fernald A & Mazzie C (1991). Prosody and Focus in Speech to Infants and Adults. Developmental Psychology 27: 209-221. © 1991 the American Psychological Association.

We communicate our emotions to our pets through our voice tone, and the voice tone is also what makes baby-talk attractive to infants.[2] By contrast, the enunciation and pauses of baby-talk are presumably important for teaching language and for comprehending it. When talking to our dog, we automatically and unconsciously know not

1 Burnham D, Kitamura C, Vollmer-Conna U (2002). What's new, pussycat? On talking to babies and animals. *Science* 296(5572): 1435-1435.
2 Fernald A & Kuhl P (1987). Acoustic Determinants of Infant Preference for Motherese Speech. *Infant Behavior and Development* 10: 279-293

to bother speaking more clearly so that our pet can understand what we are saying. As if by magic, our adjustment of our speaking patterns in all these situations is intuitive. Compare those situations to our ultra-slow enunciation when we speak in our native language to foreign tourists who do not speak the language — we speak more slowly and with more articulation, because we want them to understand our language, but tourist-talk is not as emotionally high pitched as baby-talk, or even pet-talk. We do not talk baby-talk to tourists because we do not attempt to emotionally bond with them. They do not bring out the music in us.

***

Judging by our emotional responses, some musical notes go well together — like strawberries and cream — whilst others do not — like tuna fish and strawberry jam. Those that fit together are called consonant, and its opposite is dissonance. To the vast majority of us, persistently dissonant music often sounds *wrong*, but that did not stop classical composers over the past century from forcibly educating audiences with increasingly challenging music.

In the war between consonance and its dark twin dissonance, the atonal composer Arnold Schoenberg (1874–1951) towers above all others. His music was at the time detested by the majority of classical listeners, yet his teachings became so prestigious among the classical music establishment during much of the 20th century that composers who did not follow the path of atonal music were considered limited or even second rate.[1] For people who have never listened to Schoenberg's music before, it is worth spending a minute trying out a brief sample (e.g., online at Youtube or Amazon) because it sounds like nothing else in classical music. Baffling. Fragmentary. Nothing to hang on to.

On the one hand Schoenberg's proponents include Professor Paul Henry Lang (1901–1991), who was for many years the music critic for the *New York Herald Tribune*, as well as being the editor of *The Musical Quarterly* from 1945 to 1973. As an author Lang's most well-known book is the ambitiously entitled *Music in Western Civilization* (1941). Lang's support of Schoenberg was equally epic:

> Schoenberg's innovation is the greatest single event in the music of the first half of our century.[2]

On the other hand, there are traditionalists such as the conductor, composer and pianist Leonard Bernstein (1918–1990), who is best known as the music director of the New York Philharmonic, as well as for writing the music for *West Side Story*, *Candide*, *Wonderful Town*, and *On the Town*. Bernstein applauded one violinist's performance of Schoen-

---

1 See Boulez P (1991). "Possibly..." (1952). In *Stocktakings from an Apprenticeship*, collected and presented by Paule Thévenin, translated by Stephen Walsh, with an introduction by Robert Piencikowski, Oxford: Clarendon Press, pp. 111–40. His work has since been conducted by some of the most respected conductors including Simon Rattle and Daniel Barenboim.

2 Lang PH (1958). *Musical Quarterly* 44(4): 507-8. Lang was a professor at Columbia University. He is cited in Mitchell D (1993) *The Language of Modern Music* London: Faber and Faber, p.60.

berg and then joked with her, "But every time I hear Schoenberg, I just want to run to the nearest window and jump out!"[1]

These polar opposites suggest that whatever Schoenberg was doing to music, it was impossible to ignore. Schoenberg started a musical revolution — a system of composing that made it impossible to be pleasant or soothing to the untutored ear. Schoenberg's radical canon of dissonant sounds is so jarring that it still drives mainstream classical audiences into retreat fifty years after his death. The reception was much more violent when he first presented it.

His Second String Quartet was greeted with outrage in Vienna — as the soprano sang out the first atonal line, a prominent critic jumped up and shouted, "Stop it, that's enough!" whilst another yelled, "Be quiet, carry on playing!"[2] The vocalist at another premiere left the stage in tears. The audience response was one of such outrage that tickets to the repeat performance warned the bearer that they were entitled to listen silently, but not to express an opinion until the music was over.[3] Most of them *hated* it. These were not simply responses of disapproval, as if the quality of the music was poor. The musical establishment in bourgeois Vienna just before the Great War felt *violated*, as if their territory was being urinated upon. A Viennese reporter felt so intruded upon as to declare Schoenberg a 'public nuisance.'[4] At a performance of *Pierrot Lunaire*, an audience member was seen to point at Schoenberg and yell, "Shoot him! Shoot him!" At more than one concert his friends were left with no option but to shield him from projectiles thrown by the audience or to evacuate him from the theatre. In Berlin's *Financial Times*, German composer and critic Otto Taubmann put words to the general sentiment greeting Schoenberg's new discordant music: "If that is the music of the future, then I have a prayer to my Maker: please never make me endure another performance."[5]

What could drive Schoenberg to make such music when it was so hated?

The first of Schoenberg's compositions that relinquished any reference at all to a key — "You lean against a silver-willow" (*Du lehnest wider eine Silberweide*) — was written during the summer of 1908. That summer was a particularly important time in Schoenberg's personal life, as it was when he was betrayed and abandoned by the people he loved most. Schoenberg's wife Mathilde had just left him for his admirer and companion, the young Austrian painter Richard Gerstl (1883–1908). Gerstl — an aspiring expressionist painter often in conflict with his tutors — introduced himself in 1906 to the decade-older Schoenberg because he was inspired by the music. After inspecting Gerstl's abilities as a painter at Heinrich Lefler's School of painting, Schoenberg commissioned Gerstl to paint his portrait. Later Schoenberg deepened their relationship, and made further painting commissions, including one of his wife Mathilde. The three became intimately acquainted, conversing on painting and music and ultimately sum-

---

1 Chang L (2002). Letter to the Editor: Leonard Bernstein; Phantasy? Phooey. *The New York Times*, 16 June.

2 Reich W (1971). *Schoenberg: A Critical Biography*, trans. Leo Black, London: Longman Group Ltd., p.35.

3 Lebrecht N (2001). Why We're Still Afraid of Schoenberg. *La Scena Musicale*, 8 July.

4 From a Viennese daily in its local news section, as cited by Reich W (1971). *Schoenberg: A Critical Biography*, trans. Leo Black, London: Longman Group Ltd., p.35.

5 Börsenkurier, Nov 1912. Quoted in Reich W (1971). *Schoenberg: A Critical Biography*, trans. Leo Black. London: Longman Group Ltd., p. 78.

mering together. Gerstl was often seen at musical events with Mathilde Schoenberg, and her husband knew about it. Presumably during one summer Mathilde Schoenberg and Richard Gerstl became lovers, and in June 1908 Schoenberg caught Gerstl and his wife *in flagrante delicto*.[1] Mathilde moved in with Gerstl, leaving Schoenberg behind with their children. The bewildered husband reports thinking of suicide regularly during this period, and he wrote daily letters to his wife begging her to come home for the sake of the children — which after a few months she did. After Gerstl lost Mathilde, he burned the contents of his studio and committed suicide with melodramatic style: while hanging himself naked in front of a mirror he stabbed himself in the heart.[2]

It would be unfair to suggest that Mathilde's abandoning him and the children combined with Gerstl's gruesome death were the inspiration of Schoenberg's subsequent dedication to music that is never innately pleasant;[3] however, the events of that fateful summer would have left even the most emotionally intelligent individual in a state of trauma. Perhaps despairing dreadful experiences bring about dissonant discordant music.

But that is not how Schoenberg saw it. Rejecting any suggestion that his life and work be compared, he developed a theoretical framework for this new music. Schoenberg and his followers were effectively suggesting that the traditions of harmony and consonance were cultural, and that any set of musical rules could emerge as a cultural standard of beauty. This rationale for his twelve tone music became a defense against his ferociously negative critics. Schoenberg's explanation was that the listener's lack of enthusiasm for dissonance was caused by their own short-sightedness — they were simply not musically educated enough to appreciate it.[4] One famous Schoenberg quote, which might be wishful thinking or territorial bravado, has him making the now discredited claim:

"I can wait... One day, milkmen will whistle my tunes like Puccini."[5]

---

1 Simms BR (2003). "My dear Hagerl": self-representation in Schoenberg's String Quartet No. 2. *19-th Century Music* 26: 258-277.

2 MacDonald M (2008). *Schoenberg* 2nd edition. New York: Oxford University Press USA: 6-8.

3 Schoenberg had been incorporating increasing amounts of dissonance into his compositions for some time, although the works of 1908 definitely represent a turning point, including the first time he (or anyone of that stature in the previous 500 years of Western classical music) abandoned a key signature. A controversial article that makes the argument (based on a "suicidal" will that Schoenberg wrote while Mathilde was with Gerstl) that the atonality was triggered by her infidelity appears in Lebrecht N (2003). Arnold Schoenberg's Second String Quartet. *La Scena Musicale* 9(4): p. 46.

4 In his application to teach at the Academy of Fine Arts in Vienna in 1910, Schoenberg underscores the exclusivity of his sophistication with the following: "I write a kind of music that does not appeal to those who do not understand anything about it. On the other hand, it must be admitted that it does appeal to those who do understand it." Schoenberg A (1958). *Arnold Schoenberg Letters*, edited by Stein E. London: Faber and Faber.

5 The quote is from: McSmith A (2008) Sublime — or ridiculous? The art of noise. *The Telegraph* newspaper (London), 3 January. As an interesting response, Puccini said of Schoenberg, "Who can say that Schoenberg will not be a point of departure to a goal in the distant future? But at present — unless I understand nothing — we are as far

In defending his own compositions, Schoenberg touched on a rather old question: how much of music is innate to us? By suggesting that the public conception of musicality could change so much that his avant-garde atonal pieces would one day be whistled by milkmen, he implies that a culture could make up any musical schema which, if promulgated ubiquitously, would charm and engage the public.

Behind Schoenberg's seemingly arrogant statement lies one unshakable belief: the *essence* of music can change. That is, the sounds that people deem as musical are determined entirely by experience: what they heard in the womb, what their parents listened to at home, and the music approved of by their culture and peer group. Not only do your peers and previous experience determine whether you like Bach or the Beatles, but it completely shapes what you think music is — even so far as what you find to be harmonious, or consonant. If a person does not appreciate an atonal chord, it is not because of an innate human reflex, but because their musical ear is not accustomed to such a note. Schoenberg believed that in the future musical education would change and his compositions would be seen in a new light. In a quote ascribed to Schoenberg his views on musical education are writ large: "*I have today made a discovery which will ensure the supremacy of German music for the next hundred years.*"[1] While Schoenberg may have been quite tongue-in-cheek about the territorial and jingoistic aspirations for his music, his followers took it as the gospel. As Pierre Boulez, a well-established composer and Schoenberg follower, said, "Any musician who has not experienced — I do not say understood, but truly experienced — the necessity of dodecaphonic music is useless."[2]

***

All cultures can and do differentiate between music and noise.[3] However, the definition each culture arrives at is dramatically different. The Suya tribe of the Amazonian rainforests produce songs without instruments that sound to Western ears surprisingly like a bunch of people talking.[4] Plainly the essence of music, if there is such a thing, is quite elusive, but that does not necessarily exclude dissonance, tribal rainforest songs, or German industrial music.

Ethnomusicologists are in a position to establish scientifically whether some aspects of music are innate to all humans by comparing the music of different cultures, hoping to find some attributes of music, such as certain keys or rhythms, that are the

from a concrete artistic realization of it as Mars is from Earth." Originally in Carner M (1958) *Puccini, A Critical Biography*. London, p.161 — Cited in Donald Mitchell (1993) *The Language of Modern Music*. London: Faber and Faber, p.21.

1 The quote is attributed to Schoenberg in Stuckenschmidt HH (1977). *Schoenberg: His Life, World and Work*. Translated by Humphrey Searle. New York: Schirmer Books. However, there is much debate as to whether this quote was said with intense irony, or if it was actually said by Schoenberg at all.

2 Boulez P (1991). "Possibly..." (1952). In *Stocktakings from an Apprenticeship*, collected and presented by Paule Thévenin, translated by Stephen Walsh, with an introduction by Robert Piencikowski. Oxford: Clarendon Press, p. 111–40.

3 Merriam AP (1964). *The Anthropology of Music*. Evanston, Illinois: Northwestern University Press.

4 Nercessian A (2007). *Defining Music: An Ethnomusicological and Philosophical Approach*. Lewiston, N.Y.: Edwin Mellen Press.

same in every culture, no matter where you go. Yet, even though music is culturally ubiquitous, it has assumed so many different forms that it is hard to find anything that all songs (and thus their singers) have in common all over the world. At first sight, the available evidence would seem to support Schoenberg entirely.

In an experiment designed to find out how easily humans can detect mistuning in types of music that are not part of their own culture,[1] scientists found that Western adult listeners generally have less trouble to detect mistuning in familiar contexts (i.e., from their own culture), such as the major or minor scale, than in unfamiliar ones, such as in the Javanese pelog scale. The scientists then asked their participants to judge tunes based on the Western major scale and the rarely heard Western augmented scale. The latter is composed of a symmetrical sequence of alternating minor thirds and semitones, and as such is structurally even simpler than the major scale. The listeners still performed better if the melodies they heard were based on the familiar major scale. These findings clearly testify that acculturation is more important that simplicity — much of what we take for granted in music we have actually learned.

But in reality, there might be something instinctive about musical taste that goes beyond cultural learning. This is important, because if musical taste is 100% learned, then it is culturally relative, which would mean that *crash-boing* music is no better or worse than Mozart. However, if you claimed that there is *no* essence to music, it would mean that any system of composition could sound good to your ear, so long as you had suitable training from childhood. The advantage of defining music is that we may find that some music is more "musick-y" than other music. If we knew the essence of music, we could make better music — for everyone.

The first recorded scientific investigation into what makes music sound *good* was supposedly performed by the ancient Greek philosopher Pythagoras (c. 570-495 BC),[2] famed for his "triangle" theorem. Legend has it that as he passed a blacksmith one day, he realized that the sounds that two hammers made when hitting their anvils could sometimes be pleasant and sometimes be grating. Intrigued, he measured the weight of the hammers and found that the pairs that harmonized pleasantly always weighed a multiple of one another (e.g., twice as heavy, three times as heavy, etc.). Continuing his experiments with different materials, Pythagoras found that two strings, one of them being exactly twice as long as the other, produced two notes separated by exactly an octave. From this and his other findings, he concluded that consonance and dissonance were dependent on the ratio of the length strings that were used. Consonance, according to him, would only occur if the ratios of the lengths of the strings were simple fractions of one another: 2:1, 3:2, 4:3, etc.. In short, Pythagoras showed that what made noises (e.g., hammering) that sounded pleasant was an essential property of mathematics and physics.

More than two thousand years later, the great Italian astronomer Galileo Galilei (1564–1642) picked up on these ideas. Galileo found that when comparing two vi-

---

1 Lynch MP, Eiler RE, Oller KD, Urbano RC & Wilson P (1991). Influences of acculturation and musical sophistication on perception of musical interval patterns. *Journal of Experimental Psychology: Human Perception and Performance* 17: 967-975.

2 Caleon IS & Subramaniam R (2007). From Pythagoras to Sauveur: tracing the history of ideas about the nature of sound. *Physics Education* 42: 173-179.

brating strings, the relationships between the *frequencies* of the vibrations determined whether the two sounds were consonant, as opposed to the *lengths* of the strings. The frequency of a sound is the number of vibrations per second made by the string, which does depend partly on the string's length, but also on the thickness and the tension of a string. If you have one string twice the size of another and they sound good together because they are an octave apart, you can make them sound discordant by just tightening one of the strings. Galileo's insight may seem a minor revision, but it was a real breakthrough because he linked music to air motion and vibrations, rather than to the string — which would not emit sound if plucked in a vacuum.

Two centuries later, the famous German physicist and physician Hermann von Helmholtz (1821–1894) put forth his own ideas regarding the consonance of two sounds.[1] He knew that when two sounds with slightly different frequencies are played together and the vibrations causing the sounds coincide, they reinforce each other, resulting in a momentary increase in intensity. On the other hand, when these vibrations do not coincide or work against each other, the intensity of the sound is diminished. These periodic fluctuations in the intensity of a sound are known as *sensory beats* and their number depends on how often the vibrations of the two notes coincide (see Figure 4.2).

Helmholtz theorized that hearing occasional beats was disturbing and lowered the quality of the sound, making it unpleasant (or dissonant).[2] On the other hand, if the beats are at too high a frequency to be heard, as in the case of frequency pairs in simple integer ratios, the overall sound experience should be more agreeable (or consonant) — the end result being as Pythagoras and Galileo had described centuries before. Helmholtz's theory is still around and has even received some support recently,[3] but it has some severe shortcomings as well. One of the most important criticisms is the necessity for both notes to make sound simultaneously if any beats are to occur. Yet it is obvious that even if two notes are played one after another we can still judge them to be consonant or dissonant. Helmholtz's thoughts are not the final verdict.

Helmholtz believed that the physical characteristics of consonance found in a pair of tones would operate on innate properties of the auditory system.[4] His demonstration that consonance was of a physical, measurable nature certainly undermines the notion that consonance is a mere construct of human culture, yet the question of whether humans can innately distinguish between consonance and dissonance, or even prefer one over the other, can only be settled unequivocally by means of a biological proof.

---

1 Cazden N (1962). Sensory theories of musical consonance. *The Journal of Aesthetics and Art Criticism* 20: 301-319.
2 In the real world an instrument does not have one frequency; a plucked string would have a fundamental frequency (which is loudest and lowest) and many overtones, which are typically multiples of the fundamental frequency. When two strings are played, if the numerical ratio of all the frequencies from both strings is simple, coincidences of vibrations become very numerous, enough to either cancel each other out or become too rapid to be perceptible.
3 Fishman YI, Volkov IO, Noh MD et al. (2001).Consonance and dissonance of musical chords: neural correlates in auditory cortex of monkeys and humans. *Journal of Neurophysiology* 86: 2761-2788.
4 Zentner MR, Kagan J (1998). Infant's perception of consonance and dissonance in music. *Infant Behavior & Development* 21: 483-492.

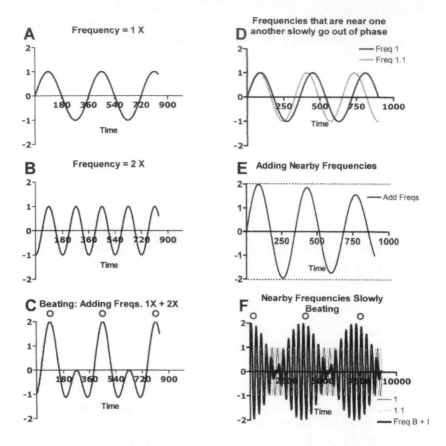

Figure 4.2 - How sensory beats arise from two different frequencies.[1] Graphs on the left (A-C) show how two frequencies that are consonant would create regular sensory beats (panel C, circles) at a fast frequency that would still sound pleasant, while graphs on the right (D-F) show how two dissonant frequencies would create beats at a much slower frequency (panel F, circles), which would sound dissonant. In graph A (top left) is a schematic of the vibrations of a perfect string; in this ideal case its frequency is X. In graph B is a schematic of the vibrations of another string whose frequency is twice that of the first (2X). At the bottom would be the net vibrations the ear would detect if the two strings were plucked at once; the air vibrations would add, and in this case there would be beats (marked by circles) at the same frequency of the top string (i.e. at the lower frequency). These beats occur at such a fast frequency (the same frequency as the lowest fundamental tone) that the beats sound

---

1 A much more thorough account of the traditional physics-based explanation behind consonance can be found in the chapter on "Tutti: All Together Now" in Ball P (2010). *The Music Instinct: How Music Works and Why We Can't Do Without It.* London: The Bodley Head.

consonant. If the frequency of the vibrations of the two strings were related by a non-integer ratio (graph D), the frequencies would slowly go out of phase (i.e. their peaks would not always co-occur). In fact, the timing of the peaks would change with respect to each other, resulting in the total vibration (graph E) having its peak diminish (and later increase). Graph F shows graph D and graph E superimposed but with a compressed time scale. The low frequency beats (circles) result when the two waves manage to align; directly in between beats they are exactly out of phase, such that when one wave hits it peak, the other wave is hitting its low-point. In this case the frequencies would not be a simple ratio, and the beats would be comparatively rare (approximately 1/10 of the frequency of the fundamental tone, a much lower frequency of beats compared to graph C), so the overall sound would be buzzy or unpleasant.

The anthropological finding that humans of all cultures can distinguish between and prefer consonant over dissonant music makes it a rather old human trait — rather than being a feature of a recently emerged culture. It makes sense that if there were a biological essence (or a *least common denominator*) to music, it should be present in animals. Because of their close relationship to us, other primates are the natural choice when starting to investigate into this question, and they do not disappoint. In 2000 a study reported the results of an experiment in which Japanese monkeys (*Macaca fuscata*) were first trained to discriminate between two chords, consisting of a consonant octave and a less consonant major seventh.[1] Once the monkeys had learned to perform well on this test, they were presented with two consonant and dissonant chords (perfect fifth and major seventh; perfect fourth and minor second) and their ability to distinguish between them was tested. Monkeys performed much better when a consonant chord changed into a dissonant one, rather than the other way round. Although this preferential success may have been an artifact caused by the way the monkeys were trained, the results at the very least showed that monkeys do have the ability to discriminate consonant and dissonant chords.[2]

Monkeys have even more surprising qualities. We humans have the ability to recognize a tune even if it is transposed (moved up or down in pitch) by an octave. In an attempt to find out whether other primates may be able to do the same, a team of researchers placed two male rhesus monkeys into a modified cage, with three speakers placed around it.[3] Whenever the monkeys touched the central speaker, they heard a tune, after which a second test tune was played. The monkeys were trained to touch the speaker to their right when the tests sample was the same as the first sound sample they had heard. When the two samples were different, the monkeys had to touch the left speaker.

1 Izumi A (2000). Japanese monkeys perceive sensory consonance of chords. *Journal of the Acoustical Society of America* 108: 3073-3078.

2 Monkeys are not the only animals possessing this skill. In another study, European starlings (*Sturnus vulgaris*) tuned out to have it as well; see Hulse SH, Bernard DJ & Braaten RF (1995). Auditory discrimination of chord-based spectral structures by European starlings (*Sturnus vulgaris*). *Journal of Experimental Psychology: General* 124: 409-423.

3 Wright AA, Rivera JJ, Hulse SH, Shyan M & Neiworth JJ (2000). Music perception and octave generalisation in rhesus monkeys. *Journal of Experimental Psychology: General* 129: 291-307

At first, the monkeys performed rather poorly — they simply did not recognize the synthetic melodies after the music had been transposed. This radically changed, however, when the researchers resorted to what they thought to be more memorable songs: *Old MacDonald* and *Yankee Doodle*. It turned out that in general the monkeys were only able to reliably recognize a transposed tune when the melody was tonal — they got it right in 80% of the trials. Whenever an atonal tune was used, their performance dropped back to mere chance levels. It is very unlikely that these results can be accounted for by previous musical experience of the monkeys — their exposure to music certainly was considerably less than that of any human. The monkeys appear to perceive, process and store music in a way similar to how we do it.

Yet, surprising as these results are, they do not answer the question whether non-human animals actually prefer consonant over dissonant chords. To answer this, scientists at Harvard designed a simple apparatus to test the sound preferences of cotton-top tamarins that had never heard music.[1] The tamarins were put in a V-shaped cage (see Figure 4.3), and they were played different sounds depending upon which arm of the maze they occupied. The tamarins, therefore, controlled the sound stimuli, and the time spent in each arm of the maze was taken as the sonic preference of the tamarin. For example, in one experiment if a tamarin was in the left arm of the maze the speaker played recordings of tamarin feeding noises, while the right arm of the maze had tamarin distress calls (that the tamarins spontaneously made while being held by the veterinarian during routine check ups) played at the same volume; the tamarins spent 60% of their time on the side with the feeding noises, compared to 40% of their time with the distress calls. This shows that for relevant sounds the tamarins had a preference for pleasant ones, and they would move around in the maze to keep the auditory environment nice.

Figure 4.3 - The apparatus used for testing the auditory preferences of cotton-top tamarins. Each side of the maze has a hidden speaker at the end, and when a tamarin remained on one side, the speaker on that side was active and played a particular sound

1 McDermott J & Hauser M (2004). Are consonant intervals music to their ears? Spontaneous acoustic preferences in a nonhuman primate. *Cognition* 94: B11–B21.

(e.g., a screeching noise similar to fingernails on a blackboard). Movement to the other side resulted in the other speaker being active instead and playing a different noise (e.g., white noise). Tamarins showed no preference between the screeching and white noise, although Harvard undergraduate students did. From McDermott J & Hauser M (2004). Are consonant intervals music to their ears? Spontaneous acoustic preferences in a nonhuman primate. Cognition 94: B11–B21. Copyright 2004 Elsevier. Reprinted with permission.

The main experiment the scientists then performed compared whether the tamarins preferred consonant musical chords to dissonant musical chords. The tamarins showed no preference for consonant over dissonant chords. The same type of experiment was then repeated with Harvard undergraduate students. An empty room with hidden speakers had a stripe down the center of the room, and if the students remained on the left side they heard consonant chords, and on the right side they were played the dissonant chords; before entering the room, the students were given no explanations or instructions except that they must remain in the room for five minutes. As expected, the Harvard undergraduates spent almost all their time on the left side of the room (90% vs. 10%). This shows that the Harvard undergraduates had a clear preference for the consonant chords, thus distinguishing them from cotton-top tamarins.

***

People put all sorts of junk onto Youtube. That being the case, cognitive scientists in San Diego were amazed to find that among the many home movies claiming that "my pet can dance," there was a white 12-year-old sulphur-crested cockatoo named Snowball (*Cacatua galerita eleonora*) who performed head bobs and foot steps that were remarkably well-synchronized to the beat of a pop song. The scientists tracked down the bird and did a statistically controlled experiment to test how well it could dance to the song "Everybody" by the Backstreet Boys, but to make sure the dancing was to the music and not a coincidental movement, they repeatedly changed the tempo of the song.[1] Snowball was able to adjust to the different tempi, providing the first verified example of a non-human animal that can keep time to the music.

Despite the many claims by pet owners that their dogs can dance, scientists surveying the evidence have found that the only animals that seem able to keep time to music are from species that learn complex vocal expression by mimicking sound, especially parrots;[2] it is theorized that other vocal learners (vocal birds, seals, dolphins) would be able to develop this skill, but that vocal nonlearners (dogs, cats, nonhuman primates) would not. The fact that the capering cockatoos dance recurrently suggests that they find music and dancing rewarding — allowing them to recognize and entrain to a regular beat.

1 Patel AD, Iversen JR, Bregman MR, Schulz I (2009). Experimental Evidence for Synchronization to a Musical Beat in a Nonhuman Animal. *Current Biology* 19(10): 827–830.
2 Schachner A., Brady TF, Pepperberg IM, and Hauser MD (2009). Spontaneous motor entrainment to music in multiple vocal mimicking species. *Current Biology* 19(10): 831–836.

In humans a regular beat is rewarding as soon as a baby is born; rocking a baby's crib is often used by mothers to soothe babies even when they are napping. This essential aspect of music is so fundamental to the human mind that it can even be recognized by newborn babies in their sleep. Scientists in Hungary measured the brain waves (electroencephalograms) of sleeping infants and found that when a simple rock drum beat in 4/4 time was missing the downbeat (but not other beats), the infants' brains responded as though something was missing.[1]

Infants not only prefer regular beats — they also prefer consonant over dissonant music, just like adults usually do. Scientists at Harvard University tested four-month-old babies for the preference of consonance over dissonance by comparing their responses to two 35-second melodies, composed on a computer synthesizer — one melody in parallel thirds (which is consistently perceived as consonant), and a manipulated version in parallel minor seconds (usually perceived as rather dissonant).[2] Seating the babies in an infant seat, the scientists played the tunes from speakers covered with "attractively patterned concentric circles." Each baby's looking time was used as a measure of attention, and the scientists compared how long the babies looked at the patterned speakers to establish if they had a bias for listening to the consonant melodies. They also watched how the babies behaved during both tunes. They found that the babies were consistently content to listen to the consonant versions, watching the speaker, babbling and smiling. But during versions in which dissonant intervals were introduced, the babies showed clear signs of distress: turning their gaze away, squirming and fussing, and even grimacing. The strength of their reaction surprised the researchers — "We thought it would be subtle," one of them said, "but it was so striking."[3]

But even using very young babies does not prove conclusively that the human love of music is genetic and not learned. The objection remains that the infants might have received enough musical and language input during their brief lives — or even prior to birth — to explain their distress at dissonant music. It has been shown using a microphone implanted in a woman's uterus that it is possible to hear music from the womb, and that some babies can prenatally develop a preference a particular song (e.g., the theme tune from the Australian soap opera *Neighbours*) if it is heard hundreds of times before birth.[4] How could it be possible to prove that a baby may have a genetic preference for consonance, irrespective of any sounds heard while still in the womb?

---

1 The sleeping neonates were played synthesized drum beats, which in some cases were missing the downbeat (1), and compared to normal rhythms or rhythms missing other "less important" beats, in an "oddball" paradigm; see Winkler I, Háden GP, Ladinig O, Sziller I, Honing H (2009). Newborn infants detect the beat in music. *Proceedings of the National Academy of Sciences USA* 106 (7): 2468-71. The main result was a negative signal at -200 ms, which is surprisingly similar to mismatch negativity found in awake adults when auditory "deviations" are presented; see Näätänen R, Paavilainen P, Rinne T, & Alho K (2007). The mismatch negativity (MMN) in basic research of central auditory processing: A review. *Clinical Neurophysiology* 118: 2544-2590.

2 Zentner MR, Kagan J (1996). Perception of music by infants. *Nature* 383, p. 29.

3 Zentner quoted from Parker SG. (Nov-Dec 1996). Tiny Music Critics. Right Now, *Harvard Magazine*

4 Hepper PG (1991). An examination of foetal learning before and after birth, *The Irish Journal of Psychology* 12: 95-107.

A scientist working at the Japan Science and Technology Agency believed he had the answer.[1] Some of the original notes from Mozart's minuet in C Major were altered to produce a second, dissonant version of the tune. Playing both the original and altered versions of the minuet to newborns (first-born two-day-old babies with almost no possibility for musical experience, except in the womb) the study compared the time the infants looked at the speaker, the source of the music. The results are by now a familiar story — the infants showed a preference for the consonant 'pleasant' version, looking longer at the speaker when the consonant version was played. To counter any argument that this preference was due to prenatal learning, an extra innovation was added to the testing: the experiment was carried out twice, comparing the responses of the "normal" infants with those of first-born two-day-old hearing newborns of *deaf* parents. The parents of this second group were congenitally deaf — the parents lived in a deaf community with no music, they did not speak, and used Japanese sign language as their first language. Remarkably it made no difference whether the babies had deaf or hearing parents: all babies liked the consonant version of Mozart more. Thus, infants prefer consonance over dissonance, the preference is present from birth, and the preference for consonant music is *not* caused by experiences before or just after birth. It is innate.

This shows that the consonant essence of music is a fundamental biological phenomenon, not simply a matter of semantics. If we banned the word *music* and used other words (e.g., melodic sounds, tinkly piano sounds, etc.), the problem of defining *music* would still exist. Whatever way we defined the word *music*, people — and especially children — would still be able to hear a difference between industrial noises and orchestral melodies. Perhaps the best way to approach the problem of defining music is by thinking linguistically about how we give names to objects. Instead of making a checklist saying, "*All* music must have: 1) a regular rhythm, 2) notes organized into keys, and 3) sounds organized to elicit emotion," the defining features of music can be described with family resemblances.[2] To see a family resemblance, you look for many possible shared traits, but you understand that no single trait is necessary or sufficient to identify whether someone is, or is not, a member of the family: for instance, the Habsburg family of monarchs were distinctive because of their protruding lower jaw, protruding lower lip ('Habsburg lip'), and their nose having a hump (Figure 4.4), but not all members of the family had all these physical features.[3] Family resemblances can be used to categorize concepts (e.g., music) as well as people.

1 Masataka N (2006). Preference for consonance over dissonance by hearing newborns of deaf parents and of hearing parents. *Developmental Science* 9: 46-50.

2 This can also be referred to as "prototype theory." Its origins come from Wittgenstein and Eleanor Rosch, but the populist view that I am working from was from a course at University of California at Berkeley in the 1980s centered on the book: Lakoff G (1987). *Women, Fire, and Dangerous Things: What Categories Reveal About the Mind.* Chicago: University of Chicago Press.

3 The official term for the protruding lower jaw is mandibular prognathism. In the case of Charles V the "deformity" made the Habsburg King of Spain appear as if his mouth was open, implying that he was stupid; he was taunted for his appearance and constantly reminded of it. See Grabb WC, Hodge GP, Dingman RO, Oneal RM (1968). The Habsburg Jaw. *Plastic and Reconstructive Surgery* 42(5): 442-445.

A clear example of using family resemblances to define a concept is the word *breakfast*. In your own mind, what is breakfast? If you answered that breakfast is a meal in the morning, how would you describe the cafés in the USA advertising, "Breakfast served all day?" This implies that breakfast does not have to be eaten in the morning, so long as the meal includes greasy eggs, bacon and sausage. But then how would you make sense of the phrase, "I had pizza for breakfast." We implicitly understand the word's meaning, but it challenges our hypothesis about what breakfast is. Defining objects using family resemblances (rather than by using a checklist) results in a more nuanced view of what music is. Family resemblances are more flexible because they have a prototype (e.g., grand dad) that the instances (e.g., his descendants) may resemble to a greater or lesser degree. For example, in your minds' eye there is a Platonic ideal of breakfast, where toast and cornflakes are always served at exactly eight in the morning; the closer a meal (a potential member of the family) comes to this Platonic ideal, the more "breakfast-like" that meal is. So it may be with music; there may be an ideal of music which includes traditional rhythms, keys and harmonies. However, having a perfect example does not exclude less prototypical sounds from being defined as music, in which case, Schoenberg may turn out to be cold pizza at 7 AM.

Figure 4.4 - The Habsburg Facial Features. This medal of Charles V (1500–1558) accentuates the Habsburg lip, jaw and nose.

The most central facet of music would be the deliberate organization of sound in order to affect the emotions of most listeners — yet there are musical exceptions to this, including Schoenberg. We might expect that all human cultures would base their music upon sounds that communicate emotions, which should make music similar in different cultures. However, it may not be so straightforward, as shown in the following thought-experiment. Imagine if you invented a computer program called *Tune-Perfect* that composed the most "musical" tunes possible,[1] a program that could create tunes that children loved and adults couldn't forget, what music would it come up

---

1 This is not such a hypothetical question. Such computer programs have been developed for several decades, although the results are not necessarily beautiful. It goes without saying that the musical results are based on the specific program used, and can be anything from classical to jazz solos. See Jacob BL (1996). Algorithmic composition as a model of creativity. *Organised Sound* 1 (3): 157-165. See also Biles JA (1994). GenJam: A genetic algorithm for generating jazz solos. In *Proceedings of the 1994 International Computer Music Conference*. San Francisco: International Computer Music Association: 131-137.

with? Beethoven's Fifth? The Beatles' "Hey Jude"? Actually, it would not be long before your computer came up with *Twinkle Twinkle Little Star*. It has it all. Major key. An absolutely rigid rhythm. Pauses at the end of every phrase. Pitches that are bunched together. The melody moves up and down like a cat on a stairway. It's so easy to sing. It's even easier to remember.

Twinkle Twinkle Little Star: 10 Reasons Why It Represents the Essence of Music
1) It is in the major key
2) It has no notes outside its key
3) It starts on the tonic
4) It ends on the tonic
5) It has an absolutely regular rhythm (4/4 time)
6) It only pauses at the end of musical phrases
7) It begins phrases on a stressed beat
8) It ends phrases on a stressed beat
9) Downward pitch steps are always one step (the next note on the scale).
10) The only upward steps are either a single step higher or a jump from the tonic to the dominant (fifth)

But if you polled 10,000 people of all ages, old veterans from the war, young mothers with toddlers, teenagers with piercings, and you asked them what was the most perfectly musical song of all time, not one of them would even consider Twinkle Twinkle.

Ah, you say, but that is because the lyrics are rubbish. You would explain, "Real songs have themes of love, faith, or justice. A diminutive star just doesn't cut the mustard." But, of course, it does. The word *star* is in the top fifty most popular words in the titles of pop songs listed in Billboard magazine's top 40,[1] and *star* is one of the most poetic words in the English-speaking world. The only explanation for *Twinkle Twinkle Little Star* is this: it's kid stuff. Too boring for anyone over the age of five. For music to be really popular, it needs to have more than the essence of children's music; it also needs some spice.

***

The reason children's music is not everyone's favorite music, even if it comprises the most universal features of musicality, is because a person's musical taste can become more *sophisticated*. Being that there is no official scientific definition for *sophistication* — concerning music or anything else — I will give my own crude definition here.[2]

---

1   The data is based around an illegal data set called The Whitburn Project, which is a use-net based database of every song in Billboard's top 40 songs since 1890 (not a typo, really 120 years ago). The database, which includes over 25 megabytes of data, includes song titles, chart positions, weeks on the chart, tempo (in beats per minute), and many other parameters. Andy Baio did a preliminary analysis of the data (http://musicthing.blogspot.com/2008/05/100-greatest-ever-cliches-in-pop-song.html), and identified the top 100 words in pop song titles, and *Star* appears in the top 50 (not including you, am, the, a, etc.). Not surprisingly, the word *Love* was number 1.

2   This definition is *not* "the correct definition," and I am completely averse to making polemics based on terms that the author has himself defined, as my experience is that

Sophistication is an acquired state (it is not naïve or simple) involving an advance in perception. It usually refers to complicated stimuli, so sophisticated things are expected to be subtle, and not obvious. In the scientific literature sophistication is sometimes contrasted with *acculturation*:[1] both sophistication and acculturation are learned, but acculturation can be acquired implicitly and unconsciously, whereas sophistication seems to be mastered explicitly. For example, when a baby born in Athens learns to speak Greek, that is acculturation, but when a man born in London learns to read and enjoy Greek poetry, that is sophistication. Because sophistication is more developed, it can be described as *refined*, although that sounds value-laden. I personally am not making a judgment about better or worse, although "snobby" people may.[2]

Sophisticated stimuli are often designed for people with sophisticated tastes, so sophistication is often the opposite of what comes naturally, or even of the mainstream. The most prototypical sophistication involves taking genuine pleasure in what is interesting rather than in what is nice.[3] A simple example is traditional beer, which is sophisticated compared to lemonade — it is an acquired taste because it is bitter and not sweet. So are Shakespeare's tragedies (compared to cartoons). So is Schoenberg's music (compared to lullabies). Here is my working definition:

> Sophistication is a perceptual development (based on experience and transcendence) resulting in the conscious rejection of naïve or natural tastes, typically in favor of more complex, subtle or rare tastes. It can include a rationale for rejecting things because your aesthetics are (as you see it) superior or better-informed.

It seems simple, but keeping it non-judgmental is nearly impossible, because it invites comparisons that invariably open a can of worms. Rock and classical music are both sophisticated compared to lullabies, but when compared to each other, an argument ensues. It is stereotypical to imagine a rock fan in their twenties becoming a listener of gentler classical music in their forties. Certainly plenty of rock musicians move onward to classical: in 1999 the heavy metal band Metallica released an album

---

such arguments end up being circular. If you do not like the term *sophistication* and its connotations, please feel free to substitute your own term, and I hereby reiterate that I do *not* believe that sophisticated music is better than unsophisticated music.

1 Lynch MP, Eiler RE, Oller KD, Urbano RC & Wilson P (1991). Influences of acculturation and musical sophistication on perception of musical interval patterns. *Journal of Experimental Psychology: Human Perception and Performance* 17: 967-975.

2 Pierre Bourdieu uses the term *La distinction* (translated in English as "distinction"), which has similar features to sophistication as described here; however, Bourdieu is not avoiding value judgments, but instead is making a political and sociological polemic in which these value judgments are central in the function of societal control. The physiological and learning aspects of sophistication mentioned here may fit to some extent within Bourdieu's concept of habitus. See Bourdieu P (1984). *Distinction: A Social Critique of the Judgement of Taste*. Translated by Nice R. London: Routledge.

3 I acknowledge that one can transcend toughness and ugliness and end up back appreciating *nice* things, i.e., there can be further sophistications on initial sophistication, such that you can learn to genuinely appreciate all the fine details of being nice. This argument reminds me of the 12-step programs where, unless you have previously hit rock bottom, you lack street credibility when succeeding at being mainstream, cf. Iggy Pop vs. James Blunt. Plainly, to develop this polemic would be a book unto itself.

and a concert film with the San Francisco Symphony Orchestra entitled *S&M* (symphony and Metallica), and at the 2007 Classical Brit Awards Sir Paul McCartney won the Album of the Year for his album *Ecce Cor Meum*. However, these instances in which a taste for orchestral music supplants rock do not imply that classical is necessarily more sophisticated than rock; I am acquainted with more than one formerly sheltered boy taught violin from an early age suddenly discovering rock music at age 13 and then rejecting classical because it does not reflect the reality of sexual activity. The violinist Nigel Kennedy became famous for making the transition from classical to more popular genres, with a similar transition in his speaking accent; between discipline and freedom or between social grace and fun — those transitions could go in either direction, and neither one seems to me intrinsically more sophisticated. The evolution of a person's preferred emotions — as opposed to the evolution of their perceptual abilities — often dictates their progression in taste; this tends to manifest itself in territories with values and poses. The fact that McCartney entitled a classical album in Latin underscores the prejudices surrounding sophistication.

This raises the question as to whether the Schoenberg lovers enjoy twelve tone music because of its sonic qualities or because of its territorial pose. After all, it seems paradoxical that serialism is not universally considered bad music, given that the negative response to dissonant music is innate, and that the response happens in babies of multiple cultures. How is it that musical responses that are natural to us can disappear but only in some people? It is a greater reversal of your natural impulses than learning to stick your finger in your eyes after getting your first pair of contact lenses. The dissonance aficionados not only leave behind the hatred of dissonance, but they attain an appreciation of it and even crave its sophistication. They are not being contrary, lying when they say they like dissonance, to the point where they convince themselves that they actually do like dissonance. Some psychology experiments have shown objectively that people with substantially more musical training actually perceive aspects of twelve tone music that go over the heads of everyone else.[1]

This suggests that somehow intellect and familiarity can cause people to like music they might biologically dislike — even Schoenberg's. His music has many of the standard indicators of sophistication that people acquire.[2] One of the relatively uncontroversial indicators of sophistication is less repetition. Simple songs tend to take the form *verse-chorus-verse-chorus*-etc., whereas classical music might be considered more sophisticated because its archetypal form is *theme ==> development*. As the comedian Kin Hubbard (1868–1930) said, "Classical music is the kind we keep thinking will turn into a tune." Because Schoenberg prohibited the repetition of a note until all 12 notes of a scale are played in a tone row, in each bar there is less repetition of notes.[3]

---

1 Krumhansl C, Sandell G, and Sergeant D (1987). The Perception of Tone Hierarchies and Mirror Forms in Twelve-Tone Serial Music *Music Perception* 5: 153–184.

2 Schoenberg almost explicitly makes this argument about sophistication, familiarity and perception when he writes, "if an idea presupposes experiences that cannot have been everyone's or that are not familiar to everyone, then some people will be quite unable to follow." See Schoenberg A (1975) *Style and Idea: Selected Writings* , edited by Stein L, Belmont: London, p. 99.

3 As Schoenberg says, "This method consists primarily of the constant and exclusive use of a set of twelve tones. This means, of course, that no tone is repeated within the

Another characteristic of sophisticated music is that it uses a greater variety of components;[1] again using 12-tone rows forces variety on a bar by bar basis. Compared to the average interval size in most music from around the world, the average interval size in Schoenberg's twelve tone works is double — the melodies of Schoenberg jump around more than any type of music except for Swiss yodeling.[2] Even in more main-stream classical music, using a wide variety of harmonies can be considered sophisti-cated, although this can come across as quite judgmental. As Joni Mitchell said,

> I don't understand why Europeans and South Americans can take more sophistication. Why is it that Americans [sic] need to hear their happiness major and their tragedy minor, and as jazzy as they can handle is a seventh chord? Are they not experiencing complex emotions?[3]

The simple answer is that North Americans have very different musical rules for reinforcing their territory. While it is *partly* true that a person's response to music fol-lows from their favorite emotions (see figure 3.8 in chapter three), it also depends on a person's territory, and both of these influence what the listener expects — their *gram-mar* for music. "Playing with the ear's expectations" is what makes music pleasant to the seasoned ear. Tension and resolution. Music definitely has rules, but part of the fun is breaking them. The enigma inherent in trying to compose music loved by every-one is choosing which rules to play by. There is no point in breaking a rule from one song the listener has heard only once, whereas a composer would feel obliged to break many of the rules from a song the listener has heard a thousand times since childhood (e.g., *Twinkle Twinkle Little Star*). The progression through these violated rules parallels sophistication. Schoenberg transcended so many of music's rules, including the goal of coordinating emotions; ironically, the emotions provoked in his Viennese audiences were coordinated into attacking him. He took sophistication to its ultimate conclusion.

The problem is that there is a complete spectrum of sophistication, such that some rules can be broken often, while others probably need to be adhered to almost all the time. If each person has different rules, depending on what music they regularly listen to, then there can be no least common denominator for sophistication: even if every-

---

series and that it uses all twelve tones of the chromatic scale, though in a different order." Schoenberg A (1975). *Style and Idea: Selected Writings*, edited by Leonard Stein, Belmont: London, p. 218.

1 In one study Schellenberg and Trehub showed that both infants' and children's per-ceptual abilities were improved by repetition of tones, whereas the abilities of adults were not. They attributed this to acculturation rather than sophistication, because it was not done through deliberate learning. By the definition in this book the effects of sophistication and acculturation are nearly the same except that sophistication is deliberate and it also leads to preference, whereas acculturation is passive and it can lead to changes in perceptual abilities that are not necessarily accompanied by chang-es in preference or taste. Schellenberg EG and Trehub SE (1999). Culture-General and Culture-Specific Factors in the Discrimination of Melodies. *Journal of Experimental Child Psychology* 74: 107–127.

2 Huron D (2006). *Sweet anticipation: music and the psychology of expectation*. Cambridge, Mass: The MIT Press, p. 344.

3 Berson M (2010). "Fiddle and the Drum" presents a new facet of songsmith Joni Mitchell. *The Seattle Times* newspaper, 20 February.

---

one listened to the same genre of music, at the very least, compared to young children, adults would want a different set of rules broken.

It also stands to reason that the more you know about music, the more you like breaking the rules — or making up your own rules. It is no coincidence that in his life-time Schoenberg was known as a great teacher — not just of 20th century music, but of Mozart and Bach — and his exhaustive knowledge of the great masters almost certainly fuelled his radical musical departure from our conventional perceptions of music.

This implies that there can be no such thing as "the best music," because the word *best* cannot substitute for *natural* or even *representative*. The most archetypal music is not going to be liked by everyone, so, almost by definition, there is no music that can appeal to everyone. Conventional music, like humor, can become too familiar or too simple, thus becoming saccharine or boring. The only exception would be for newborn human babies, because they have so little experience.

So who is right: Helmholtz's theory that music comes from the essence of the sounds' vibrations, or Schoenberg's implicit assumption that everything about music is simply based on learning and association? Well, both are partly right. There can be no objective line between music and non-music; the line will always be blurred when a soundscape has only a partial family resemblance to music that we recognize. The most important issue is that sound has a powerful ability to touch our emotions. As it happens, humans have a natural predisposition from infancy for musicality, and this includes a natural preference for consonant sounds (which we share with some birds but not with most nonhuman primates). According to Jerome Kagan at Harvard, com-posers such as Schoenberg are literally "fighting biology" — as unsophisticated babies we prefer consonance, so the 'grimacing and fussing' provoked in Viennese music critics unfamiliar with Schoenberg's dissonant compositions is hardly surprising. But, "*Biology isn't destiny.*"[1] Culture and customs can overwhelm our biological predispositions from childhood. At the individual level, there cannot be a "best" music for everyone because the listener and his or her previous experience is a fundamental part of the process of determining what is good. Schoenberg is just another example showing that we can learn to genuinely enjoy sophisticated (and even bitter) tastes — why else would so many people enjoy coffee, beer or *King Lear*?

---

1 Jerome Kagan from Harvard, quoted from Parker SG (1996). Tiny Music Critics. Right Now, *Harvard Magazine*, November-December.

CHAPTER 5. WHY DO AGGRESSIVE YOUNG MEN BLARE OUT BOOMING MUSIC FROM THEIR CARS?

YOUR RESPONSE TO MUSIC DEPENDS ON YOUR PERSONALITY.

"If it's too loud, you're too old."[1]
—Ted Nugent

In the winter of 1964, the up and coming band the Detours were playing their Thursday night residency at the Oldfield just outside London. On a break between sets, a pint-sized 17-year-old in a little brown suit, brown shirt, brown shoes and a helmet of lacquered hair approached the leather-clad musicians. The unlikely lad told the lead guitarist that he could play the drums better than the band's current drummer.[2] They offhandedly gave him a shot and chose for him to play Bo Diddley's "Roadrunner." Not only did the kid know the song, he laid into it like a hurricane — breaking the bass pedal, tearing a drum skin and even denting the metal hi-hat. The band hired him on the spot, and in doing so changed the history of rock and roll. That unmanageable boy was legendary drummer Keith Moon, and the Detours soon changed their name to The Who.

After "Moon the Loon" joined the band, The Who became famous for smashing their instruments at the end of their concerts and flinging the broken bits of gear at their audience, showing they had given it all they had. Fans scrambled for pieces of splintered guitar wood to take home, which they gathered like territorial relics of each irretrievable performance. For their American TV debut in 1967, Moon planned something extra

---

1 Barnes M (2009). Come on, feel the noise. *The Guardian* newspaper (London, UK), 09 January.
2 Van Every, D (2009). "Rock Drum Greats — Keith Moon of The Who" Jan. 16th. Accessed. 8th Feb, 2010; http://biographiesmemoirs.suite101.com/article.cfm/rock_drum_greats_keith_moon_of_the_who

special. While Townshend was smashing his guitar into oblivion, Moon — who had bribed a roadie to load his drum-set with triple the normal amount of explosives — unleashed chaos. The resulting blast briefly knocked the network off the air and inflicted Townshend with permanent, severe ear damage.[1]

The band stuck to their guns with this devastation for most of their early career despite it costing more than they were earning. Moon, who was a teetotaler before joining The Who, was desperate to destroy his drum kit night after night. It wasn't just a gimmick; destruction and disinhibition heightened the loud music to new levels of magnetic frenzy. Why would such loud demolition enlist fans desperate to cling to the tangible remnants of performances?

The simplest answer is some people need a lot of arousal. Moon, like Kurt Cobain, suffered from behaviors resembling attention deficit disorder.[2] While Cobain would run up and down his street as a child, beating his toy drum, Moon became professionally enthralled with the "loud." There are a lot people who find it arousing and captivating to play and listen to music raucously, and it fit with his sensual lifestyle of booze, drugs, and women.

For decades, there were fans the world over who sought to baptize themselves in the pressure blasting from The Who's amps. As with Manowar in chapter two, The Who's loudness was conquering territory. This is hardly unique to The Who. How often have you pulled up to a stop light only to hear the bass in an adjacent car seeping through closed windows and locked doors? They find it arousing, invigorating, and as shown in chapter one, it is a method some people choose to mark their territory. But if music is for reinforcing territory, and loudness can conquer territory, why isn't *all* music loud? Why doesn't everyone want loud music? And why is it mostly younger men who do?

***

Since ancient times intense thrills have always clubbed together with loud music.[3] While "sex, drugs and rock and roll" is a relatively new experience in human history, war is not.[4] War may be ugly, but it can also be thrilling. In Chapter 1, music and war were shown to be linked, but the kind of music was not classified, because battle music has varied so much over history. From AC/DC's *Highway to Hell* to Turkish Janissary music, it only has one thing in common: it is loud. Drums, trumpets, horns, and cymbals.[5] Music for war has to energize people. Standing in a field soon to be littered with the bodies of friends and enemies, the battle march booms. There are no quiet strings in this

---

1 Van Every D (2009). Rock Drum Greats — Keith Moon of The Who. Suite101.com. 16th January. Accessed. 8th Feb, 2010; http://biographiesmemoirs.suite101.com/article. cfm/rock_drum_greats_keith_moon_of_the_who

2 Lusk J (2000). The Real Keith Moon. Accessed: Feb 8th, 2010; http://www.channel4. com/history/microsites/R/real_lives/moon.html

3 In addition to being loud, arousing music can be fast, high and varying in pitch, unexpected (e.g., dissonant), or glissando. A wide variety of timbres can also lead to arousal, for example whispering (compared to speaking in a low and quiet voice).

4 For an engaging history of how ubiquitous war can be in primitive societies, see Keegan J (1993). *A History of Warfare*. London: Pimlico.

5 Farmer HG (1949). Crusading martial music. *Music and Letters* XXX(3):243-249.

tune; the music is all drum and brass. The emblazoned flurry of notes strikes fear into your enemies and strengthens your resolve.

But war was not the only thrilling experience of ancient cultures. Religious ceremonies have been performed in huge, stone temples, from the Acropolis to Medieval cathedrals, where the music would echo and reverberate, amplifying the experience time and again. Large choirs heightened the sensations while the church organ (which shares many traits with a brass section) blasted the holy songs upwards toward their mighty inspiration. The religious rites required such loud praise — a breathless singer and a solo fiddle would never have been loud enough to make everyone raise their hands in the air shouting, "Praise the Lord!" Whether staring at your enemy from across a field, or contemplating the stains of sin on your immortal soul, fear could only be drowned out by reverberations you could feel on your chest.

Then the amplifier changed the music of thrills and adventure. For millennia stringed instruments were overpowered by voices, noises and almost any other instrument. Then, during the 20th century, the amplifier evolved.[1] Suddenly the quietest acoustic guitar could be heard cheek by jowl with a rowdy horn section. It is no coincidence that heavy metal progenitors Led Zeppelin refurbished fanfares as rock anthems. The loudness of the amplifier in and of itself would have drastically altered musical history, but an extra consequence immediately followed. No sooner had the amplifier been invented than a drunken genius decided to turn the volume all the way up. The sine waves of sounds were heightened beyond the fidelity limits of the amplifier, and then there was *clipping* — the tall sine waves were beheaded so all were the same height. The unnatural result was distortion — and the distortion was *mighty*. No longer confined to the quiet and dainty, the guitar found its voice, and it could squeal and scream.

But why does feeling thrills demand harmfully loud decibels? A well-publicized survey carried out by researchers from the Massachusetts Eye and Ear Infirmary in 2002 asked visitors to MTV's website whether they were concerned by the danger of hearing loss as a symptom of listening to loud music. Most of the 6,148 females and 3,310 males who responded expressed no concern whatsoever — despite three out of five of them reporting ringing in their ears after concerts or clubbing. Their average age was 19. Loud music seems a perennial attraction for teenagers. Why would teenagers (who have excellent hearing) need the music to be cranked up so loud to feel the emotion?

***

On June 13th 1926, while New York blistered under the molten sun, an aging London professor of classical music, Nicolas Coviello, and his young nephews decided to take a late afternoon constitutional through Coney Island.[2] A local jazz band flared up nearby and they decided to approach it. Coviello listened imperturbably as the band

---

1 Although technically the amplifier was invented in 1906 by Lee DeForrest with the invention of the vacuum tube, the issues of sound distortion and availability meant that amplifiers were not commonly available to musicians until after World War I. Loudspeakers dated back to the mid-1800s (e.g., the telephone), but the electric guitar did not appear until 1932, and the first commercially successful guitar was the Fender Esquire, which appeared in 1950.

2 Wallechinsky D, Wallace A (2005). *The New Book of Lists: The Original Compendium of Curious Information*. Edinburgh: Canongate Books.

members tickled, scratched and clawed at their strings with furious passion. The brass instruments pumped up the volume and the band gyrated to the vigorous beat. Coviello, whose coloring had been shifting to a bright red, turned and declared to his nephews, "That isn't music. Stop it!" He then swayed for a moment and keeled over dead. "Killed by Jazz?" cried the headline of London's *Daily Mirror* the next day. While it may not be surprising that a classical musician from an older generation would not appreciate jazz, what exactly inspired such a dramatic protest?

In the 1920s, jazz was the music that thrilled the young and baffled the old. In the 1950s history repeated itself with Rock and Roll, except this time it was the former jazz fans that were baffled. Time and again older generations have complained about the volume of young people's music. The only difference is that now we can fit super bass rigs into a car, allowing young men to indulge in volume, speed and defiance all at once.

Why is being young entangled with rebelliousness, thrill-seeking and risk? Is it logical, or biological? Maybe when one does not have very much to lose, risky behavior is pragmatic. Certainly the youth typically have fewer assets and minimal family responsibilities compared to their parents. However, thrill-seeking cannot simply be ascribed to having nothing to lose, because not all thrill-seekers lack territory.

Take the case of Stefano Casiraghi, who was in line to inherit an entire country. He was already leading a charmed life as the son of a Milan millionaire before he married Princess Caroline of Monaco. He had everything. His wealth and royal ties created a well-established social scene and a path straight towards success. Nitpicking journalists had a difficult time finding ammunition as his past was essentially unblemished. The closest thing to a scandal in which Casiraghi found himself was that he once lied about a genital tumor in order avoid a stint in the Italian military. Even his marriage appeared all but perfect. Stefano once mentioned that there was only one item that Caroline and he ever argued over: high speed motor racing.

Casiraghi's need for speed started early, and he indulged his craving at first by racing his Ferrari on mountain roads. When he graduated from university, he set up a real-estate construction company, but he devoted a significant amount of his time to his racing. Eventually he found his *raison d'être* on Italy's Lake Como: speedboat racing. Despite having once escaped death when his boat's engine exploded off the Isle of Guernsey, Casiraghi pursued his undying passion. He said of himself, "I am what they call a throttle man." [1]

Casiraghi's exploits kept people's attention, and a blasé journalist once joked, "Well, Casiraghi hasn't killed himself yet. Maybe that's for next year." [2] Unfortunately, the light-hearted prophecy turned out to be a bitter truth. Casiraghi died at the age of thirty while defending his speedboat racing title in the World Offshore Championships. At 108 mph, his catamaran went airborne, hit a wave, flipped, and his neck was snapped.

But Casiraghi's is not the only story of death claiming a young daredevil who had everything. Clearly thrill-seeking is not a psychological paradigm induced by poverty or lack of territory. Even in the upper echelon of social and personal success, thrill-seeking pushes individuals toward the precipice necessary to induce the next high. It seems as

---

1 Reed JD, Stratte-McClure J and Bentley L (1990). Another tragedy for Monaco. *People* magazine 34(15): 86-87. October 15.
2 Kurth P (1993). In The House of Grimaldi. *Cosmopolitan* magazine, July.

though Casirhagi was bored with his perfect life and jazzed up his emotions by thrill-seeking. For Stefano Casiraghi thrill-seeking was his ticket to a young death, and both his passion and his death were incredibly loud.

***

Just before Johnny Ace's (1929–1954) posthumous number one hit single "Pledging my Love" (1955) broke the color lines between black and white musicians, he became the first fatality of the Rock and Roll lifestyle. On Christmas Day of 1954, in a drink-fuelled revel backstage at his Houston City Auditorium concert, Ace aimed his .22 automatic at two people and pulled the trigger without effect before changing the rules of his dangerous game to Russian roulette. Ace fired the hidden bullet into his head at point blank range, in front of his girlfriend, fans, and blues-legend Big Mama Thornton. He was twenty-five.

Ace's obsession with firearms explains why he had an automatic with him. Guitar-ist Milton Hopkins said that Ace's idea of excitement was driving his Oldsmobile at 90 miles per hour with his pistol in his hand shooting at road signs warning of the speed-limit.[1] By the time of his death, Ace was an unmitigated thrill-seeker. His suicide was the culmination of a life of uninterrupted excitement. Music was just more stimulation for his bottomless appetite. A natural-born thrill-seeker like Ace was always on the watch for the next best thing — if his music didn't produce thrills, then he would find something else that did. On the day of his death, he bet on Russian roulette.

Psychologists would call Johnny Ace a Sensation Seeker. Sensation Seeking is a psychologically-validated, measurable personality trait. Sensation seeking makes people obsessed with thrill-seeking and boredom aversion, and it is epitomized by fast cars, loose women, illegal drugs and dangerous living. It was first described in the early 1960s by American psychologist and godfather of thrill-seeking Marvin Zucker-man, who conducted a series of experiments to discover how different people cope with the effects of sensory deprivation. Imagine the following experiment: you are placed in an empty, soundproof water tank for an indefinite period of time, possible hours. You are in complete isolation, complete darkness, and you are forbidden to whistle, sing or make any sounds at all to entertain yourself. When Zuckerman carried out exactly this experiment, he found that some volunteers were much more vulnerable than others to isolation — suffering from extreme restlessness, anxiety, and even hallucinations. He speculated that such stark variations between different people's reactions arose be-cause each person has their own optimal level of stimulation. If a person does not need much stimulation, then they can survive longer periods in isolation. But people who need lots of stimulation will begin to suffer from paranoia, and their minds will start playing tricks on them.

Zuckerman wondered whether this need for sensory stimulation was the very thing that drives people to carry out thrill-seeking activities such as skydiving and motor-cycle racing. In order to compare each volunteer's reactions to sensory deprivation with their thrill-seeking tendencies, he asked each participant to complete a personality

---

1 *Houston Chronicle* (1999), November 28, p. Zest-23.

questionnaire which he designed, called the Sensation Seeking Scale (SSS).[1] This scale not only measured Thrill-seeking tendencies, but also the three other aspects of sensation seeking: Disinhibition, Experience Seeking, and Boredom Aversion.

Disinhibition is that aspect of personality that lets people do all the things they have been unequivocally told not to do: taking drugs, risky sex practices, even being rude; it is characterized by a disregard for social conventions. Experience seeking is the desire to try new things and to enjoy sensual experiences; anything that involves trying something for the first time or sensations that may be unpleasant but different, like body odor or earthiness. Boredom aversion is the spur to action if boredom comes anywhere nearby.

This concurrent need for thrills and avoidance of boredom fit with Zuckerman's idea that each person has an optimal level of stimulation that they want to achieve. It turned out that of all of Zuckerman's experimental volunteers, the ones who were the most freaked out by the dark, were also the ones who wanted to jump out of airplanes. Ironically, this group of Zuckerman's volunteers, with their long straggly hair and leather biker jackets, was also the toughest looking bunch.

All the actions of Keith Moon, not just the drum-smashing, illustrate the full spectrum of sensation seeking in his personality: youth, disinhibition, defiance. In the likes and dislikes column of the NME's June 1965 "Life Lines" featurette, Keith Moon, with usual precision, summed up the interests of all teenage male musicians.

Miscellaneous Likes?	"Birds"
Professional Ambition?	To smash 100 drum kits
Personal Ambition?	To stay young forever.

Violent tendencies, such as Moon's instrument destruction, are not the only potentially destructive tendency associated with youthful sensation seeking. In a series of experiments I looked at a wide range of activities to determine what gives people pleasure. I wanted to find out if there was something intrinsic, possibly even something biological, behind why some people get pleasure from some activities — such as seeing a beautiful scene or place in nature — while other people prefer completely different pastimes — such as extreme activities (e.g., bungee jumping). I created a simple questionnaire that asked, "How much pleasure would you get from this activity?," followed by 45 highly varied activities, such as "Knowing my child/friend has achieved something wonderful," "Having a really good laugh," "Doing good deeds for people, helping," and "Going for a run." For each activity the participants had to circle a number between 1 (None) to 7 (makes life worth living). Having accumulated literally thousands of responses, to make sense of it all I used a statistical method called factor analysis, which tries to boil down the 45 different activities into a handful of categories by looking for

---

1 You can take this test on the following website: http://www.bbc.co.uk/science/humanbody/mind/surveys/sensation/

groups of activities that were liked by the same subgroup of people. For example, the people who rated highly "Sitting and chatting with friends" were also the same group of people who enjoyed "Meeting new people," and they also tended to favor "Traveling to a new place"; these activities (along with 6 other activities) formed the category of activities I ended up calling "extroverted pleasures."[1]

The computer picked out that there were at least seven categories of activities that give people pleasure: sensation seeking, gentle pleasures, extroversion, outdoors, work (and getting things done), exercise, and indoor violence.[2] One provocative finding was that in whatever cohort of people that I analyzed, "listening to a great piece of music," which appeared consistently in the top 5 activities that induce pleasure, was always in a different category from "Loud music (which is to your taste)." People's tastes in pleasurable activities were both coherent and particular. "Listening to a great piece of music" was almost invariably associated with a grouping that I would describe as "gentle pleasures." In this category the participants consistently chose gentle activities. "Seeing a beautiful work of art," "Listening to the birds, nature or quiet," and "Seeing a beautiful scene or place in nature."

By contrast, "Loud music (which is to your taste)" appeared in another grouping that the computer always picked out, which I called the "sensation seeking" category. It is worth remembering that I did not tell the computer to find such a category, but based on what people said they liked, the computer grouped together "extreme sports (e.g., bungee jumping)," "Riding amusement park rides," "'Experimental' sex," "Going fast (e.g., skiing, cars, boats)," "Taking or experimenting with illicit (or mind-altering) drugs," and "a brilliant night out drinking with friends." [3] Just as Zuckerman noted a connection between high sensation seekers and a preference for "generally loud rock music,"[4] the results of my experiment also showed "loud music" as an activity was linked consistently with other pleasures related to sensation seeking. Can the personality trait of sensation seeking explain why aggressive young men blare out booming music from their cars?

***

The science of personality is controversial and its results difficult to reproduce, but there is one aspect that appears reliably — sensation seeking. But can personality ever

---

1 The other six core members of the extroversion factor were: "Having a really good laugh," "Pleasant or exciting dreams," "Kissing (assuming love, lust or attraction)," "Receiving a heart-felt compliment from someone you like or respect," "cuddling," and "family gatherings."

2 The "Indoor violence" factor was a strange combination of mostly indoor activities (appearing repeatedly in different cohorts) consisting of the following: "Video/ Computer games," "Martial arts," "Watching television," "Yoga or related discipline," "Surfing the web," and even "Doing crossword puzzles." It tended to appear among younger groups, and was skewed toward males.

3 According to the individual item correlations, the most central members of the sensation seeking factor were wild parties followed by experimental sex. While it did involve some aspects of thrill and adventure seeking, it would not be surprising if the category was centered upon disinhibition.

4 Litle P & Zuckerman M (1986). Sensation seeking and music preferences. *Personality and Individual Differences.* 7, 575-577.

explain your actions? In academic circles, this question is called the person-versus-situation conundrum:[1] are a person's actions determined by his predispositions or by the particular situation in which he finds himself? It's certainly not your personality that wills you to go to the grocery store, but your personality may determine how quickly you try to get in and out.

If you see a stranger looking forlornly out to sea, would you diagnose the stranger as having a depressive personality, or is it simply that he is having a bad day?[2] Certainly you can't tell the difference when only running into someone once. For personality scientists, a pattern must exist in order to ascribe actions to a personality. Over time a personality trait must have three attributes: it must be *repeatable*, *stable*, and *generalizable*. In essence, personality would function like a so-called black box, which gets its name from the opaque nature of the personality's inner workings. The important fact is that a black box has a consistent output based on its input.[3] If you provide input "A," you will always receive output "B." So, when a person has a highly demonstrative and sincere personality, if input "A" was the death of a close friend, then output "B" would *always* be sadness and tears. However, with some people the genesis of their sadness is complicated.

Franz Schubert (1797–1828) is considered one of the greatest composers to have ever lived.[4] According to the great pianist and music teacher Harold Bauer,[5]

> In some ways, the music of this amazing genius is more indispensable to us than that of any other composer.[6]

Unfortunately, Schubert died in relative obscurity, decades before the public recognized the value of his work. He may have suffered from depression during most of his short life,[7] and in a letter to Leopold Kupelweiser dated 31 March 1824 he says, "I feel like the unhappiest and most wretched person in the world."[8]

---

1 Barenbaum NB, Winter DG (2008). History of Modern Personality Theory and Research. In (Eds.) John OP, Robins RW, Pervin LA, *Handbook of Personality: Theory and Research*. New York: The Guilford Press, pp. 3-28.

2 According to the American bible of psychiatric diagnosis, (American Psychiatric Association (2000). *Diagnostic and Statistical Manual Edition IV-TR*, Arlington, Virginia: American Psychiatric Association) to be diagnosed as depressed a person must have a lowered mood (or loss of interest) lasting for at least two weeks.

3 Friedenberg J, Silverman G (2006). "Mind as a Black Box: The Behaviorist Approach," In *Cognitive Science: An Introduction to the Study of Mind*, London: Sage Publications, pp 85-88.

4 Woodford P (1978). *Schubert*. London: Omnibus Press.

5 In addition to performing internationally on both violin and piano from the age of 9, Bauer founded the Beethoven Society of New York, was president of the Friends of Music of the Library of Congress, and was the head of the piano department at the Manhattan School of Music. Highlights of his performing career include giving the Paris premiere of Debussy's Children's Corner suite and the New York premiere of Ravel's Concerto in G major. Ravel dedicated his Ondine to Bauer.

6 Schauffler RH (1949). *Franz Schubert: the Ariel of Music*. New York: Putnam's, p. 202.

7 Gibbs CH (2000). *The Life of Schubert*. Cambridge, UK: Cambridge University Press. pp. 95-97.

8 Letter from Schubert to Kupelweiser in Rome 31 March 1824. In Deutsch OE (1947). *The Schubert Reader*, (trans. Eric Blom). New York: Norton.

Schubert's agonizing disappointments in life were the stuff of soap operas.[1] Son of a parish schoolmaster and a housemaid, nine of Schubert's thirteen siblings died before the age of six. Schubert attended music class from an early age, and he was recognized as having some talent. However, for most of his life he was barely able to make ends meet. Introverted and shy, he avoided large (and potentially profitable) performances, instead concentrating his performances on songs and chamber music for a small group of close friends. In 1814, Schubert met a young soprano by the name of Therese Grob. After composing several songs for her, Schubert planned on asking Grob for her hand in marriage. As such, it was most inopportune that in 1815, a law was passed which required proof of the monetary means of supporting a family before one could marry; Schubert had to sacrifice love to gain employment — doing teaching, which he loathed. In 1824 he fell in love again, this time with one of his music pupils, Countess Karoline Eszterházy. The situation was impossible, and in any event his love was unrequited, so he never revealed to her the depth of his feelings.

Schubert was remarkably prolific, composing for 5 hours at the start of each day. In the 18 years of his adult life he composed over 1000 works.[2] Just as his music was beginning to become appreciated, he fell ill at the age of 31. While typhoid fever eventually killed Schubert, he had been suffering from symptoms of mercury poisoning for quite some time. Mercury was used at that time for treating syphilis, and it is theorized that Schubert had been suffering from the disease for several years.[3]

If you saw Schubert staring forlornly out to the sea, you might give him the benefit of a doubt: maybe he's having a bad day. But if you bumped into him again, and again, and he was always just staring off, you might start to believe that Schubert had a depressed personality. However, Schubert did not have a bad day — he had a bad life. Maybe he was born a happy young lad, before watching all of his siblings perish, his music career falter, and love escape him while sex killed him. You'd be depressed too... though you probably wouldn't be buried next to Beethoven for it.

So, as personality traits go, ascribing depression to personality or environment is difficult. The person could be morose, or their life could be tragic. Situational factors could conceivably justify depression. Thrill-seeking is a much more clear cut personality trait because there are no situations that justify taking a risk with your life just for fun. Unlike being depressed and staring out to sea, speedboat racing is not a natural emotional response to a disappointment in love, the birth of a child, the death of a sibling, or any particular life event — it is a manifestation of the sensation seeking personality trait.

Studies show that people between the ages of 16 to 20 happen to be the highest sensation seekers; they are more likely to get involved in car accidents — accident rates being highest among males in this group — and more often convicted for driving of-

---

1 The psychological effects of key events in Schubert's life are touched upon in the chapter on Schubert in Neumayr A (1994). *Music and Medicine*, Volume 1, translated by Clarke BC. Bloomington, Illinois: Medi-Ed Press.

2 See Newbould B (1997). *Schubert: The Music and the Man.* Berkeley, California: University of California Press.

3 Neumayr A (1994). *Music and Medicine*, Volume 1, translated by Clarke BC. Bloomington, Illinois: Medi-Ed Press.

fences.[1] Sensation seeking is not only associated with taking pleasure in "experimental sex" on my survey; it is even associated with the propensity to download internet porn.[2] Perhaps the sensation seeking personality trait is the connection between adolescence and loud music. If sensation seeking responded to that burst of teenage hormones, it would explain how loud music, thrill seeking and sexual frenzy hit teenagers at once like a car crash.

***

In 1966, a 20 year old, Cynthia Albritton, was not much different from many young women of that era. She loved art and the gorgeous men of rock and roll. That year, she decided to mix the two. Her college art class had assigned her the task of plaster cast-ing "something solid that could retain its shape." [3] Art was about to turn a corner, and it would never be the same again. Cynthia and her best friend grabbed their plaster and went to a gig of Paul Revere and the Raiders. There, the two of them requested the honor of immortalizing the band members' genitals in a mould. Cynthia's request was rejected, but she could console herself because she lost her virginity to the lead singer.

Was her vision to capture the metaphorical erections of rock music one member at a time? No. Cynthia used it as a gimmick to compete with all the other groupies.[4] Even though it was just a talking point, it was her backstage pass to getting intimately close to her heroes of rock and roll. For all the talk about plaster casting, two years drifted by before she convinced anyone famous to place such sensitive material into her vase of plaster.

In an unanticipated venture into the annals of history, the first rock star to acqui-esce was Jimi Hendrix. When they first met and accosted Hendrix outside of his hotel, he had already heard of the plaster casters and immediately invited them up to his hotel room. As her partner Dianne orally "prepared" Hendrix for the experience, Cynthia mixed the plaster. According to Jimi's bassist Noel Redding (who also had his member cast for posterity), the encounter was actually more clinical than erotic.[5] However, the mould was a success, and a career was born. Over the years Cynthia has managed to immortalize over ninety artists, including the Dead Kennedys' Jello Biafra and singer-songwriter Anthony Newly. In this mixture of sex, loud music and experience seeking, her first rock star, Hendrix was probably her biggest success.

Things changed as Cynthia aged. She found that the call of loud music and endless sensation seeking was waning. Never losing her artistic vision, however, she drifted to

1 Stradling S, Meadows M, Beatty S (2004). Characteristics and crash involvement of speeding, violating and thrill-seeking drivers. In Rothengatter T, Huguenin RD (eds.) *Traffic and transport psychology: theory and application.* Oxford: Elsevier, pp. 177-194.

2 Weisskirch RS, Murphy LC. (2004). Friends, porn, and punk: sensation seeking in personal relationships, internet activities, and music preference among college stu-dents. *Adolescence* 39(154): 189-201.

3 Albritton C. "The Official Cynthia Plaster Caster Website." Accessed March, 15, 2010; http://www.cynthiaplastercaster.com/flash/home.html.

4 Albritton C. "The Official Cynthia Plaster Caster Website." Accessed March, 15, 2010; http://www.cynthiaplastercaster.com/flash/home.html.

5 Cross CR. (2005). *Room full of mirrors: a biography of Jimi Hendrix.* London: Hodder & Stoughton Ltd.

filmmakers and other territories that are more linked to status than sensation seeking. Why is this move away from the loud so prototypical? Why is it mostly in the young that we see such exaggerated sensation seeking?

In the summer of 1998, a fifteen year old Billie Piper unleashed her UK number 1 hit, "Because We Want To." The chorus chants:

> Why you gotta play that song so loud?
> Because we want to! Because we want to!
> Why d'you always run around in crowds?
> Because we want to! Because we want to!

She may not have been a rocket scientist, but she definitely said it loud and clear. Young adults not only want to play their music loud and run around in crowds, but they want to have wild sex, drink, shoot things, drive as fast as possible and leave pretty corpses. However, some of us older folk can't help but ask — why Billie? Why?

Because science says so. In repeated tests on different cultures, sensation seeking has been found to vary with age, reaching a peak at late adolescence. While it is difficult to compare adults to children because the tests for sensation seeking are different for children, the scientific consensus is that males have higher sensation seeking levels than females, and that for both sexes sensation seeking increases throughout out childhood, reaches a peak in adolescence and then rolls downhill thereafter to a cowardly and silent old age (see figure 5.1).

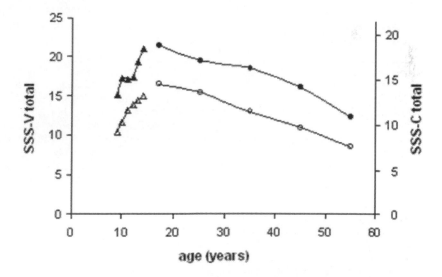

Figure 5.1 - Total sensation seeking scores for adults (SSS-V, circles) and children (SSS-C, triangles). Solid symbols are males, clear symbols females.[1]

---

1 Note that in some studies the peak in sensation seeking is reached slightly later, in the twenties. Children's data from Russo MF, Stokes GS, Lahey BB, Christ MAG, McBurnett K, Loeber R, Stouthamer-Loeber M, & Green SM (1993). A sensation seeking

People argue over whether psychology is a product of nature or nurture, but personality is not only a consequence of both genetics and environment, but also of age. Just as height and hair color — or even whether we have hair — changes with age, so too does personality. The changes with age are a fundamental biological process. Of course environment, nutrition and your family upbringing can modify what age does to your personality, but age remains one of the primary determinants. The levels of sensation seeking may be chronicled in a person's genes, but its expression will depend on a person's age. Although there is much argument within psychology as to whether a static or consistent *personality* even exists,[1] sensation seeking is one of the best-established personality traits because it is measurable, consistent and heritable — almost like height or blood pressure.

There is good evidence that sensation-seeking is a highly genetic personality trait. In studies comparing identical to fraternal twins, statistics can tease apart the contributions of genetics vs. environment/upbringing to a personality trait; comparing the influence of nature versus nurture shows that 58% of the sensation-seeking trait is heritable.[2] This is just about the highest level of genetic determination that a personality trait can normally achieve, given that the range of heritability calculated for most personality traits is between 40-60%.[3]

There is also physiological evidence that sensation seeking is biological. When presenting individuals with a loud noise (60 decibels), their body's level of arousal changes; this arousal can be measured as a change in heart rate, which is an objective measure of a physical response outside of conscious control. Amazingly, the average response to the tone is completely different depending on whether the person is high in sensation seeking or low in sensation seeking; the low sensation seekers have a sudden increase in heart rate (arousal), while the high sensation seekers have a sudden decrease in heart

---

scale in children: Further refinement and psychometric development. *Journal of Psychopathology and Behavioral Assessment*, 15: 69-86. Adult data from Zuckerman M, Eysenck SBG, Eysenck HJ (1978). Sensation seeking in England and America: Cross-cultural, age, and sex comparisons. *Journal of Consulting and Clinical Psychology* 46: 143.

1 There are many criticisms of personality in general. For example, behavior can be made to change by changes in diet. Other proponents of personality view it in a positive (and highly flexible) perspective. See Rogers C (1959). A theory of therapy, personality and interpersonal relationships as developed in the client-centered framework. In Koch S (Ed.). *Psychology: A study of a science*. Vol. 3: Formulations of the person and the social context. New York: McGraw Hill.

2 This study which compared 442 pairs of twins, half of which were identical twins — who have all their genes in common — and half of which were fraternal twins — who share about 50% of their genes — enabling scientists to measure the extent to which genetic and environmental factors contribute towards shaping personality. Fulker DW, Eysenck SBG, & Zuckerman M (1980). A genetic and environmental analysis of sensation seeking. *Journal of Research in Personality*, 14: 261-281 quoted in Zuckerman M (1994). *Behavioral Expressions and Biosocial Bases of Sensation Seeking*, Cambridge: Cambridge University Press, p. 291.

3 While genes are commonly referred to as the recipe for humanity, the environmental contribution to an individual's personality continues (in an ever-diminishing level) throughout adulthood. This is where the nature versus nurture debate can really get going; perhaps there is no such thing as a genetic personality trait, merely biological susceptibilities to ways of thinking.

rate (calming). Musical taste also varies with age, and this data suggests that sensation seeking may explain why older generations often prefer much quieter music than their children do.

Sensation seeking is also manifested (at least in part) biochemically. High sensation seekers statistically have lower levels of the enzyme monoamine oxidase B (MAO-B) in their blood platelets.[1] In the brain this enzyme can breakdown monoamine neurotransmitters in order to reduce the transfer of information between neurons, which may imply that high sensation seekers are more habituated to feeling intense emotions. Having lower quantities of the enzyme MAO-B, means that dopamine (the reward chemical) exists in increased amounts, enhancing social and sexual rewards. Dopamine, one neurotransmitter that MAO-B breaks down, is responsible for activity directed at gaining rewards such as food and sex.

A study contrasting high and low MAO-B monkeys living in a natural environment found that low MAO-B monkeys (presumably the high sensation seekers) were more active, aggressive, dominant, sexually active, and social than high MAO-B monkeys of both sexes.[2] The difference in sociability among monkeys suggests that low MAO-B (high sensation seeking) might also be associated with extroversion in humans. Studies show that low MAO-B male and female college students reported spending more time socializing on an average weekday and weekend than high MAO-B students.[3] This suggests that sensation-seeking behavior has a physiological component.

But, if sensation seeking is a consistent, biologically-determined personality trait, why does it peak between the ages of 16 to 20? One explanation is that people between these ages are also at their hormonal peak, so that listening to and playing loud music is simply a manifestation of what is going on in their bodies biologically. This means that for a given person, their level of sensation seeking depends on a mixture of their age, gender, and genetic predisposition. If sensation seeking peaks during male adolescence and early manhood, and if high scores in sensation seeking are often accompanied by a preference for loud music, then we have found the answer to our question: why do aggressive young men blare out booming music from their cars? Because that is when

1   Zuckerman M (1994). *Behavioral Expressions and Biosocial Bases of Sensation Seeking* Cambridge: Cambridge University Press, pp.291-301. Studies show that there is a significant negative correlation between the General SSS and blood platelet MAO, with 9 out of 13 correlations being significant for the general SSS. Zuckerman quotes: Schooler C, Zahn TP, Murphy DL & Green SB. (1978). Psychological correlates of monoamine oxidase activity in normals. *Journal of Nervous and mental Disease*. 166: 177-186; Murphy DL, Belmaker RH, Buchsbaum MS, Martin NF, Ciaranello R & Wyatt RJ. Biogenic amine related enzymes and personality variations in normals. *Psychological Medicine*. 7: 149-157.

2   Redmond DE, Murphy DL, & Baulu J (1979). Platelet monoamine oxidase activity correlates with social affiliative and agonistic behaviors in normal rhesus monkeys. *Psychosomatic Medicine, 41,* 87-100 quoted in Zuckerman M (1994). *Behavioral Expressions and Biosocial Bases of Sensation Seeking.* Cambridge: Cambridge University Press, 300.

3   Coursey RD, Buchsbaum MS, Murphy DL (1979). Platelet MAO activity and evoked potentials in the identification of subjects biologically at risk for psychiatric disorders. *British Journal of Psychiatry,* 134: 372-381 quoted in Zuckerman M (1994). *Behavioral Expressions and Biosocial Bases of Sensation Seeking.* Cambridge: Cambridge University Press, p. 300.

they are highest in sensation seeking. But this begs the real question of why sensation seeking, risk taking and loud music would evolutionarily be linked to hormones such that they peak in adolescence.

***

For a young man growing up in the middle class in the West, growing up is fairly easy. Admittedly, most teenagers will argue this point, but in retrospect, life is pretty good. A warm bed, hot meals, and lazy summers form a prototypical example. Drama, such as a two-week romance or not having a car, is the closest they ever get to tragedy. It's the period often remembered as "my salad days." Yet sensation seeking is genetically predisposed to peak around this time. Why is that?

Adolescence holds within it the kernel of its own destruction. Eventually Daddy stops paying for the lazy summers. The young man has to leave home. He starts marking out the territory of his new home with loads of dirty laundry, overfilled rubbish bins, and mold...along with loud music, loud clothes, and underwear lying all over the floor, often belonging to both sexes.

Regardless of an individual's circumstances, in our species the creation of a young man's territory is biologically-programmed to occur around late adolescence. This would have been imperative in the primitive cultures from which man evolved. This territorial need coincides with the peak in sensation seeking; the same kind of peak occurs in women, but it is more petite. As in many other animals, staking out territory is not for the faint of heart. It takes a certain amount of reckless abandon to challenge the alphas. The inner experience is probably identical to that of a kob fighting for a territory in the lek. In humans this would determine who would fight their way to the best territory. Usually someone with a little bit of craziness in his eyes. Even if one is not trying to supplant the king of the mountain, even if one is trying to stake out a modest little plot to attract a modest little girl who shares one's dream of a well-maintained vegetable garden, there's always some jerk who wants it all for himself.

The need for territory and the peak of sensation seeking would have collided in adolescence in our forerunners. Like the rudder on the Titanic, evolution ten thousand years ago would not have directed adolescent behavior toward pacifism. Stefano Casirhagi may not have *needed* to conquer territory, but his teenage ancestors definitely would have. The late-adolescent territorial venture is competitive and risky, so traits such as high energy and risk taking are advantageous.

And loud music advertises just such a bold attitude. It announces that one does not care who hears it. If someone does not like it, what are they going to do about it? It takes bravery to confront the social norms, whether one is a human or a wolf. In evolution bravery will be delineated from stupidity based on the ability to survive. If you are brave but weak, you'll perish; if you are brave and strong, you will conquer territory. Not surprisingly, bravery and confrontation attract women and other followers because the survivors are winners. Applying the same argument to music, when a young man's bass woofers are thumping out of his car, he is demanding the respect that heralds social territory. The individual is then well on his way to establishing a throne that will not be called into question — until some newfangled music strikes him down in front of his young nephews.

Thus, territory has both inward and outward benefits. The outward signs of territory make you attractive, which helps to gain sex. Inwardly, territory has emotional correlates that make you feel empowered — either to enjoy what you have got, or to make your next conquest. As shown in chapter two, having sex helps you to feel this empowerment. This is all very well for the man with territory and sex, because each sustains the other, but it is a Catch-22 for the boy or girl without territory. Biologically, the final piece of the puzzle is sensation seeking, which drives you to do those activities that will land you in your first territory. Loud music advertises that territory-gaining attitude, even if the interior of a Ford is the sum total of all you have conquered so far.

CHAPTER 6. WHY DO WE LISTEN TO SAD MUSIC?

THE RESPONSE TO MUSIC DEPENDS ON CONTEXT.

What came first, the music or the misery? People worry about kids playing with guns, or watching violent videos, that some sort of culture of violence will take them over. Nobody worries about kids listening to thousands, literally thousands of songs about heartbreak, rejection, pain, misery and loss. Do I listen to pop music because I'm miserable or am I miserable because I listen to pop music?
—John Cusack, from *High Fidelity* (2000)

Los Angeles, 2003. A sun-bleached landscape stretches toward the horizon. Buildings and cars glisten in the heat. In a swimming pool overlooking the city, a tall and lanky English man is paddling alone in the shallow end of the pool while waiting for lunch. Cut to flashback fifteen years before. The same Englishman, now electric on stage, is dolefully singing into a microphone while adoring fans are showering him with long-stemmed red roses. The shy superstar is Steven Patrick Morrissey, former singer with the iconic 80's band, The Smiths. By the early 1990s, the gloomy and wistful pop star had been exhausted by Britain. Explaining his move to Los Angeles, he says, "Britin's a terribly negative place. And it hammers people down and it pulls you back and it prevents you."[1]

But there is something decidedly incongruent about Morrissey's move. Of all places, why Los Angeles? Even Morrissey himself recognized this peculiarity: "I normally live in LA, if you can call it normal living," he quipped.[2] It seems perverse that Morrissey would

---

1 Times Online (2007). Morrissey complains that immigration has led to the loss of Britain's identity. *Times Online* (London, UK), 29 November.
2 Simpson M (2003). Return of the lone stranger. *The Guardian* newspaper (London, UK), 31 May.

---

want to be in LA, given that he is the lyricist who penned the line: "A dreaded sunny day so I meet you at the cemetery gates." Such lugubrious words just shrivel up and die in the scorching California heat. Hemmed in by LA's vast roadway culture, Morrissey might be forgiven for contemplating his lyric, "If a ten-ton truck kills the both of us, to die by your side, well, the pleasure — the privilege is mine."

Poor Morrissey. After years of baring his melancholic soul, the only way to buoy his newfound happiness was to leave the wellspring of his downcast muse. Whether or not his censure of the British psyche is fair, his implicit premise is that his own mood is precariously sustained by his environment. This raises a question about music. Morrissey's music shaped a decade by being the most conspicuous testimony for the maxim, "Misery loves company." Is his adoption of Los Angeles an admission that, "Your milieu, including your music, is what props up your happiness?" After all, many people would agree with the statement, "Music is the secret to happiness." When people are surveyed about what they do to improve their mood, listening to music is the second most effective method.[1] If music can make you happy, why would you willingly listen to music that might make you sad? Why not avoid sadness altogether and immerse yourself in happy music? The trivial answer is that sad music does not make you sad, it makes you happy.

To prove this catch-22 — that sad music makes people happy — a scientist would say that you need an experiment in which each participant's happiness is measured before and after listening to sad music, but this is not as straightforward as it sounds.[2] How can you know, let alone measure, when somebody is *really* happy? If you ask people directly, they may give you the answer they think you want; if you play sad music and then ask, "So, now how do you feel?" many people will say "sadder" even if they don't feel much of anything. One way of surreptitiously revealing a person's emotional response to a stimulus is to ask them to appraise something else that is ostensibly unconnected to it. For example, in one experiment shoppers were handed a small gift (such as notepads or fingernail clippers) in a shopping center. Their pleasure spilled over into their thinking generally, as later testified by an apparently unrelated survey; the gift recipients rated how well their TVs were working as higher than did those people who had not been given a small present.[3]

Similarly, when psychologists asked cinema-goers for their opinions on their quality of life, their careers, their future and some controversial public figures, they found that people's assessments were generally more positive after happy films, but negative after sad films. Watching films like *Back to the Future* (1985) caused people to become more satisfied, more optimistic and, interestingly, more favorable towards their politicians, while sad films such as *The Killing Fields* (1985) made people more pessimistic

---

1 Exercise is number one. See Thayer RE, Newman JR, and McClain TM (1994). Self-regulation of mood: strategies for changing a bad mood raising energy, and reducing tension. *Journal of Personality and Social Psychology*, 67(5): 910-925.

2 The measurement of happiness cannot be done in any one way, so scientists have developed a plethora of approaches for making these measurements, each having its advantages and weaknesses. See chapter 2 for more details.

3 Isen AM, Shalker T, Clark M & Karp L (1978). Affect, accessibility of material in memory and behavior: A cognitive loop? *Journal of Personality and Social Psychology* 36: 1-12.

about the future performance of the economy.[1] This implies that emotions displayed in a film do not purge you of those feelings. This seems to disprove the idea that works of art are supposed to engender catharsis; the emotions in the performance are purported to vent your pent up emotions, thus making you more emotionally balanced. Not so with cinema. Sad films do not make you happier — they temporarily make you appraise your life more negatively.

So, is music different from film? Does sad music actually make you happy? This question is less like a scientific hypothesis and more like a philosophical enigma. It is reminiscent of a kōan, the Buddhist riddles such as "What is the sound of one hand clapping?" because there is a paradox in listening to something sad to make yourself happy. The question, "Does sad music actually make you happy?" is rarely attacked scientifically, but when it is, the answer is, "Sometimes yes, but sometimes no." In one Japanese study entitled, "Why do people listen to sad music: effects of music on sad mood," the effect of sad music on a person's mood depended on their mood in the first place: people in a very sad mood did feel happier, but listeners in a neutral mood felt sadder and those in slightly sad mood were left unchanged.[2] In fact, in that study both sad and not-sad individuals were made substantially less sad by doing geometry problems — proof that distraction works.

A long-standing study from Canada claimed that sad music changed the physical responses of people's bodies into a sad configuration.[3] In my own studies on the effects of sad music on mood, we used Samuel Barber's *Adagio for Strings* because, in terms of eliciting an unambiguous emotional response, it was one of the most consistent. In 2004, a BBC Radio 4 survey in search of the world's saddest music found that this one piece towered over all others.[4] With a majority of more than 50%, the voters chose Barber's *Adagio for Strings* performed by the London Symphony Orchestra as the saddest piece they had ever heard. It out-gloomed Dido's Lament *"When I am laid in Earth"* by Purcell, the *Adagietto* from Gustav Mahler's Symphony No. 5, and Richard Strauss' *Metamorphosen*. Two years later, Barber's *Adagio* became the bestselling classical download on iTunes[5]. In the USA, the incredible sadness ascribed to the *Adagio* has elevated it to the status of 'national funeral music'.[6] First used during the national mourning for John F. Kennedy after his untimely death, it formed the soundtrack in Oliver Stone's *Platoon* for scenes of doomed American soldiers fighting for their lives in the Vietnam War. The most memorable recent appearance of Barber's masterpiece as a focus for international mourning was during the Last Night of the Proms in 2001, when the piece was per-

---

1 Forgas JP & Moylan SJ (1987). After the movies: Transient mood and social judgment. *Personality and Social Psychology Bulletin* 13: 467-477.

2 Matsumoto J (2002). Why do people listen to sad music: effects of music on sad mood. *Japanese Journal of Educational Psychology* 50: 23-32.

3 Krumhansl CL (1997). An Exploratory Study of Musical Emotions and Psychophysiology. *Canadian Journal of Experimental Psychology* 51(4): 336-353.

4 Howard L (2007). The popular reception of Samuel Barber's 'Adagio for Strings'. *American Music* 25: 50-80.

5 Higgins C (2006). Big demand for classical downloads is music to ears of record industry. *The Guardian* newspaper (London, UK), 28th March.

6 Hillman R (2003). Cultural memory on film soundtracks. *Journal of European Studies* 33: 323-332.

formed by the BBC Symphony Orchestra just days after the 9/11 attacks on the World Trade Center in New York.

The piece is undeniably sad, yet, in my studies, Barber's *Adagio* engendered a cocktail of diametrically opposed emotions in participants, who filled in subjective question-naires divulging that they felt *both* more sadness *and* more happiness. Time and again we see that sad music does not simply make people "happy" *per se*, although it does have a powerful effect on people. Something astonishingly paradoxical is happening to people when they listen to sad music. What is it?

***

At the height of the Great Depression, *Gloomy Sunday* (1933), the lethal masterpiece of self-taught Hungarian composer Rezső Seress (spelled "Seres" in Hungarian), became known as the "suicide song" after compelling at least seventeen listeners to end their own lives.[1] *Gloomy Sunday* is a morbid love song in which a man declares that the only way to prove his devotion to his sweetheart, who refuses to believe he really loves her, is by killing himself one gloomy Sunday. Although mired in controversy, the song has had a variety of suicidal effects. In 1936 Joseph Keller, a shoemaker in Budapest, included the lyrics in his suicide note, while a young shopkeeper in Berlin hung herself with a copy of "Gloomy Sunday" at her feet, and in New York, "Gloomy Sunday" was the funeral music resolved upon by a pretty typist who gassed herself. An epidemic of song-inspired sui-cides provoked the chiefs at the BBC to ban the song from the airwaves, only lifting the ban in 2002. In the US, some radio stations and nightclubs adopted a similar boycott.[2]

As fate would have it, not even Rezső Seress would escape the bizarre effects of his song. Seress, who had been unsuccessful in making a living in Paris as a songwriter, had many rows with his girlfriend who questioned the stability of his career choices. The couple finally parted with angry words. The Sunday following their quarrel, Seress found himself fingering a strange and melancholy tune as he sat at his piano, gazing mo-rosely through his apartment window at the Parisian skyline. Storm-clouds gathered in the grey sky, and heavy rain poured. "What a gloomy Sunday" he said, and scribbled down the notes to his new song. The translation for the lyrics he wrote is:

> It is autumn and the leaves are falling
> All love has died on earth
> The wind is weeping with sorrowful tears
> My heart will never hope for a new spring again
> My tears and my sorrows are all in vain
> People are heartless, greedy and wicked...[3]

---

1 The facts surrounding "Gloomy Sunday" are poorly documented and sometimes dis-puted. For an academic discussion see: Stack S, Krysinskad K, & Lester D (2007). Gloomy Sunday: did the "Hungarian suicide song" really create a suicide epidemic? *Omega* 56(4): 349-358.
2 Lax R & Smith F (1989). *The Great Song Thesaurus*, 2nd edition, New York: Oxford University Press, p. 243.
3 These are the original despairing lyrics written by Seress, with the caveat that these lyrics for Gloomy Sunday have been translated into English. Historically speaking, in the released version of the song Seress's original lyrics were rewritten (again in Hun-garian) by Seress's friend László Jávor. Javor's lyrics when translated are more artistic

Not surprisingly, Seress originally had a hard time getting a record deal for *Gloomy Sunday*. One music publisher seems to have anticipated its morbid effects when he rejected the song:

> It is not that the song is sad, there is a sort of terrible compelling despair about it. I don't think it would do anyone any good to hear a song like that.

But when Seress finally sold the song to a music publisher, its phenomenal success led him to contact his ex-lover, the muse of *Gloomy Sunday*, to arrange their reconciliation. The very next day, however, his sweetheart was found dead. She had poisoned herself, and next to her was a suicide note with just two words: "Gloomy Sunday." In America music producers attempted to mitigate the depressing tone of the song by adding a third stanza to the Billie Holiday version, which began "Dreaming, I was only dreaming." This fooled no one and only increased the song's popularity — and there appeared still more accounts of music-possessed lovers jumping from their damaged lives into oblivion.

When questioned about the effects of his song, Seress replied, "I stand in the midst of this deadly success as an accused man. This fatal fame hurts me. I cried all of the disappointments of my heart into this song, and it seems that others with feelings like mine have found their own hurt in it." [1] In 1968, in a final surrender to the curse of his

---

"Budapest, January 13. Rezsoe Seres, whose dirge-like song hit, "Gloomy Sunday" was blamed for touching off a wave of suicides during the nineteen-thirties, has ended his own life as a suicide it was learned today. Authorities disclosed today that Mr. Seres jumped from a window of his small apartment here last Sunday, shortly after his 69th birthday. The decade of the nineteen-thirties was marked by severe economic depression and the political upheaval that was to lead to World War II. The melancholy song written by Mr. Seres, with words by his friend, Ladislas Javor, a poet, declares at its climax, "My heart and I have decided to end it all." It was blamed for a sharp increase in suicides, and Hungarian officials finally prohibited it. In America, where Paul Robeson introduced an English version, some radio stations and nightclubs forbade its performance. Mr. Seres complained that the success of "Gloomy Sunday" actually increased his unhappiness, because he knew he would never be able to write a second hit."
— New York Times, 1968

---

but equally morbid: "This last Sunday, my darling please come to me / There'll be a priest, a coffin, a catafalque and a winding-sheet / There'll be flowers for you, flowers and a coffin / Under the blossoming trees it will be my last journey / My eyes will be open, so that I could see you for a last time / Don't be afraid of my eyes, I'm blessing you even in my death..." The original Seress lyrics in Hungarian are: szomorú vasárnap / Ősz van és peregnek a sárgult levelek / Meghalt a földön az emberi szeretet / Bánatos könnyekkel zokog az öszi szél / Szívem már új tavaszt nem vár és nem remél / Hiába sírok és hiába szenvedek / Szívtelen rosszak és kapzsik az emberek...

1 *Time* Magazine (1936). Letters, April 13.

song, Rezsó Seress jumped out the window of his apartment and plunged to his death. It was a Sunday.

So if we ask, "Did Gloomy Sunday make these suicidal people happy or sad?" plainly the answer is, "Probably neither." As for sad, there is not enough information, so we can only guess whether the song made them sad, or if they chose the song because they were already miserable. A conservative guess would be that by the time they started playing the song over and over they were not in a great mood. We can only speculate as to whether playing the recording made them even sadder. The only thing we can say for certain is it definitely did not make these depressed people happy.

But maybe it made them feel "better." There are other ways of feeling better than by being happier. Consolation. Communion. Resolved to a bad end. You could split hairs about the word *happiness* and claim that all of three of these emotions lead to happiness, and from a psychological perspective they do bring about *greater positive affect*, but, as I see it, "resolved to a bad end" does not resemble "happiness" *per se*. It sounds more like the sort of emotion one experiences from being in one's own territory, like a captain going down with his ship.

***

Ever since Freud's *Beyond the Pleasure Principle* rejected the idea that all motivations could be distilled down to the pursuit of pleasure or the rejection of pain, psychology has struggled to explain why people willingly do horrific things to themselves. For instance in 1963 the Buddhist monk Thich Quang Duc lit himself on fire (while surrounded by hundreds of his fellow Buddhists) in protest against the repressive policies of the Catholic Diem regime that controlled South Vietnam — dousing yourself in gasoline and striking a match to die a motionless, speechless death is difficult to explain in terms of the simple seeking of pleasure or avoidance of pain. Unlike most suicides, which justify themselves as the end of unbearable pain, a suicide in protest is painful on the outside, but an act of strength, and of territory, on the inside. If melancholy music also did not make you feel bad, but made you feel territory, that would explain the paradox of why people voluntarily listen to sad music.

Most people assume that there is a simple pathway for how music makes you feel an emotion: you hear music you remember related memories ⇒ you feel the relevant emotion. This seeming truism is called *emotivism* by music psychologists. The one-liner from philosophy would be, "the sadness is to the music rather more like the redness to the apple than the burp to the cider." [1] What if people do not really feel the emotions — instead they only *figure out* the emotions that should be communicated by the music? Consider a St. Bernard's sad face: the face is not expressing sadness, because the dog's emotions are expressed at the other end; we merely interpret its facial features as sad. [2] For a piece of music, this would mean that people could perceive an emotion that is totally manufactured within the listener, which would explain why people feel different emotions to the same music; however, a by-product of this would be that people might be lying or kidding themselves about how the music makes them feel. Imagine a toddler

1 Bouwsma OK (1965). The Expression Theory of Art. In *Philosophical Essays*. University of Nebraska Press. 21-50.
2 Kivy P (2002). *Introduction to a Philosophy of Music*. Oxford: Oxford University Press.

who falls down and stands back up unflustered, until the parents ask him if he is all right, at which point the child starts to cry. This possibility is taken very seriously in the aesthetic philosophy of music, and it is called *cognitivism*.[1] Cognitivists believe that the emotions "in" music are more like a grimace than a punch in the nose. The emotivist position holds that when listening to emotionally provocative music you engage in a *real* emotional response to it, just as you would do to the news of the death of a loved one. The cognitivist position contends, however, that when you listen to a musical extract, you can unconsciously decode the emotion that is being portrayed, but you do not actually "feel" the emotion — then when asked how you feel, you confound the emotions communicated by the piece with your own feelings (see Figure 6.1). If cognitivism were true, that would answer why people listen to sad music — because it does not really make them feel sad. It makes them feel *moved by its beauty*.

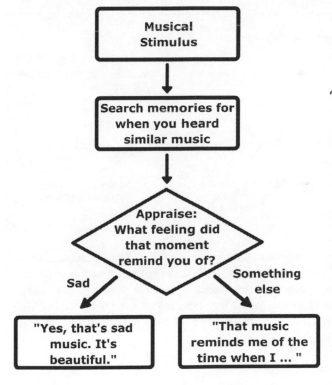

Figure 6.1 - Cognitivism: how music could communicate emotions that "do not hurt." If you appraise the music as being similar to other sad music, that could result in a cognitive recognition of sadness without a concurrent sad mood. Instead you may conflate the emotions from the reference memory with the emotions you currently have (which are more based on beauty and being moved than on sadness *per se*).

---

1 I am taking the "hard" cognitivist position here, rendering it almost absurd for clarity. Obviously Peter Kivy feels emotions when he listens to music or he would not have dedicated his career to becoming one of the foremost philosophers of music. Kivy P (2002). *Introduction to a Philosophy of Music*. Oxford: Oxford University Press.

At first glance cognitivism does not seem like a very satisfactory answer to why people listen to sad music. The problem with cognitivism is that the entire thing is counter-intuitive: people are very rarely mistaken about their own emotions. But, hang on. Most of the time when we listen to music, do we actually feel its "intrinsic" emotion? Think about Muzak or a neighbor's noisy stereo, then compare that to getting punched; every time you are punched makes you feel an emotion. Music seems much more context-dependent, almost like language. As Shelley said, "Our sweetest songs are those that *tell* of saddest thought." [1] The emotivist argument that music makes us feel emotions seems to be the exception rather than the rule, and the evidence for music having intrinsic emotions is mixed. Psychobiologists have wheedled their way into the argument by attempting to measure the physiological responses (e.g., heart rate) to music; this presumes that if music changes your heart rate, then you must be feeling an emotion.

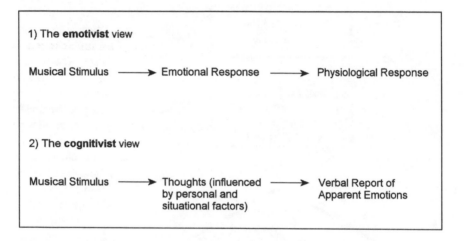

Figure 6.2 - How detecting music-induced physiological changes supports the emotivist theory. If music leads directly to thoughts (but not emotions, as per cognitivism), then one might not expect a change in physiology (e.g., heart rate). This assumes that thoughts are less likely than emotions to lead to physiological responses, which has been assumed since the early days of psychology but may not be the case.

Figure 6.2 shows the role psychobiology apparently plays in the argument between the emotivists and the cognitivists. Several research groups have successfully observed biological changes in response to the emotions in music.[2] But the cognitivists would

1 Shelley PB (1820). To a Skylark. Accessed 10 April 2010; http://classiclit.about.com/library/bl-etexts/pshelley/bl-pshel-sky.htm.
2 Krumhansl CL (1997). An exploratory study of musical emotions and psychophysiology. *Canadian Journal of Experimental Psychology* 51(4): 336-353. See also Lundqvist LO, Carlsson F, Hilmersson P, Juslin PN (2009). Emotional responses to music: experience, expression, and physiology. *Psychology of Music* 37(1): 61-90.

respond that music acts only as a messenger, and that thinking about the emotion (or empathy, given that music is a social substitute) is the real prime mover.[1]

Oh dear. How could music scholars get themselves in such a muddle? First someone denies the existence of the intense emotions that everyone knows come from music. Then other academics start finding reasons to take the argument seriously. For example, our intuitive feeling that music elicits emotions is based on our very selective memories. If you ask "when did you hear music last, and what did it make you feel?" a person is much more likely to access a memory of a powerful musical experience, while forgetting the twenty times they listened to Muzak when on hold on the telephone. This selective memory compounds the problem caused by the measurements of emotions being subjective.[2] Scientists crave objective evidence, such as smiling for happiness or raising the inner brow in sadness, but these facial expressions are often missing when people are listening to music. The kings of hard, reductive evidence are the physiologists; they have measured changes in blood pressure and breathing that correspond to different emotions in music, so theoretically that must prove that emotivism is true.[3]

But not necessarily. What we can be sure of is that sometimes music does seem to have a fairly direct effect on emotions. Most people would agree that the idea that music *never* engenders emotions (so-called "hard" cognitivism) is pretty difficult to defend. However, any single piece of music may have radically different effects in different people, and sometimes even in the same person. Thus, "hard" emotivism is also difficult to defend, because the purported emotions contained *inside* the music are not always communicated successfully, which makes music much less clear in communicating emotions than language. One way to get around the problems of both hard cognitivism and hard emotivism is to take the middle path: there must be a compromise falling partway between cognitivism and emotivism. What is that compromise?

***

Country music has created a problem for scientists. Steven Stack, an expert in suicidology who has published over 250 scientific papers on that and related topics, did an analysis of the relationship between country music and metropolitan suicide rates

---

1 This kind of empathy, where seeing somebody else's emotion makes you think "as if" you were having a weaker version of the same emotion, is supported by neuroscience. See Morris JS, Frith CD, Perrett DI, et al (1996). A differential neural response in the human amygdala to fearful and happy facial expressions. *Nature* 383:812-5. For a description of relating to smiling based on mirror neurons, see Leslie KR, Johnson-Frey & SH Grafton ST (2004). Functional imaging of face and hand imitation: towards a motor theory of empathy. *Neuroimage* 21: 601-7.

2 To get round the selective-memory argument, people have used the Experience Sampling Method (ESM), which relies on having people wearing beepers repeatedly fill in questionnaires throughout the day. See Sloboda JA, O'Neill SA (2001). Emotions in everyday listening to music. *Music and Emotion: Theory and Research* (Oxford University Press: Oxford, pp. 415-430.

3 Krumhansl CL (1997). An exploratory study of musical emotions and psychophysiology. *Canadian Journal of Experimental Psychology* 51(4): 336-353. See also Lundqvist LO, Carlsson F, Hilmersson P and Juslin PN (2009). Emotional responses to music: experience, expression, and physiology. *Psychology of Music* 37(1): 61-90.

among whites.[1] The hypothesis was simple: with its themes of marital discord, alcohol abuse and job dissatisfaction, country music should nurture a suicidal mood — not just among its detractors, but amongst its fans. Plainly the lyrics of country music concern lost love and human downfall — a downward movement into the gutter, the prison, the grave or the bottle[2] — but is the music itself sad? In a statistical analysis of what made a country music song a hit, the only factor that was consistent for both male and female singers was slow tempo.[3] The most successful country music seems to be musically sad.

But not every scientist agreed that country music causes people to kill themselves. Another four papers came out quibbling over the statistics, claiming that country music tended to be broadcast in white areas where divorce rates were already high — so suicide rates would be high anyway.[4] The only thing the scientists could agree on was that country music, which by many standards is a "sad" genre, tends to appear in the same urban areas in the USA where suicide rates are high. Blues players would laugh at the battling scientists because in blues circles it is axiomatic that sad music only thrives where life is hard and disappointing — to play the blues, you got to have been covered in mud.[5] It remains controversial whether sad music is a cause or consequence.

Funerals crystallize this conundrum. The conventional explanation for why we listen to sad music is that sometimes sad music is simply the only appropriate music. Can you imagine the public outcry at the funeral of Princess Diana if Elton John had performed, in place of his sorrowful *Candle in the Wind*, a triumphant rendition of *Saturday Night's Alright for Fighting*? This fits with the idea that feeling sadness leads people to select sad music, making sad music a consequence. While this makes intuitive sense, it is at odds with a worldview where we do things to maximize pleasure and minimize pain. If you already feel a sense of loss, and you are hanging out with a crowd of people who by and large also feel miserable, listening to sad music will not help you all to feel more cheerful. However, using music to communicate a sad mood that was *homogeneous*, a sad

1 Stack S and Gundlach J (1992). The effect of country music on suicide. *Social Forces* 71(1): 211-218.
2 Stewart K (1993). Engendering narratives of lament in country music. In Lewis GH (ed.), *All that Glitters: Country Music in America.* Bowling Green State University Popular Press: Bowling Green, USA.
3 In this study the single most important determinant of a successful song was the artist's stature and fame. Male artists (and to a lesser extent females) had success with songs of a sexual theme. Among male artists (but not among female artists) songs with a honky-tonking theme were notably successful, while female artists (but not male artists) had hits that centered around themes of rambling and sad love. See Jaret C (1993). Characteristics of successful and unsuccessful country music songs. In Lewis GH (ed.), *All that glitters: Country music in America*, Bowling Green State University Popular Press: Bowling Green, USA.
4 Maguire ER, Snipes JB (1994). Reassessing the Link between Country Music and Suicide. *Social Forces*, 72: 1239-1243. Stack S, Gundlach J (1995). Country Music and Suicide — Individual, Indirect, and Interaction Effects: A Reply to Snipes and Maguire. *Social Forces*, 74(1): 331-335. Snipes JB, Maguire ER (1995). Country Music, Suicide, and Spuriousness. *Social Forces*, 74(1): 327-329. Mauk GW, Taylor MJ, White KR and Allen TS (1994). Comments on Stack and Gundlach's "The Effect of Country Music on Suicide:" An "Achy Breaky Heart" May Not Kill You. *Social Forces*, 72(4): 1249-1255.
5 Cross CR (2005). *Room full of mirrors: a biography of Jimi Hendrix.* London: Hodder & Stoughton.

social territory, could help everyone, by kindling territorial feelings such as "things are as they should be" and "confidence to take the next step onward."

Scientists have shown that people in a sad mood prefer to socialize with other people in a sad mood, and they derive more satisfaction from such conversations. In one study psychology students at Stanford University who did not know one another were randomly put into pairs and asked to take 10 turns being either the speaker or a listener in a conversation.[1] Initially each participant was assessed for *dysphoria* (an emotional state characterized by depression, anxiety, or unease). The conversational subject matter was then freely selected by each speaker from a list of 90 topics including both positive subjects ("things I like about my mother") and negative ones ("situations which make me impatient"). If both the speaker and listener were dysphoric, they rated the conversation as more satisfying than if one person was dysphoric and the other was not. If they were both dysphoric, they also rated their partner as warmer than if the partners were mixed. Most tellingly, in the mixed pairs the conversations became more depressing over time; in the first half of the experiment all the participants were much more likely to choose positive, low-intimacy topics, but in the second half a substantial number of sad participants talking to happy listeners chose to talk about "How often I have spells of the blues and what they are about" and "Long-range worries or concerns I have about my health." Sad participants talking to other sad participants simply did not do this. This fits with what happens at a funeral; people in a sad mood tend to be buoyed by those who have a mood that matches theirs.

Far from being "self-torment," sad music may serve an important social function by engendering a sense of belonging in sad situations — a social territory that "starts where people already are." At a funeral the leading mourners are the family and close friends of the dead, and they establish an "appropriate" territory that all other grievers must conform to. By controlling the music, dress code, and style of service, they create a fitting mood to respect their loved one. Most importantly, they forge a territory united by their grief. So misery does love company, *and* music does make people feel better, if not exactly happier. As the lyrics of REM's 1993 hit single promise: "Everybody hurts. You are not alone."[2] In terms of evolution this makes sense if your tribe is making music together, but now when listening alone to recordings of sad music, surprisingly it still can give you a sense of having company in misery, even though you have no company. The inexplicable feeling of solace is subjectively so similar to having a friend that it is hard to recognize it for what it truly is: a sense of social territory. As Robert Browning consolingly declared: "He who hears music, feels his solitude peopled at once."[3] This sounds just like emotivism; however, in this case the emotion contained in the music is not happiness or sadness, but *belonging* and social territory.

---

1 Locke KD, Horowitz LM (1990). Satisfaction in Interpersonal Interactions as a Function of Similarity in Level of Dysphoria. *Journal of Personality and Social Psychology* 58(5): 823-831.

2 REM's song "Everybody Hurts" appeared on their 1992 album "Automatic for the People." It was also released as a single in 1993, and it peaked at number 29 on the Billboard Hot 100.

3 Browning R (1871, collected 1894). Balaustion's Adventure, line 323. *The Poetical Works of Robert Browning*, Volume 6. London: Macmillan and co., p. 18.

The bigger mystery is why people would listen to this music when they are not at a funeral. No one believes only sad people listen to sad music. If listening on your own to sad music was always depressing, then country music cities would be inundated with car drivers dreaming of head-on collisions. But the vast majority of people on earth are pretty happy,[1] even in cities where country music is mainstream. This suggests that sad music must *not* be communicating sadness, but is communicating something else instead — such as territory. An example of when a sound's meaning is territorial rather than denotative is "Valspeak," the youth-culture lingo immortalized by the Frank Zappa song "Valley Girls" with the words, "Oh my God!" A young woman who is from the San Fernando Valley region of Los Angeles will end almost all her sentences with an upward inflection of her voice — as if asking a question. But she is not questioning everything she says, as if her party girl existence is a camouflage for a deeply philosophical soul. Like the upward voice tones used in Australia, this "uptalk" functions socially in aligning the speaker and listener in conversation.[2] The cognitivists would claim that you translate the sound's meaning in your mind, and part of that meaning would be that you are surrounded by like-minded people. This would be a good feeling, contrary to emotivist theories claiming that sounds (such as sad music) communicate the inherent emotions within them.

Think of your favorite song — one that makes you feel like a school kid let out of school early on a summer afternoon — that makes you smile from ear to ear — then think of the same song blaring from your neighbor's sound system at 3 am on a Monday morning. There must be more than meets the ear, if your emotional response to music can fluctuate so dramatically.

The paradox in music is that both the cognitivists and emotivists are right. Music is both part fable *and* part heartfelt emotion. You are a cognitivist when you are casually or distractedly listening to sad music; you feel the territory but not the rending of your own humanity. But when you are in a stirring context and you hear moving music that matches it, something else happens to you. If the mood of the music fits the moment, and the music is in your territory, then you are beckoned to it like an emotivist: sucked into the troubled rivers of your circumstances, the music takes you deeper than your airy body could go without its heavy emotions.[3] The context in which you hear the music changes everything, as does its relationship to your territory (see Figure 6.3). The context could be an event, like a lover leaving, or a disposition, like a doomed artist in a garret. Sad music in the right context can bring a man to tears.

Scientific studies have repeatedly proven the role of one's emotional context on whether music influences your mood. For example, if university students are asked to tell a story about a painting while listening to background music, the music's emotion is absorbed if the participants are telling a neutral story, but if they tell a happy or a sad

---

1 Happiness studies consistently show that most people rate their subjective well being as being quite happy. See Diener E & Diener C (1996). Most people are happy. *Psychological Science*, 7:181-185 and Myers DG & Diener E (1995). Who is happy? *Psychological Science*, 6: 10-19.

2 Guy G, Horvath B, Vonwiller J, Daisley E, and Rogers I (1986). An intonation change in progress in Australian English. *Language in Society* 15: 23–52.

3 Context here can be defined very broadly. A discrete event such as a funeral can be a context for sadness, but so can sitting by yourself while doing nothing but focusing on the music. Depression, or a susceptibility to waves of sadness, is an amorphous context that might make someone vulnerable to sad music's charms.

story, the volunteers' emotions are determined by the story, irrespective of the mood of the music.[1]

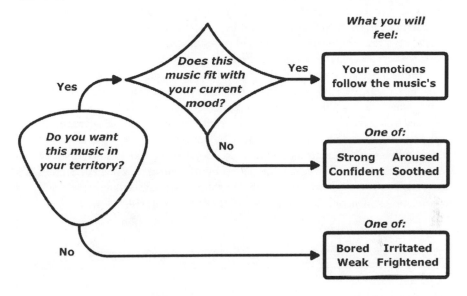

Figure 6.3 - The emotions elicited by music depend on both whether the music fits into your territory and whether it fits into your current context or mood. If music does not fit into your territory, it might elicit any one of the following emotions: frightened, weak, irritated, or bored. Likewise, if music does fit into your territory but does not fit with your mood, it could elicit any one of the following four emotions: strong (empowered), aroused, confident, or soothed. If the music does fit into your territory and it also fits with your mood or the current context, then your emotions will follow the emotions in the music, and your emotions may become much deeper than they would otherwise be.

Combining the effects of sad music and emotional context has solved another scientific problem: how to consistently elicit sadness in people during psychological experiments.[2] You can show them sad movies or ask them to remember a time when they were sad, but people progressively habituate — each time the stimulus is repeated, it affects the person less and less.[3] One laboratory stimulus that works repeatedly is to combine

1 Stratton V and Zalanowski A (1991). The Effects of Music and Cognition on Mood. *Psychology of Music* 19:121-127.

2 Hernandez S, Vander Wal JS, Spring B (2003). A Negative Mood Induction Procedure with Efficacy Across Repeated Administrations in Women. *Journal of Psychopathology and Behavioral Assessment* 25(1): 49-55.

3 Of course you could also show people sad photographs (such as in the International Affective Photographic System — IAPS) or play them sad music, but in my experience the effects of these stimuli are (objectively speaking) very muted. People sometimes cry at sad movies, but they almost never cry because of sad music or sad photos.

a sad autobiographical script with sad music. You obtain the autobiographical script by asking the participant to tell you about a time when they were really sad. When they are asked to concentrate on this sad memory while listening to the sad music, they do not habituate in the same way they would by just reading the script, and it certainly works better than the music alone.[1] For the same reason, the cheesy overdone music in movie soundtracks works brilliantly in the context of the film. The context of what else you are doing determines whether the music works its magic — or not.

Which finally explains why so many people listen to sad music without crowds of country music-lovers jumping like lemmings off the nearest cliff: sad music does not normally make you sad. On a normal day, without a sad context, *your* sad music affirms your territory — and you — thus empowering you. In most cases, people will not be depressed by regularly listening to sad music, because the distance conferred by cognitivism will protect them against the sadness in the music. But in a sad context like lost love, emotivism unsheathes the sadness in the music. The emotions elicited by sad music have a dual nature: one genuinely sad, the other territorial.

---

1   Hernandez S, VanderWal JS, Spring B (2003). A Negative Mood Induction Procedure with Efficacy Across Repeated Administrations in Women. *Journal of Psychopathology and Behavioral Assessment* 25(1): 49-55.

CHAPTER 7. DOES VIOLENT MUSIC LEAD TO VIOLENT BEHAVIOR?

DISTINGUISHING WHETHER MUSIC IS A CAUSE, A SYMPTOM, OR A REMEDY

"Anything that starts with Duke Ellington ends with an attack on the Fuhrer's life."
— A Gestapo officer[1]

Two days before Christmas 1985 two recently unemployed Nevada youths took turns putting a .12 gauge shotgun to their heads and pulling the trigger.[2] Ray Belknap successfully blew his brains out. James Vance survived, but he shot away his lower face leaving him grossly disfigured. The catalyst for their violent self-destruction? An afternoon of drinking, marijuana and the critical ingredient: the heavy metal music of Judas Priest. For their parents and prosecuting lawyers, there was an incontrovertible link: Judas Priest's music fuelled the boys' violent exit from the world. The parents sued the band and their record company, CBS. Attorney Vivian Lynch, prosecutor in the tragic case, argued that music with lyrics like theirs is capable of *"meddling in the mysteries of the human mind."* But can just listening to heavy metal music make you violent?

In a study of 200 Australian high school students, 20% of the males and 60% of the females regularly listening to heavy metal had tried to kill or hurt themselves in the previous six months, vastly more than among pop music listeners.[3] But this does not prove heavy metal is the cause. The issue is whether the music is the root of self-harm or a sign of something else that could turn violent — although there are millions of heavy

---

1 Savage J (2008). *Teenage: The Creation of Youth — 1875–1945*. Pimlico: London.
2 Henry WA & Pappa E (1990). Did The Music Say Do It? *Time Magazine*, July 30.
3 This is vastly more than among pop music fans, where it was only 8% of males and 14% of females. Martin G, Clarke P & Pearce C (1993). Adolescent suicide: music preference as an indicator of vulnerability. *Journal of the American Academy of Child Adolescent Psychology*, 32: 530-535.

metal fans who are not violent or criminals, young offenders in juvenile detention are three times more likely to be heavy metal fans.[1] The expert consensus was, *"if we know a youth is white, male, 15 years old, drug involved, and in trouble with the law, then the odds are very high indeed that his music of choice will be some form of hard rock or heavy metal."*[2]

Perhaps there is something about the personalities of these troubled young men, such as sensation seeking, that makes them choose heavy metal for their territory. Certainly the squealing, distorted guitar sounds have the tonal qualities of the voice during arousal. When a person or animal feels both arousal and that they are on their own territory, their confidence is pumped up — potentially to the level of violence. But not all arousal is bad or violent; people can be highly aroused while dancing, laughing, or doing all manner of "nice" activities.

So, just because Judas Priest's music is arousing does not make it the motivation for Belknap's and Vance's suicide attempt.[3] Not only can arousal lead to non-violent behaviors, but the music may have been a symptom rather than a cause — other aspects of their lives may have been the real source of their suicidal fury. Belknap and Vance were already sufficiently angry with life to have had thoughts of suicide, whether they were listening to Judas Priest or Jingle Bells. Eighteen-year-old Belknap had just been fired from his job and twenty-year-old Vance had just quit his, leading to an angry confrontation with his mother. The afternoon of their suicide pact, they jumped out of a first floor window with a sawn-off shotgun and ran to a nearby church yard, yelling "life sucks!" Their aroused state may simply have given them the willpower to actualize their fantasies. The question is: does heavy metal cause trouble, or do troubled kids seek out heavy metal?

The argument is complicated by the fact that troubled kids supposedly look for trouble anyway. Heavy metal might actually reduce the fury they would have otherwise unleashed. For example, Freud popularized the idea of *catharsis*. This is the theory that misfortune and discord cause a build up of aggressive impulses that will explode unless they are vented.[4] This was the sort of rationale that priests would use when teaching young men boxing — the fighting would "get it out of their system" and prevent them from engaging in socially unacceptable violence. As far back as Aristotle it was proposed that art, particularly art depicting violence, might be one way that negative emotions can be vented safely. Perhaps listening to Judas Priest is a remedy that helps

---

1 Wass H, Miller DM & Reditt CA (1991). Adolescent and Destructive Themes in Rock Music: A Follow Up. *OMEGA: Journal of Death and Dying* 23: 199-206.

2 Roberts DF, Christenson PG & Gentile DA (2003). The effects of violent music on children and adolescents. In Gentile DA (ed.), *Media Violence and Children*. Westport, CT: Praeger.

3 Heavy metal music is definitely arousing, but its effects on anger depend on the personality of the listener. Gowensmith WN & Bloom LJ (1997). The effects of heavy metal music on arousal and anger, *Journal of Music Therapy* 1: 33-45.

4 Bushman BJ (2002). Does venting anger feed or extinguish the flame? Catharsis, rumination, distraction, anger, and aggressive responding. *Personality and Social Psychology Bulletin*, 28: 724–731. The original work by Freud is in: Breuer J & Freud S (1895, translated 1955). Studies in hysteria, Volume 2, Brill AA (Trans.). London: Hogarth. (Original work published 1893-1895).

to keep the millions of law-abiding (but potentially troubled) metal-heads from doing something genuinely violent.

***

Marvin Gaye (1939–1984) was shot dead on 1 April 1984 by his father, with two bullets from a Smith and Wesson .38 — which Marvin had bought for him.[1] The verdict of the trial of Marvin Pentz Gay (Senior, 1914–1998, no *e* in his surname) for the murder of his son created more questions than it answered. Although Gaye's father claimed that he had acted in self-defense, just beforehand the young Marvin was not even in the same room — the murder actually took place when Marvin Senior entered the bedroom where Mrs. Gay and the young Marvin were sitting and talking. Gay Senior was originally charged with first degree murder, but ultimately pleaded no contest to voluntary manslaughter. However, the judge did not sentence the 70-year-old father to any prison time; instead Gay received a six year suspended sentence and five years of probation. Not only was Gay Senior an old man with various physical ailments who was no threat to the community, but the judge cited the evidence that Marvin Junior provoked the entire incident by severely beating and kicking his father just beforehand. The enormous bruises all over Marvin Senior's back and forearms testified to the extent of the provocation.

His father may have pulled the trigger, but what really caused Marvin Gaye's death? Was it the PCP (angel dust) mixed with cocaine, which was in Marvin's system when he died — and when he severely beat his father? Was it his body guards, who helped source the illegal gun for Gay Senior — on Marvin's orders? Was it his paranoia and auditory hallucinations? He thought people were out to get him and his family, which is why he ordered the gun for his then 68-year-old father, who had never owned one before. Or was it Gaye's own will? According to his bigger than life bodyguard Andre White, Marvin may have provoked the attack, secretly hoping to commit suicide by proxy. During their last phone conversation, White reminded the younger Marvin of Gay Senior's oft repeated threat, "I brought you into this world, and if you lay a hand on me, I'll take you out." Marvin responded, "He means it too." Then White said, "If you keep fucking with your daddy, he's told you what he will do," and then in White's own words, "Marvin paused when I said that, and it was like a light bulb lit up. He wanted to die, but he couldn't do it himself. He got his daddy to do it." [2] Young Marvin had repeatedly made statements of suicidal intent, but is that proof that he manipulated his father into doing the deed?

When investigating a disease, scientists love a clean demonstration of the cause. The best cause is one that is both *necessary and sufficient*: this means that without that cause, the disease would not happen, *and* if you add the cause, it should be enough to cause the disease. In the case of diabetes being caused by a lack of insulin, the scientists who are credited with figuring it all out, Frederick Banting (Nobel Prize 1923) and Charles Best, assembled three pieces of evidence that showed insulin from the pancreas

---

1 Turner S (1998). *Trouble Man: The Life and Death of Marvin Gaye*. London: Michael Joseph. pp. 211-232.

2 Turner S (1998). *Trouble Man: The Life and Death of Marvin Gaye*. London: Michael Joseph. p. 5.

was both necessary and sufficient to prevent diabetes. 1) They knew that degeneration of the pancreas was often associated with diabetes, 2) when they removed the pancreas from a dog, the dog ended up with symptoms identical to diabetes, and 3) when they injected that diabetic dog with an extract of the pancreas from cows (later purified into insulin), the dog became healthier. Those three steps (associate, remove, reintroduce) are the clearest proof that a cause is necessary and sufficient.

However, life is rarely so simple. As the murder of Marvin Gaye shows, there can be myriad complicating factors and many contributing causes. Often there is no single cause that is both necessary and sufficient. Sometimes partisans argue about causes in terms of the solution they propose (e.g., gun control), but there can be as many solutions to a problem as there are causes. With all these contributory causes, scientists often talk about risk factors.[1] Whether or not you believe that Marvin Gaye was responsible for his own murder, it seems clear that his drug-taking, paranoia and suicidal yearnings certainly fostered every aspect of the shooting. The purchase of the gun was (for the younger Marvin) a remedy for his paranoid fears. The drug-fuelled beating young Marvin gave his 70-year-old father was the proximate cause of the incident. And Marvin's own mother and bodyguard suggested that the shooting was the result of Marvin's death-wish.[2]

***

There is little evidence that violent music, even with violent lyrics, can *in and of itself* inflame teenagers to brutal acts.[3] By contrast there is strong evidence that violent television and music videos are associated with a host of delinquent tendencies — from failing school and abuse of women, all the way to a life of crime. But associations do not prove that music videos are the cause. That can only be shown by comparing one group that watches the violent video to a similar group that does not. While it would be preferable to have an objective measurement of violence in such experiments, having the students fill out questionnaires about their attitudes toward violence is the only way to detect the elicited "violence." After all, ten minutes of MTV is usually not enough to start a punch-up in the lab. However, one objection to these experiments is that the students could guess the purpose of the experiment (to measure violent thoughts) and then simply answer the questionnaires accordingly. As such, several experiments have been designed to prevent the experimental subject from guessing the purpose of the experiment, and these also support the idea that violent music videos make young people more violent.[4]

---

1 For a complete discussion of the types of evidence needed to designate a putative risk factor as a cause, see "Evans's Postulates," e.g. Evans AS (1976). Causation and disease: the Henle-Koch postulates revisited. *Yale Journal of Biology and Medicine* 49(2): 175–195.

2 Turner S (1998). *Trouble Man: The Life and Death of Marvin Gaye*. London: Michael Joseph. pp. 211-232.

3 American Academy of Pediatrics: Committee on Communication (2001). Impact of Music Lyrics and Music Videos on Children and Youth. *Pediatrics*, 108: 1222-1226.

4 Greeson LE & Williams RA (1986). Social implications of music video for youth. *Youth and Society*, 18: 177-189. Johnson JD, Jackson LA & Gatto L (1995). Violent attitudes and deferred academic aspirations: deleterious effects of the exposure to rap music. *Basic and Applied Social Psychology*, 16: 27-41. Peterson DL & Pfost KS (1989) In-

For example, in one study of university students, each subject was told that they were going to rate potential hosts for a TV show about rock music.[1] The experimental subject then sat in a room with the ostensible music show presenters, unaware that they were in fact confederates of the researcher. While they were all waiting for the interviews, they passed the time by watching either antisocial or neutral music videos. After that, the experimental subject witnessed one potential host telling a joke to the other, which was interrupted when an authority figure briefly entered the room and brusquely warned the joke-teller to "settle down." Then the scolded joke-teller made an obscene gesture at the retreating authority figure's back; in the control condition he merely adjusted his clothing. After that, the two contenders for TV host left the room and tapes of their "live interviews" were shown to the experimental subject, who then rated them on honesty, politeness and how much he liked them.

When the TV host made an obscene gesture, the students liked him less and ascribed fewer positive traits to him — but only if they had watched the neutral videos. When the students watched the antisocial videos first, their ratings of the job applicant were the same whether or not he had made the gesture. This shows that even a short exposure to violent videos was enough to effectively eliminate the natural inclination to dislike rude and defiant people. In another interventional study, removing MTV from a forensic inpatient ward resulted in a significant decrease in aggressive behavior among the patients.[2] This small study suggests that MTV may actually be part of the cause of violence, at least among psychiatric patients. These types of findings are not replicated when simply violent music (as opposed to violent music videos) is tested. While music videos can plainly increase how violent impulses are acted upon, music alone tends to limit itself to reinforcing group allegiance. But the fact that music inspires allegiance does not necessarily imply it also has the power to inspire acts of violence.

The social territory of music is most powerfully made by the beat, which listeners express though dancing, singing or keeping time.[3] Certainly the beat is often more recognizable to listeners than the lyrics.[4] This fits with an experiment that I ran in 2007 comparing ten songs for how happy each one made people feel. The song that was rated as most happy was Lily Allen's recently released *LDN*, which was a cheery tune with lyrics describing pimps, crack whores and muggings of the elderly.[5] The dark lyrics did not seem to affect the experimental subjects' happy reception of the song, which triumphed

---

fluence of rock videos on attitudes of violence against women. *Psychological Reports*, 64: 319-322.
1 Hansen CH & Hansen RD (1990). Rock music videos and antisocial behaviour. *Basic and Applied Social Psychology*, 11(4): 357-369.
2 Waite BM, Hillbrand M & Foster HG (1992). Reduction of aggressive behavior after removal of Music Television. *Hospital and Community Psychiatry*, 43: 173-175.
3 Shepherd J (1990). *Music as a social text*. Cambridge, UK: Polity Press.
4 Gunderson R (1985). *An investigation of the effects of rock music videos on the values and self-perceptions of adolescents*. Doctoral dissertation, Ann Arbor, MI, USA: United States International University. Rouner D (1990). Rock music use as a socializing function. *Popular Music and Society*, 14: 97-107. Strasburger V & Wilson B (2002). *Children, adolescents and the media*. London: Sage Press.
5 Kirby T (2006). "If you're happy and you know it, listen to Lily. If not, it's the Verve." *The Independent* (London) newspaper, 11 December.

over cheery ditties *She Loves You* by the Beatles and *Dancing Queen* by ABBA. However, that was pop music; heavy metal and its fans may represent a special case. Fans of violent music, especially heavy metal or rap, pay much more attention to the lyrics than do other adolescents,[1] which could contribute to violent behavior; in one study 16% of high school students ranked music amongst the top three sources of moral guidance, whilst 24% rated it in the top three for information on social interaction.[2]

Even so, there has been some doubt as to whether the lyrics can be such potent influences. In many cases, the violent lyrics are so garbled that it is impossible to understand them. In one study, for example, less than 30% of the adolescents tested knew the words to their favorite song.[3] Another study found that adolescents rated lyrics as the least important reason for liking a song, surpassed by rhythm, vocals, music and melody.[4] Even if young people neither rate nor comprehend lyrics, there is evidence that music with violent lyrics can affect people without their being conscious of it.

To demonstrate that violent lyrics can increase the ability to access violent thoughts, participants of one experiment were asked to read and pronounce aggressive and neutral words, and after listening to violent songs they read and pronounced the aggressive words more quickly.[5] In the same study subjects were asked to judge how related were words that were definitely violent — words such as *blood*, *hatchet*, and *kill* — to words that might or might not be construed as violent — such as *alley*, *drugs*, and *police*. If they listened to music with violent lyrics beforehand, participants rated the ambiguous words as more similar to clearly violent words. Thus, music with violent lyrics may prime the mind with aggressive thoughts and feelings[6]. Evidence of this sort has debunked the notion of catharsis. Violent lyrics do not calm the subconscious mind — at least not on a short-term basis.

But the question in the case against Judas Priest was: can music make you do something you don't want to do? Science has all but discredited the possibility that a subtle message buried in the lyrics can secretly overwhelm your will.[7] But heavy metal comes

1   Arnett J (1991). Adolescence and heavy metal music: from the mouths of metalheads. *Youth and Society* 23: 76-98. Kuwahara Y (1992). Power to the people y'all: rap music, resistance and black college students. *Humanity and Society*, 16: 54-73. Christenson PG & Roberts DF (1998). *It's not only rock & roll: Popular music in the lives of adolescents*. Cresskill, NJ: Hampton Press.

2   Rouner D (1990). Rock music use as a socializing function. *Popular Music and Society*, 14: 97-107.

3   Greenfield PM, Bruzzone L & Koyamatsu K et al (1987). What is rock music doing to the minds of our youth? A first experimental look at the effects of rock music lyrics and music videos. *Journal of Early Adolescence*, 7: 315-329.

4   Ballard M, Dodson A & Bazzini D (1999). Genre of music and lyrical content: expectation effects. *Journal of Genetic Psychology*, 160: 476-487.

5   Anderson CA, Carnagey NL & Eubanks J (2003). Exposure to violent media: the effects of songs with violent lyrics on aggressive thoughts and feelings. *Journal of Personality and Social Psychology*, 84: 960-971.

6   Anderson CA, Carnagey NL & Eubanks J (2003). Exposure to violent media: the effects of songs with violent lyrics on aggressive thoughts and feelings. *Journal of Personality and Social Psychology*, 84: 960-971.

7   The original experiments promulgated by James Vicary concerning subliminal advertising in films have been admitted to be fabrications, and no other experimenters have

with baggage — the music itself might turn a young person into a violent person. This was shown in a study of Christian heavy metal. When it was compared to traditional, nihilistic heavy metal, psychologists at Jackson State University found that exposure to heavy metal music, irrespective of lyrical content, increased males' sex-role stereotyping and negative attitudes toward women.[1] Even if they do not perceive it as such, troubled youths may use violent music as a mood- or emotion-regulator — amplifying their depression and anger,[2] repeating destructive thought patterns, and reinforcing negative attitudes. Music alone might not put suicidal thoughts into your head, but it can deepen a violent or hopeless state of mind.[3] As was shown in the chapter on sad music (see Figure 6.3), your music leads to territorial feelings when it does not match your current mood, but when the music's mood matches your own, your emotions follow the music's emotions, which can then amplify your mood far beyond where it would normally go.

In Belknap and Vance's case, their mood was already one of nihilistic outrage: Vance had just had a huge argument with his mother, and both of them had lost their jobs recently, Vance only hours before. So on the fateful day, the youths hit a new low. They were ready to follow angry music to extremes of emotion. The mood from Judas Priest's *Stained Class* album they had been listening to was suicidal but in an empowered and self-affirming way, with lyrics such as these from "Beyond the Realms of Death":

> This is my life, this is my life
> I'll decide not you
> Keep the world with all its sin
> It's not fit for livin' in
> Yeah! I will start again[4]

Just after the gruesome shooting, Vance had used hand gestures to tell the police that he had mutilated himself because "life sucks." This statement was not one of despair but of wrath and resentment. You can imagine them saying "life sucks" as a battle cry, with their fists pumping the air.

The court ruled that although the music might have had a toxic influence, there were many other aspects of their lives that contributed to their self-destruction. The teenagers' families had histories of alcoholism, drug use, gambling problems, domestic violence, petty crimes and suicide attempts that had nothing to do with music. The row

---

succeeded in producing the originally claimed results. See Pratkanis AR (1992). The Cargo-Cult Science of Subliminal Persuasion. *Skeptical Inquirer.* Amherst, New York: Committee for Skeptical Inquiry, 16.3. However, there is a well-established psychology literature showing that stimuli below the threshold of conscious awareness can affect your preferences. See Kunst-Wilson WR & Zajonc RB (1980). Affective discrimination of stimuli that cannot be recognized. *Science,* 207: 557-558.

1 The control condition was exposure to easy-listening classical music. St. Lawrence JS & Joyner DJ (1991). The effects of sexually violent rock on males' acceptance of violence against women. *Psychology of Women Quarterly,* 15: 49-63.

2 Gordon T, Hakanen E & Wells A (1992). Music preferences and the use of music to manage emotional states: correlates with self-concept among adolescents. Paper presented at the *Annual Meeting of the International Communication Association,* Miami, FL.

3 Goleman D (1995). *Emotional Intelligence.* New York: Bantam Books.

4 By Les Binks and Rob Halford. © ebonytree; EMI April Music Inc

between Vance and his mother — on the day of the boys' suicide mission — was not unprecedented. On one occasion Vance had tried to choke his mother and on another he had hit her with a hammer. Belknap had stolen money and a van and had exposed himself to women. Both talked of leaving their hometown of Sparks, Nevada, to become mercenaries. Heavy metal was just one part of their rebellious lifestyle that included suicidal fantasies.

Yet a couple of months later Vance changed his story, insisting that he and Belknap were driven by the lyrics of Judas Priest. *"All of a sudden,"* he said, *"we got a suicide message, and we got tired of life."* Four of the five members of Judas Priest, who perform in metal mesh and studded leather, sat at the defendants' table dressed in business suits hearing themselves accused of "mind control." In an interview, guitarist Glenn Tipton revealed "We were shocked. Nothing in the album says, 'Go do this, go do that.'" Which is true, although the prosecution claimed that one song does subliminally say, "Do it!" over and over. Three years later, Vance took an overdose of the drugs doctors had prescribed him for his injuries and died. The songs of Judas Priest did not drive him to suicide — his abiding hatred of life did.

But committing suicide takes mental energy. Judas Priest contributed to Belknap and Vance's suicide pact by giving them the mutual confidence to actually "Do it." Music of one's own territory has a profound ability to arouse. Indeed, once aroused, emotions are supercharged, taking people to places of ecstasy, rage and shame. That means that the same music can arouse emotions that could lead two dissimilar people to opposite actions. Compare James Vance to Glenn Tipton. The Judas Priest guitarist did not try to blow his own head off with a shotgun. For him the territory was clad in rich, studded leather and filled with fans that idolized him.

CHAPTER 8. DOES LISTENING TO MOZART MAKE YOU SMARTER OR JUST HAPPIER?

THE POWER OF MUSIC DEPENDS ON ITS RELATIONSHIP TO YOUR TERRITORY.

"Rap music is just computerized crap... After three songs I feel like killing someone."

— George Harrison, guitarist & Eastern religion devotee

In 1998 Zell Miller, then Governor of the State of Georgia, started giving away free CDs of Mozart to every baby born in the state. This government-education program was sparked by the news that you can increase your baby's intelligence by playing specially-selected pieces of Mozart to your baby — the Mozart Effect.[1] As the New York Times described it, "Researchers have determined that listening to Mozart actually makes you smarter,"[2] despite the fact that the original researchers were quick to highlight that they made no such claims.[3] Judging from the continued success of books

---

1 Note that the term "The Mozart Effect" is used loosely by the media to refer to two completely different effects: 1) the idea that listening to music transiently improves your spatial temporal abilities and 2) receiving musical instruction for extended periods increases overall intelligence — this chapter refers exclusively to (1) while chapter nine in this book explains (2). For a complete explanation of how these two "Mozart Effects" differ in both their conclusions and scientific investigation, see the recent review: Rauscher FH (2006). The Mozart Effect: Music Listening is Not Music Instruction. *Educational Psychologist*, 41(4): 233-238.
2 New York Times music columnist Alex Ross, in a light-hearted 1994 article, this was presented as the final piece of evidence that Mozart has dethroned Beethoven as "the world's greatest composer."
3 Rauscher FH, in her 1999 reply to Chabris and Steele et al. In Chabris, CF (1999). Prelude or requiem for the "Mozart effect"? *Nature*, 400: 827–828.

and tapes — there are all manner of web sites selling specially selected Mozart tapes for making your baby brighter[1] — this conclusion seems to prevail in the public consciousness. The popular fascination for the Mozart Effect did not materialize in some New Age weekly or in *The News of the World*. A ground-breaking report appeared in 1993 in the scientific journal *Nature*, authored by an academic psychologist and a theoretical physicist from the University of California at Irvine.[2] Not surprisingly, the research immediately attracted widespread attention in the international press. The news spawned a crop of bizarre "Mozart-enhanced" products, as well as claims that the Mozart Effect also worked on animals, ranging from cows that produce more milk when serenaded with Mozart[3] to Japanese yeast whose density increases ten-fold above normal during the brewing of a "Mozart sake."[4]

Here is what really happened: Frances Rauscher, a psychologist and cellist, Gordon Shaw, a physicist turned neuroscientist, and a student named Katherine Ky, set out to conduct a long-term experiment on the effects of *studying* music on intelligence. However, such experiments would require following experimental participants for months; as the researchers were restricted by their funding, for their first experimental series they were forced to limit themselves to a quick experiment on the effects of passive music *listening*. They played ten minutes of Mozart's Sonata for Two Pianos in D Major to thirty-six University of California undergraduate science students, with the plan to test the students' intelligence afterward. The scientists at the University of California chose this piece specifically because Mozart was a child-prodigy, excelling not only in music but also in billiards. He was obsessed with mathematics, to the point where the furniture in his house was covered in etched numbers. Much of Mozart's music is systematically structured, and the Sonata for two pianos in D has many instances of symmetrical patterns. The volunteers were given tests that measure core intellectual capabilities, such as a standardized spatial relations test called the Paper Folding and Cutting test, which is a part of the Stanford Binet IQ test. This test involves a series of diagrams testing one's imagination of complicated movements in space; for example there is one of a sheet of paper that is folded horizontally, then along the vertical axis, and then another fold on the horizontal axis, followed by one corner being cut off; the examinee is then asked what the paper would look like if it was unfolded, with the answer choices showing various paper-cutouts with assorted diamonds and triangles cut out of them (See Figure 8.1).

Listening to Mozart caused an improvement in test scores corresponding to an increase in IQ of 8-9 points, but the improvement only lasted for fifteen minutes. Psychologists were stunned by this finding, because the explanation for how it worked challenged the textbooks. In 1995, the team from California claimed that the Mozart Ef-

---

1 For example, as of July 2006, www.babyexperiences.co.uk has a CD called "The Mozart effect" for stimulating babies' brains.

2 Rauscher FH, Shaw GL & Ky KN (1993). Music and spatial task performance. *Nature*, 365: 611.

3 Tomatis A (1991). *Pourquoi Mozart*. Paris: Fixot.

4 In northern Japan, Ohara Brewery finds that Mozart makes the best Sake. The density of yeast used in brewing the traditional beverage (a measure of quality) increases by a factor of ten. Campbell D (2001). *The Mozart Effect: Tapping the Power of Music to Heal the Body, Strengthen the Mind, and Unlock the Creative Spirit*. Harper Collins: New York.

fect was an example of priming, or 'warming up the brain'.[1] Priming is a well-established psychological phenomenon in which a person's performance of a task can improve if the scientist prepares them by stimulating them beforehand. For example, in a timed test for how long it takes for you to recognize and identify a face, you will be faster at recognizing Princess Diana's face if immediately beforehand you are shown Prince Charles's; by previously showing a relevant stimulus, the brain activates an appropriate memory just before it is needed. Gordon Shaw, the theoretical physicist on the research team, explained, "We suspect that complex music facilitates certain complex neuronal patterns involved in high brain activities like math and chess. By contrast, simple repetitive music could have the opposite effect." So, given its repetitive structure, unassuming melodies, and tendency to attract outlandish dancing, does disco make you stupid?

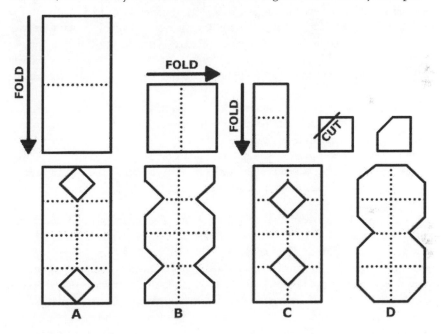

Figure 8.1 – Example of the question type from a paper folding and cutting test. A sheet of paper is folded as shown as per the arrows on the upper figures. A single cut is made with scissors as shown using the diagonal line. Choose which of the lower figures matches the resulting pattern when the paper is unfolded. Note that being tested on a series of questions similar to this in a timed examination setting can provide a putative measure of spatial relations abilities. The answer can be found in the notes.[2]

***

1 Rauscher FH, Shaw GL, Ky KN (1995). Listening to Mozart enhances spatial-temporal reasoning: Towards a neurophysiological basis. *Neuroscience Letters* 185: 44–47.
2 The answer is "C." If the cut corner had been on the lower right, it would have been "D," and if the cut corner had been in the upper right, it would have been "B."

In the scientific community, the experiments generated both excitement and skepticism. Academic psychologists have an axiom that a sound can prime an auditory task, and an image can prime a visual task, but something you see cannot usually prime your brain for what you hear. The Mozart Effect was iconoclastic because it involves an auditory stimulus priming a visual task. The team from California explained this at the brain level. They proposed that listening to complex music invoked a similar brain activity to performing spatial-relation tasks; because Mozart's music was complex — and a work of genius — listening to it prepared your brain to do tasks that required similarly complex thinking. The worldwide media generalized the entire process into one idea: Mozart makes you smarter.

If true, the Mozart Effect could revolutionize not only education but improve the morale of white collar jobs. Imagine herds of formerly-depressed stockbrokers in the pit of the New York Stock Exchange, controlling the world's capital, thinking smarter thoughts while bathed in the symphonies of Mozart — buying gracefully, selling poignantly. Understandably, the media hype provoked a great deal of commercial, as well as scientific, activity, and immediately scientists around the world set out to repeat the results.

They had mixed results. In a series in *Nature* entitled "Prelude or requiem for the 'Mozart Effect'?" sixteen scientific studies compared the effect of Mozart on enhancing intelligence.[1] A heated debate followed, concerning how small the Mozart Effect was and whether it was possible to replicate it outside of Gordon Shaw's laboratory. The answer was that occasionally the Mozart Effect was replicated, and the effects were always small.[2] For scientists, this was a requiem. The Mozart Effect would never be powerful enough to lay the foundation of a new educational curriculum. However, there still remained the question of how the Mozart Effect could provoke any change whatsoever. Gordon Shaw's theory that the intricacy of Mozart's music was the source of its intellect-improving qualities needed to be tested.

If the way Mozart enhances intellect is simply via the complexity of its sounds, would it not also improve the intellect of monkeys? Scientists from the University of Helsinki tested whether the Mozart Effect influences stump-tailed macaques, a form of monkey.[3] In these studies, scientists made the macaques listen to Mozart's Piano Concerto No. 21 in C for 15 minutes before making the macaques take a memory test designed for monkeys.[4] The researchers found that listening to Mozart music did *not* improve the macaques' performance — the monkeys remembered more if beforehand they

---

1 Chabris CF (1999). Prelude or requiem for the "Mozart Effect"? *Nature*, 400: 826-827.
2 Much of the fuss concerning the Mozart Effect centers around the paper cutting and folding test, because of all the intelligence tests used, the paper-cutting and folding test was the only test to register an increase in performance consistently.
3 Carlson S, Rämä P, Artchakov D & Linnankoski I (1997). Effects of music and white noise on working memory performance in monkeys. *NeuroReport*, 8: 2853–2856.
4 The memory task they used was the delayed response task. Two identical containers are shown, a raisin is placed in one container, the containers are covered, and a screen is placed in front of the containers so that the macaque cannot see the containers during a timed delay. At the end of the timed delay, the screen is raised and the macaque can reach into one or the other container, and if it chooses the correct container, it may eat the raisin. This is done thirty times in a row, and with lengthening

listened to white noise. In fact, listening to Mozart *during* the test, as opposed to before, actually impaired the macaques' memory, while white noise during the test improved memory slightly — so in these monkeys, the Mozart Effect does not even exist.

Monkeys aside, how can we account for the Mozart Effect in humans? Gordon Shaw claimed that the *complexity* of Mozart was the X-factor that gave the music its potency. There is, however, another possible explanation: Mozart improves people's mood. It is well-known that upswings in mood can make people perform better on problem solving tests;[1] this is another of the many beneficial effects of arousal when it is positive. In the original experiments by Rauscher's team, the control group of students had either been made to sit in silence or listen to relaxation tapes. This would induce boredom or a state of relaxation, neither of which would be particularly animating.

What was needed was a direct test of whether arousal or mood was the magic ingredient behind the Mozart Effect. For this, Glenn Schellenberg and his group at the University of Toronto made a computerized MIDI version of the same Mozart sonata for two pianos and then used music sequencing software called Performer to make four different versions. The scientists varied the tempo to be either fast or slow, and the key to be either major or minor, but in all other ways the four pieces of Mozart were identical.[2] As we saw in chapter six, with the story of Kate Hevner, music that is faster and in the major key is associated with happy emotions. As predicted, students who listened to faster versions performed better on the Paper Folding and Cutting test, as did students who listened to the major key versions; overall, the *sadder*, slow-minor version resulted in an average raw test score of 8, while the fast-major version resulted in a score of nearly 16. So, only "happy" Mozart music works.

If the Mozart Effect is propelled by mood rather than by genius, then a brilliant but depressing piece of music should make you 'less smart', and sad music should decrease your test scores. To test this Schellenberg's group used the same intelligence tests, and the same upbeat Mozart piano sonata, but he compared Mozart to Albinoni's Adagio in G Minor for Organ and Strings.[3] Albinoni's adagio is sad, beautiful and complicated. If you believe that Mozart causes this increase in intelligence because Mozart's music is complicated, then you would think that Albinoni might have the same effect, but if you believe the test results depended on whether the music puts you in an upbeat mood, then you might think that the Albinoni would actually depress your test scores as well as your mood. When they did the experiment, they found that Albinoni did not make people perform better on the exam. It made them perform slightly worse. The evidence undermined Gordon Shaw's belief about complex music and suggested that mood and arousal are the basis for change when listening to music generally and Mozart in particular. They called this the 'Albinoni Effect'.

---

time delays, the macaque's accuracy for picking the container with the raisin in it will diminish.

1 Isen AM, Daubmann KA & Nowicki GP (1987). Positive affect facilitates creative problem solving. *Journal of Personality and Social Psychology*, 52: 1122–1131.
2 Husain G, Thompson WF & Schellenberg EG (2002). Effects of musical tempo and mode on arousal, mood, and spatial abilities. *Music Perception*, 20: 151-171.
3 Thompson WF, Schellenberg EG, & Husain G (2001). Arousal, mood, and the Mozart effect. *Psychological Science*, 12: 248–251.

If the mood the music causes you to feel controls your test scores, then the effects seen with Mozart may not be unique to Mozart — any happy music could do it. To answer the question — whether or not it was specifically Mozart that made these University of California undergraduates do well — Schellenberg's group compared Mozart to Schubert's Fantasia for Piano, Four Hands, in F Minor, another piece that is easy to listen to. The scientists once again found that listening to Mozart increased the volunteers' spatial-temporal abilities compared to sitting in silence, and the scientists also found a similar increase in spatial-temporal abilities after listening to Schubert. This they named the 'Schubert Effect'.[1] Did this mean the Governor of Georgia was now going to mail all newborn babies in his state a Schubert CD? If so, were they going to have to test the intellect-enhancement engendered by every single artwork?

Next the scientists compared music to non-musical entertainment. Schellenberg compared Mozart, Schubert, and silence to a tape recording of someone reading a Stephen King horror story, which had no music in it, but was potentially quite arousing.[2] The horror story could also increase the students' test scores, and some volunteers had their best test scores after listening to the story. It appeared that generally all the students performed best after listening to whichever tapes they liked most.

This has revolutionary implications. These findings vastly extend the power of territory to change not only what you decide to do, but what you are capable of doing. If you listen to your own arousing music — music that belongs in your own territory — it will make you feel aroused, encouraged and excited. By contrast, if you hear your own down beat music, it may make you more placid, and if you hear arousing music that is definitely *outside your territory*, instead of exciting you, it will enervate you (Figure 8.2).

This means that if you don't like the music, it is not going to have the intellect-enhancing effects on you. No matter what it is — ranging from upbeat to atonal — for music to make you perform better, a prerequisite is that the music makes you feel good. As with the military music in chapter one, the effects are strongest with music accepted into your own territory — only this time, instead of boosting your courage, the music is influencing your scores on part of an IQ test. This completely changes the ramifications of the so-called Mozart Effect. Instead of creating a new "civilizing" curriculum based on listening to Mozart, as parents and educators, we would have to ask the children what music they like best, even if it means incorporating music without any discernable positive attributes, such as death metal. The possibility, that young people will benefit more from the music they love than from Mozart, is so radical that the hypothesis warrants a thorough experimental test.

1 [12] Nantais KM & Schellenberg EG (1999). The Mozart effect: An artifact of preference. *Psychological Science*, 10: 370–373.
2 Nantais KM & Schellenberg EG (1999). The Mozart effect: An artifact of preference. *Psychological Science*, 10: 370–373.

The effect of music on exam performance

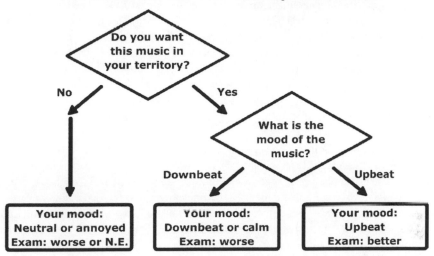

Figure 8.2 – The effect of music on exam performance depends on the mood of the music and on whether it is in your territory. People tend to perform better on exams when they are in a good mood and somewhat aroused (see Figure 10.1). Assuming you like classical music, the upbeat Mozart will make your exam results better while the downbeat Albinoni will make your exam results worse. If you do not like classical music, it may have no effect (N.E.) on your exam results, or if you really can't stand classical and it is played loudly, classical music may make your exam results worse.

On March 21, 1996 in a feat of extraordinary organization, 8,120 ten- and eleven-year-old students from 207 schools across the United Kingdom simultaneously took part in an experiment confirming that the so-called "Mozart Effect" depends on whether the kids like the music, rather than on anything intrinsic in Mozart.[1] The children, most of whom presumably liked rock music more than classical, were divided into three groups that simultaneously listened to 10 minutes of programming from three BBC radio stations featured at 11 AM that day. The first group listened to three contemporary songs then being played on BBC Radio 1: "Country House" by Blur, "Return of the Mack" by Mark Morrison, and the quickly forgotten cover of the Monkees' "Stepping Stone" by PJ and Duncan (who now grace our television screens as the comedy duo "Ant and Dec"). In contrast, the second group of ten-year-olds heard the closing 10 minutes

---

1 Note that this study *confirms* other research from Schellenberg's lab, but compared to the other experiments, this study has attracted quite a bit of methodological criticism as well. It is not surprising that if you run an experiment with over ~8,000 subjects in one morning, and you join forces with a broadcasting company as your main scientific partner, some methodological compromises are going to have to be made. I still think that simply organizing an experiment with such a large number of subjects is quite an achievement.

of Mozart's String Quintet in D major on BBC Radio 3, while the final set of students listened to a discussion about the experiment on BBC Radio 5 Live. The students then took the spatial-relations test. Contrary to the predictions of the Mozart Effect, it was not the beauty and lyrical genius of Mozart that sparked the greatest improvements in performance, but the simple repetitive rock music of Blur.[1] Behold — the Blur Effect. By showing that repetitive pop music had the most intellectual benefits, the experiment revealed the true nature of the Mozart Effect. The Mozart Effect is not perforce linked to Mozart nor to Mozart's genius; instead, the greatest enhancement of test scores depends on the listener's relationship to the music — on whether the music is in your territory.

At last, we reach solid ground. The controversial, original experiments demonstrating the Mozart Effect are true, but not for the reasons the scientists proposed. Yes, you will be temporarily better at spatial-temporal thinking — but this is because of improvements in your arousal and mood. And your mood can be enhanced by Mozart — or any genre of music — but only if you like that music. Far from reveling in the halo of Mozart's genius, you could get a similar intellectual boost from any upbeat music you like, from Abba to the Sound of Music soundtrack. This does not undermine the intellectual benefits of listening to Mozart's music — instead it correctly identifies the active ingredient as being unrelated to genius. When you hear a piece of upbeat music, it may indeed enhance your clarity of thinking, but the *real* power of music on your intellect is derived from its relationship to your territory.

---

1 Students were found to perform better in a paper folding and cutting test after listening to contemporary music over Mozart, or verbal discussion, as described by Schellenberg EG & Hallam S (2005). Music listening and cognitive abilities in 10- and 11-year-olds: The Blur Effect. In Avanzini G, Lopez L, Koelsch S, Manjo M (eds.) *The Neurosciences and Music II: From perception to performance. Annals of the New York Academy of Sciences.* 1060: 202-209.

CHAPTER 9. DOES MUSIC MAKE THE BRAIN GROW LARGER?

ACTIVE LEARNING OF MUSIC EXERCISES THE BRAIN — PASSIVE LISTENING DOES NOT.

> If I were not a physicist, I would probably be a musician. I often think in music.
> I live my daydreams in music. I see my life in terms of music.
> — Albert Einstein (1879–1955)

On the 4th of June 1809, five ominous men met in a little graveyard in Vienna.[1] A gravedigger called Jakob Demuth handed over a small parcel to the other four, containing one of the strangest relics of all time: the severed skull of the great composer Joseph Haydn. The bizarre events of that day were the mere overture of the ensuing escapade. Haydn's skull passed through the circles of Viennese society for the next 145 years before being reunited with the rest of his body. What on Earth had happened?

Haydn had died on the 31st of May 1809.[2] His death attracted the attention of Josef Karl Rosenbaum, former secretary of Prince Esterházy (Haydn's old employer) and the prison manager Johann Nepomuk Peter. Both Rosenbaum and Peter were enthusiastic followers of the teachings of phrenology, a new "science" invented by the famed neurologist Franz Joseph Gall (1758–1828).[3] In 1796, Gall had claimed that an especially gifted man, as well as insane one, could be recognized by simply feeling the bumps on

---

1 Plettenbacher EO (1990). Die Odyssee des Haydn-Schädels — Eine Criminal-Geschichte. *Mitteilungen der Gustinus Ambrosi-Gesellschaft* 7: 23-50.
2 Semmelweis K (1954). Eisenstadt erhält den Haydn-Schädel, *Wiener Zeitung* 58, 11th October.
3 Gall's unconventional teachings led to a decree of Emperor Franz II in 1801, banning Gall's lectures altogether, to defend "the first principles of religion and morality." To the emperor's dismay, his ideas continued to be popular even after Gall had moved to Napoleonic France.

the outside of his skull, which had been shaped by the brain inside.[1] Rosenbaum and Peter felt certain that Haydn's musical talents would manifest themselves from the hills and valleys on his skull, and they were determined to find out — determined enough to exhume and steal the skull once the funeral had taken place.

Figure 9.1 - Haydn's skull, as it was displayed in the museum of the Society of Friends of Music in Vienna; collections of the Society of Friends of Music, Vienna. Reproduced with permission from the Society of Friends.

But, naturally, they were not the only people fond of the old composer. In 1820 Prince Esterházy finally decided that it was time to take Haydn back to his former home, Eisenstadt, in the Austrian state of Burgenland.[2] When the grave was opened, the prince was understandably shocked to find the composer's skull was missing. The ensuing investigation was quick to identify the two malefactors, who were unwilling to hand over their treasure.[3] Having placed it in a showcase with a lyre on top (Figure 9.1), Rosenbaum even wanted to build a small mausoleum for it in his garden. Legend has it that, when a marshal arrived at his house to ask for the skull, he hid it in his wife's bed.[4] When threatened by the police, they took a gamble and simply handed over the skull of an unknown man. Content for the moment, the prince buried the skull he had received in Eisenstadt, together with the rest of Haydn's remains. Meanwhile, the real skull continued on its odyssey.

1 Von Wyhe J (2002). The authority of human nature: the Schädellehre of Franz Joseph Gall. *The British Journal for the History of Science* 35: 17-42.

2 Bahr W (2000). *Tote auf Reisen.* NP Buchverlag: St. Pölten

3 Rosenbaum also held a grudge against the Prince because he had not allowed him to marry for a long time. When he finally, under pressure from various sides, agreed to let Rosenbaum marry, the Prince fired him at the same time. See Semmelweis K (1954). Die abenteuerliche Wanderfahrt des Craniums Joseph Haydns, *Volk und Heimat* 10: 8-10.

4 Von Wyhe J (2002). The authority of human nature: the Schädellehre of Franz Joseph Gall. *The British Journal for the History of Science* 35: 17-42.

Over the following 66 years, the skull changed hands no less than seven times. Laying on his deathbed in 1829, Rosenbaum once more returned the skull to Johann Peter, asking him to bequeath it to the music conservatoire, later called the Society of Friends of Music. He agreed, but stated in his will that his wife was to pass on the skull only after his death, in order to avoid prosecution. She, however, was afraid of the men's 'hobby', as well as an investigation by the police, so after her husband's death in 1838, she secretly presented the skull to his physician, Dr. Karl Haller who was later to become the head physician of the Viennese General Hospital. He, in turn, passed it on in 1852 to the anatomist Professor Carl von Rokitansky, the founder of the science of pathological physiology, hoping that he would put the exhibit into a (yet to be built) anatomical museum. When Professor Rokitansky died in 1878, the skull found its way into the Museum of Pathology and Anatomy in Vienna, the chairman of which was the famous anatomist Richard Heschl, the eponym for Heschl's gyrus, the primary auditory cortex. The skull, however, was returned to Rokitansky's sons in 1893. Two years later, they decided to give the skull to the museum of the Society of Friends of Music in Vienna in 1895, thus finally executing Rosenbaum's will after 66 years. Exhibiting the precious head in their archive, the society guarded their new treasure jealously until 1954, when double-dealing gave way to a successful negotiation with the Prince's heirs. After a triumphal reception set up by the people of Burgenland for one their greatest countrymen, Haydn's body and skull were finally reunited in Eisenstadt.

In his last will, Johann Peter claimed to have investigated Haydn's skull and found the "sense of sound," as Gall called it.[1] We can safely assume that he indulged in some wishful thinking, since Gall's theory concerning the skull and its shape has been proved comprehensively wrong.[2] However, in the light of modern science, not all of Gall's ideas seem so far-fetched.[3] Excepting their theories about the "bumps" on the skull, phrenologists promulgated the innovation that all our mental abilities are localized in particular areas of the brain; by contrast, at that time Xavier Bichat (1771–1802), the father of modern pathology, still insisted that the brain was the seat of the intellect but not of the passions.[4] It was not until 1864 that empirical evidence showed that different parts of the brain do indeed serve different functions; the breakthrough occurred when the French physician Paul Broca demonstrated that there was an area on the cerebral cortex associated with language processing and speech production (now known as Broca's area).[5] In retrospect, phrenology at least had the right idea about the organization of the brain. In the case of Haydn, the grave robbers believed that musical genius would manifest itself as a bigger and better brain region for music. This begs the question of whether genius (or any spectacular mental talent) is too subtle to be measured in the brain's structure.

***

1 Tandler J (1909). Über den Schädel Haydns, *Mitteilungen der Anthropologischen Gesellschaft*, 39: 260-279
2 Young RM (1968). The functions of the brain: Gall to Ferrier. *Isis* 59: 261–268.
3 Livianos-Aldana L, Rojo-Moreno L, Sierra-Sanmiguel P (2007). F.J. Gall and the phrenological movement. *American Journal of Psychiatry* 164(3): 414.
4 Bichat FX (1827). *Physiological Researches on Life and Death*, trans. F. Gold. London: Longmans, pp. 62, 252.
5 Finger S (2004). Pioneers in Neurology: Paul Broca (1824-1880). *Journal of Neurology* 251: 769-770.

We now know that the phrenologists searching for signs of intelligence on the outside of the skull were doomed to failure. Of course, 1809 was a long time ago, and modern scientists would not be grave robbing to measure the "intelligence" of geniuses. Except possibly in the case of Albert Einstein. Although Einstein had made public statements that he wanted his brain given to science,[1] upon his death in Princeton on 17 April 1955, Einstein's only written instructions were that his remains should be cremated and the ashes scattered secretly in order to discourage idolaters. In an episode mirroring the bizarre travels of Haydn's skull, the duty pathologist attending Einstein's autopsy chose to remove Einstein's brain and preserve it in formalin before returning the body for the funeral.[2] After-the-fact permission for doing scientific investigations on the brain was granted by Einstein's son to Dr. Thomas Stoltz Harvey, who kept Einstein's brain for the next forty years; it ended up being stored in a box labeled Costa Cider in Harvey's office. In many ways the destiny of Harvey's entire life was determined by his acquisition of Einstein's brain, beginning with the loss of his pathology job at Princeton. Harvey's slow examination of Einstein's brain created a whirlpool of scientific notoriety concerning whether by looking at a genius's brain you can "see" the source of aptitude and virtuosity.[3]

Although scientists have never doubted learning and intelligence could create functional changes in the brain, as recently as 2004 it was dogma that these alterations would be imperceptible except at the level of the cells, which might increase in numbers or in synapses.[4] The differences between a genius brain and an average brain were expected to be quite subtle, such that they would be impossible to recognize without a microscope. Neuroscientists assumed that intellectual changes in the brain would never be large enough to be visible to the naked eye, or as changes in the folds and convolutions of the brain. For this reason charismatic Professor of Anatomy Marian Diamond from the University of California at Berkeley devised a study to compare the brain's architecture at the microscopic level in Einstein vs. normal humans.[5] Diamond was able to persuade Harvey to part with a few tiny fragments of Einstein's brain for comparison with "normal" brains, and Diamond's team found that the sizes of these brain regions were no different, nor were the number of neurons, the cells which "do the thinking." Nonetheless, Einstein's brain was different from normal in that there were comparatively more glial cells, which are the cells that nourish and support the neurons.

---

1 Clark RW (1971). *Einstein: The Life and Times.* New York: Thomas Crowell, 630.

2 For a fascinating, opinionated, and sometimes unfair journalistic description of the relationship between Thomas Harvey and Einstein's brain, see Burrell B (2005). *Postcards from the Brain Museum.* Chapter 14. New York: Broadway (Random House).

3 Burrell B (2005). *Postcards from the Brain Museum.* Chapter 14. New York: Broadway (Random House).

4 Draganski B, Gaser C, Busch V, Schuierer G, Bogdahn U, May A. (2004). Neuroplasticity: changes in grey matter induced by training. *Nature* 427(6972): 311–2. See also Draganski B, May A (2008). Training-induced structural changes in the adult human brain. *Behavioural Brain Research* 192: 137–142. See the beginning of section 4 (Dynamic changes in human brain structure).

5 The differences were seen in Brodmann's regions 9 and 39. Diamond MC, Scheibel AB, Murphy GM Jr, Harvey T (1985). On the brain of a scientist: Albert Einstein. *Experimental Neurology* 88(1):198-204.

Not surprisingly, the study appeared on national television news. Now 25 years later, it is doubted that increased numbers of glial cells are the building blocks for genius.[1] But for its time, this was still a huge advance compared to reading skull bumps, simply because this microscopic examination was much more likely to uncover the brain's recipe for genius.

In an inexplicable twist in the narrative of Einstein's brain, it turned out that his brain did have a *huge* difference from normal brains that was easily visible to the naked eye — although it could never have been seen once the brain was cut into blocks by Harvey's technician in 1956. Journalists made repeated claims that there was nothing obviously different about Einstein's brain; however, it seems that for many years Harvey was economical with the truth about the large-scale structure of Einstein's brain. The former pathologist was not able to publish his extraordinary discovery in the scientific literature until 14 years after Marian Diamond's microscopic study, and 45 years after Harvey himself had first seen what drove him to keep Einstein's brain for science and posterity.[2] Based on photographs of the brain taken in 1955, it is clear that a large segment of the Sylvian fissure is missing from both sides of Einstein's brain. Although brains vary significantly from person to person, the Sylvian fissure is one of the most obvious and consistent landmarks of the human brain, being a deep, thick and 10 cm long slit that widens into a harbor separating the temporal lobe of the brain from the parietal lobe. Even though Harvey was not a specialist or a neuropathologist, it would have been immediately obvious to him when looking at the brain that it differed enormously from normal brains and that it was somehow extraordinary. Because part of the Sylvian fissure was missing in Einstein's brain, the inferior parietal lobe (responsible for arithmetic calculation) was extraordinarily large and expanded forward into where the temporal lobe (including Wernicke's area, responsible for comprehension of language) should be. This might easily explain why Einstein learned to talk so late in childhood (after the age of three) as well as his mathematical genius.[3] The inferior parietal lobe also participates in the imagination of movement,[4] which may partly explain Einstein's unconventional thinking, such as when he first dreamed up the theory of relativity when he was 16 by imagining riding on a light beam. Einstein's cerebral cortex was so different it explains why Harvey was willing to sacrifice his job for the chance to investigate it.

All this grave robbing was finally put to rest by the advances in the past 20 years in brain scanning, especially MRI (magnetic resonance imaging). Now the individual regions of the brain can examined non-invasively while the person is still alive; this

---

1 Colombo JA, Reisin HD, Miguel-Hidalgo JJ, Rajkowska G (2006). Cerebral cortex astroglia and the brain of a genius: a propos of A. Einstein's. *Brain Research Reviews* 52(2): 257-63.

2 The photographs showing Einstein's Sylvian fissure appear in: Witelson SF, Kigar DL, Harvey T (1999). The exceptional brain of Albert Einstein. *The Lancet* 353(9170): 2149-53. Erratum in: *The Lancet* 354(9174): 258. Some journalists claimed that there was nothing unusual about the macroscopic structure of Einstein's brain, e.g. Steven Levy.

3 Burrell B (2005). *Postcards from the Brain Museum.* Chapter 14. New York: Broadway (Random House).

4 Crammond DJ (1997). Motor imagery: never in your wildest dreams. *Trends in Neuroscience* 20: 54-57.

---

means that the "specimens" are not necessarily from older donors, when the brain can undergo some shrinkage. Brain scanning living people also has the advantage of being much faster (because you do not have to wait for people to die), and it allows one to do "before and after" experiments, to question how learning can change the brain. If the basis of genius is split into what nature gives you and what you then make of it, then the explanation can be analogous to a champion runner and their muscles. Great marathoners must train and exercise their muscles to be the best, but even the most rigorous training program will not produce a champion unless the athlete starts with natural gifts that will both accommodate speed and reward diligence.

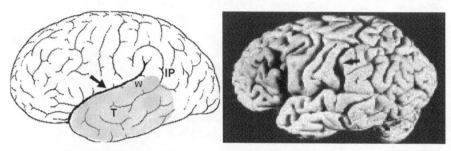

Figure 9.2 - Einstein's brain compared to an idealized brain. In the left panel is a cartoon of an idealized human brain seen from the left side of the cerebral cortex; the Sylvian Fissure is labeled with an arrow. It is normally one of the most obvious and consistent landmarks of the external brain. Below the Sylvian fissure is the Temporal lobe (T, shaded gray), which includes Wernicke's area (W), and to the right (toward the back of the head) is the inferior parietal cortex (IP). In the right panel is a photograph of Einstein's brain from the same angle. An arrow points to where the Sylvian Fissure suddenly turns upward "too soon" and combines with the post-central sulcus. As a result the temporal lobe of Einstein's brain is "squeezed forward" but the inferior parietal cortex is much larger (in the right panel, behind and below the arrow). From Witelson SF, et al. (1999). *The Lancet* 353: 2149-53. With permission from Copyright Clearance Center Rightslink.

The idea that training can change the brain to such a large extent that the changes would be visible to the naked eye was going to face significant scientific resistance. Right up until the 1970s scientists accepted the idea that neurons, the cells of the brain responsible for thinking and sending messages, are unable to divide and reproduce in adulthood, and instead fall in number over a lifetime. The first chink in the armor of this dogma was when scientists showed that some neurons could multiply in a Petri dish.[1]

---

1 See Cone CD Jr, Cone CM (1976). Induction of mitosis in mature neurons in central nervous system by sustained depolarization. *Science* 192(4235):155-8. They state, "The premise is generally accepted that mitotic activity ceases in fully differentiated neurons of the CNS and dorsal root ganglia, both in vivo and in vitro," and they cite the following references: Hogue MJ (1950). Brain cells from human fetuses and infants, cultured in vitro after death of the individuals. *The Anatomical Record* 108: 457-475;

Moving from test tubes toward whole brains, over the last twenty years neuroscientists, neurosurgeons, and psychologists alike have conceded step-by-step that parts of the brain can physically grow and regenerate as a result of their use. The changes in the use and growth of brain regions are called plasticity.

Macro-scale plasticity in humans was most clearly demonstrated by brain scanning people who were learning to juggle.[1] Juggling is a peculiar skill of hand-eye coordination, which you would expect would result in fundamental learning that was reasonably consistent between different adults. Using brain scanning to test for changes in size and structure of regions throughout the brain before and after adults learned to juggle, the German scientists found a clear difference in some visual perception areas of the brain (although not in the motor planning and coordination areas such as the cerebellum). It was as if the brain can be exercised and grow like a muscle. This description of ability fits within the more general idea that territory is created by mental association: the more you think (or do) something, the more substantial that circuit of brain activity will become.

Two other Germans, Marc Bangert and Gottfried Schlaug at Harvard University, applied this breakthrough to music. They used Magnetic Resonance Imaging (MRI) to scan and compare the brains of professional musicians and non-musicians[2]. They found that playing music at an advanced level does change the shape and increase the size of certain parts of the brain. For example, compared to non-musicians, the left Heschl's gyrus, a brain region involved in tone processing, was more developed in professional musicians and, interestingly, in amateur musicians, although to a lesser degree.[3] Not only did the professional musicians differ from non-musicians, but the brains of violinists were different from the brains of pianists. Whilst the professional violinists enjoyed an enlarged motor cortex on the right side of the brain, which is important for left finger control, the pianists had atypically large motor cortices on both sides of the brain, particularly the left side, corresponding to the intricate melody required of the right hand (Figure 9.3). The brain seems to respond to training much like a muscle, and making music is like an intensive workout for the brain.

However, while contrasting the brains of professional musicians with those of non-musicians may produce some extraordinary results, we cannot be sure that the differ-

---

Hogue MJ (1953). A study of adult human brain cells grown in tissue cultures. *American Journal of Anatomy* 93: 397-427; Lumsden CE (1959). In Russell DS, Rubenstein LT, Lumsden CE (Eds.), *The Pathology of Tumours of the Nervous System*, London: Arnold, pp. 272-309; Nakai J and Okamoto M (1963). Identification of neuroglial cells in tissue culture. In Nakai J (Ed.) *Morphology of Neuroglia*. Tokyo: Igaku Shoin, p. 65; Murray MR (1965). In Willmer EN (Ed.), *Cells and Tissues in Culture* volume 2. New York: Academic Press, p. 373; Weiss P (1956). In Ducoff HS and Ebret CF (Eds.) *Mitogenesis*, Chicago: University of Chicago Press, p. 54.

1 Draganski B, Gaser C, Busch V, Schuierer G, Bogdahn U, May A (2004). Neuroplasticity: changes in grey matter induced by training. *Nature* 427(6972): 311-2.

2 Bangert M & Schlaug G (2006). Specialization of the specialized in features of external human brain morphology. *European Journal of Neuroscience* 24: 1832-1834.

3 Gaser C & Schlaug G (2003). Brain structures differ between musicians and non-musicians. *The Journal of Neuroscience* 23: 9240-9245.

ences seen are directly caused by the process of learning music. Although the correlation between musical status and grey matter in the brain (the latter increasing with the amount of practice) suggests a causal relationship, this conclusion could still be turned on its head: having a large Heschl's gyrus might make somebody more likely to choose music as a profession. Or perhaps there is another, more fundamental cause for both, such as a genetic predisposition for dexterity that increases both the size of the relevant part of the brain and the likelihood of becoming a violinist.

Finally, size isn't necessarily everything; despite the increase in brain size caused by music, greater brain size does not in and of itself imply greater intelligence. There is a definite "correlation" between brain size and intelligence,[1] but it is not absolute. Using our favorite example, Einstein's brain weighed 10% less than average for white males of his age.[2]

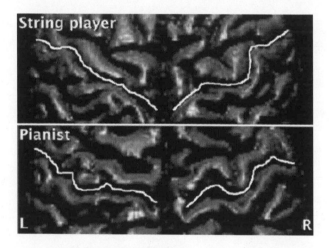

Figure 9.3 - A three dimensional rendering of the part of the pre-central gyrus associated with hand and finger skills and the central sulcus (white line). Whilst only the right gyrus is enlarged (i.e. bent and thus longer) in the string player, the pianist shows a change in both hemispheres. From Bangert M & Schlaug G (2006). Specialization of the specialized in features of external human brain morphology. Eur J Neurosci. 24(6): 1832-4. With permission from Wiley.

The most obvious explanation is that brain size depends on body size (the encephalization quotient); for instance, a brachiosaurus might have had a big brain, but as an

---

1 Rushton JP & Ankney CD (2009). Whole Brain Size and General Mental Ability: A Review. *International Journal of Neuroscience* 119: 691–731. The relationship of brain to size to intelligence (General Mental Ability, GMA) has been found from studies by Broca onwards to have a predictable, if not exact, correlation.. More recent studies have found a correlation of around 0.40 for brain size to GMA.

2 Witelson SF, Kigar DL, Harvey T (1999). The exceptional brain of Albert Einstein. *The Lancet* 353(9170): 2149-53.

animal is was not particularly "smart."[1] Nevertheless, the difference in brain weight between men and women remains whether you correct for height, weight or body surface area; the difference in size between male and female brains is not completely explained by either body size or intelligence.[2] As such, you cannot simply measure brain size and hope to understand intelligence.[3] Ultimately, to understand intelligence, you have to measure "intelligence," which in humans means an IQ test.

There has been an experiment in ten-year-old children showing that scores on simple musical tests are correlated with general intelligence,[4] but this begs the question as to whether there is such a thing as general intelligence. The alternative is that your ability in any intellectual task, such as reading or arithmetic, is unrelated to your ability on any other intellectual task. By analogy, if you want to know a person's *size*, it would be difficult to summarize their size in one number; you might measure their height, their weight, and a host of other measurements that a tailor might make. While you wouldn't want to over-generalize, because some tall people are thin and others are fat, nevertheless, it would be true to say that a baby is smaller in size than almost all four-year-olds, who are smaller than almost all adults, and it would not matter how you measured size. Most scientists attempting to measure *intelligence* make a compendium of measures that seem to vary together, called Spearman's *g*; Spearman noted a century ago when measuring a battery of different intellectual tests that, statistically speaking, for a given person the scores for all the tests seemed to be related by a common factor, which he proposed was general intelligence, or *g*.[5] Assuming general intelligence does exist, musical ability and studying music are *associated with* increased intelligence.[6]

But associating studying music with intelligence does not imply that one *causes* the other. To prove that IQ increases as a *specific result* of music lessons, one must demon-

1 Knoll F and Schwarz-Wings D (2009). Paléoneuroanatomie de Brachiosaurus (Palaeoneuroanatomy of Brachiosaurus) *Annales de Paléontologie* 95: 165–175. In fact, tools would have been well beyond the capacity of the massive Brachiosaurus, which despite having a much bigger in volume brain than a human, had a much much bigger body to control with it. The encephalization quotient of these massive beasts would have been at best 0.59, and at worst 0.70, giving it the IQ of perhaps the dumbest of crocodiles; or "restricted behavioral flexibility" as it might otherwise be put (p.174)

2 Witelson SF, Beresh H, Kigar DL. (2006). Intelligence and brain size in 100 postmortem brains: sex, lateralization and age factors. *Brain* 129(Pt 2):386-98.

3 Gould SJ (1981). *The Mismeasure of Man.* New York: W.W. Norton & Co. To this day the argument remains controversial and undecided (for socio-political as much as scientific reasons). For an opposing opinion see McDaniel MA (2005) Big-brained people are smarter: A meta-analysis of the relationship between in vivo brain volume and intelligence. *Intelligence* 33(4): 337-346. This research finds that brain size and intelligence are closely related. Haier Rex RJ, Jung E, Yeoc RA, Head K, and Alkired MT (2004). Structural brain variation and general intelligence *NeuroImage* 23(1): 425-433. This article suggests that the relationship between brain and IQ test scores might depend on the distribution of grey and white matter within the brain.

4 Lynn R, Wilson RG & Gault A (1989). Simple musical tests as measures of Spearman's *g. Personality and Individual Differences* 10: 25–28.

5 Jensen AR (1998). *The G Factor: The Science of Mental Ability.* Westport, CT: Praeger.

6 Schellenberg EG (2001). Music and Nonmusical Abilities. *The Annals of the New York Academy of Sciences* 930: 355-71.

strate that the effects observed are not due to other factors such as IQ previous to studying music, socioeconomic status, and education, and show that other types of after-school lessons (e.g., theatre, football) do not lead to a similar increase in IQ.[1]

***

Musical and mathematical abilities are often suggested to be related.[2] This is highlighted by the "Mozart effect," music's purported specific ability to improve the understanding of spatiotemporal relationships.[3] Whether you believe in the Mozart Effect or not, Mozart was definitely a keen billiards player who had his own table at home.[4] He often composed while playing at the billiards table, and it was claimed that he wrote out mathematics on the wall when playing. It has even been suggested that his debts and the fact that he was buried in a pauper's grave could only be explained, given his often good income as an internationally-famous musician, by gambling debts amassed from billiards.[5] What we are told from accounts written at the time is that he was often more passionate about billiards than he was about music:

> Whenever a famous billiard-player arrived in Vienna, it was of more interest to him than the arrival of a famous musician. The latter, he opined, would come to him all right, the former he looked up himself; he played for high stakes, whole nights long. [6]

The game that Mozart and his contemporaries played was not modern billiards, but carom, in which 3 balls are on the table and the cue ball must hit all the others; this game could demand calculations to predict the spatial relationships between the ricocheting ivory balls. Presumably Mozart found this green territory where the universe worked according to mathematical laws quite stimulating for his music.

Whatever the reason, the association of music and mathematical intelligence can sometimes be quite striking. Many famous scientists were also accomplished musicians and vice versa. Albert Einstein was famous not only for his scientific genius, but also for his 'trademark', the violin (Figure 9.4). He himself admitted that the theory of relativity "[...] occurred to me by intuition. And music is the driving force behind this intuition. My parents had me study the violin from the time I was six. My new discovery is the result of musical perception."[7] Other musical scientists include the famous astronomer

1 Ceci SJ, & Williams WM (1997). Schooling, intelligence and income. *American Psychologist*, 52: 1051–1058.

2 Vaughn K (2000). Music and Mathematics: Modest Support for the Oft-Claimed Relationship *Journal of Aesthetic Education*, 34 (3/4) pp.149-166. Vaughn suggests that more research is needed to fully proved her hypothesis that learning music improves mathematical performance.

3 Rauscher FH, Shaw GL, & Ky KN (1993). Music and spatial task performance. *Nature* 365: 611.

4 Rosselli J (1998). The Life of Mozart. Cambridge: Cambridge University Press.

5 Kraemer U (1976). 'Wer hat Mozart verhungern lassen?', *Musica* 30(3): 203-11. From United Press International (1977). Mozart a Big Gambler. 9 February.

6 This observation originally comes from Sulpiz Boisserée's diaries (1815). See Winternitz E (1958). "Gnagflow Trazom": An Essay on Mozart's Script, Pastimes, and Nonsense Letters. *Journal of the American Musicological Society* 11: 200-216.

7 Root-Bernstein RS (2001). Music, creativity and scientific thinking. *Leonardo* 34: 63-68

and composer William Herschel (who discovered Uranus), the physician, organist and Nobel Peace prize laureate Albert Schweitzer,[1] the father of abdominal surgery and accomplished musician Theodor Billroth,[2] the composer and chemist Alexander Borodin, the composer and amateur natural scientist Camille Saint-Saëns[3] and, last but not least, the composer and chemist Edward Elgar, father of Pomp and Circumstance. Charles Darwin, the founder of the theory of evolution, on the other hand, tended to avoid concerts the older he became, because he apparently could not bear the high degree of mental arousal. As he put it, they "set my mind to too rapid perambulations."[4] This raises the question of whether the modulation of arousal provided by music aids the mental processes of scientific creativity, or whether musical and scientific creativity benefit from a similar inborn talent.

Figure 9.4 - Albert Einstein playing the violin, 1921. By E.O. Hoppe.

The scientific perspective on *talent* is that it is learned by practice and hard work. It doesn't matter whether you are Tiger Woods, Pablo Picasso or Mozart; studying and rehearsal are the *sine qua non* of achieving "talent."[5] The implication is that what made these prodigies succeed so early in life is the fact that each of these whiz kids had a father who assiduously taught them their talents from an early age. Earl Woods was a golf-mad former green beret who started teaching his son to hold a golf club at the unthinkably young age of eleven months.[6] Picasso's father was a

---

1 Schweitzer A (2007). In *Encyclopædia Britannica.* Retrieved 2nd August 2007, from Encyclopædia Britannica Online: http://www.britannica.com/eb/article-9066272

2 Kazi RA & Peter RE (2004). Christian Albert Theodor Billroth — master of surgery. *Journal of Postgraduate Medicine* 50: 82-83

3 Prod'homme J-G & Martens FH (1922). Camille Saint-Saëns. *The Musical Quarterly* 8: 469-486

4 Darwin C (1958). *The Autobiography of Charles Darwin, 1809-1882.* New York: Harcourt, Brace, World.

5 Sloboda JA, Davidon JW, Howe MJ, and Moore DG (1996). The role of practice in the development of performing musicians. *British Journal of Psychology* 87: 287-309. Sloboda *et al* compiled data on hours of practice and type of practice and then compared this with their success in music examinations. Their conclusion was that unschooled "talent" never materialized as such; rather, musical ability emerged directly through hard work. Musical achievement was found to be a "direct function" of accumulated formal practice (p.306).

6 Woods E (1997). *Training a Tiger.* London: Harper Collins, p. 11. Earl Woods first put a club in his son's tiny hands at the age of 11 months. Tiger was planned as a golfer, and

painter and Professor of Art who taught his boy to draw lifelike portraits; from the age of seven young Pablo had to imitate the masters, and by the age of 13 the boy produced a sketch of a pigeon that was so good that his father threatened to give up painting.[1] Leopold Mozart was a vice-Kapellmeister (a royal music master) in the court of the Prince of Salzburg who pushed his son Wolfgang *and* his daughter Nannerl on to the performing circuit and throughout the fashionable cities of Europe, including 15 months in London, starting when they were seven and ten, respectively.[2] While you could argue that these pushy fathers had genetic talent that they passed on to their offspring, which was recognized early and nurtured, it seems more plausible that these wunderkind were weaned on a diet of military discipline and their father's dreams.

Admittedly, these are only examples. Psychologists have tried to answer this question generally by looking at the amount of practice a musician requires to become proficient. If there is such a thing as *a natural*, he or she should theoretically require less practice than someone who may be enthusiastic, but not 'musical'. Surprisingly, the increased facility for learning was not found. In one study, the best violinists attending the former Music Academy of West Berlin had each gone through ten thousand hours of practice by the age of twenty.[3] Ten thousand hours is more than the equivalent of a whole year. Imagine: twenty-four hours of practicing, seven days a week, more than twelve months in a row. It is hardly surprising that you should be an able violinist after that. Interestingly, the less able violinists from a different department of the Music Academy had only accumulated half that amount of practice. Another study compared a range of children and adolescents, some of whom attended a selective specialist music school, whilst the others showed a varying degree of proficiency in playing their chosen instrument, ranging from fairly competent to rather unsuccessful.[4] Surprisingly, all the participants took a very similar amount of practice to reach the next musical grade (on the British scale from one to eight, plus a preliminary grade to start with), regardless of the speed with which they proceeded. In other words, although they were faster, the pupils attending the music school were not naturally better at playing their instrument. It took them the same amount of practice time to improve as anyone else, despite their perceived musical talent and potential. As an interesting aside, the study also reported the average amount of time it took the participants to reach grade eight, the highest musical grade and the one many young Britons aspire to. Congratulations to anyone of you who have achieved it — it is likely to have taken you about 3300 hours (or about four and a half months) of constant practice.

Earl was determined that he should be exposed to the game at a much earlier age than he had been.

1   Wertenbaker L (1967). *The World of Picasso*. Time–Life Library of Art. Alexandria, Virginia: Time-Life Books, p. 11.
2   The Sisters of Two Great Composers (1901) *The Musical Times and Singing Class Circular*, 42 (696): 82-85. The advert for their first show in London, at the ages of seven and ten, marketed them both as "prodigies of nature."
3   Ericsson KA, Krampe RT & Tesch-Römer C (1993). The role of deliberate practice in the acquisition of expert performance. *Psychological Review* 100: 363-406
4   Sloboda JA, Davidson JW, Howe MJA, Moore DG. (1996). The role of practice in the development of performing musicians. *British Journal of Psychology* 87: 287-309.

If talent is really the result of hard work, then it becomes more difficult to support the idea that musical talent is connected to intellectual aptitude. Even direct evidence that children who study music score better on intelligence tests would not be sufficient, because it does not answer whether learning music makes children brighter or whether the brighter children study music. It is also possible that the children given music lessons also enjoy generally more supportive and encouraging family backgrounds that might give them an intelligence advantage anyway. What would really be needed is a controlled experiment with twins, where one twin is locked away and made to practice constantly, while the other goes to live happily in a hippy commune with music all around; at the age of seven we reunite them to see who has more "talent." Oddly enough, this callous experiment was unintentionally performed with the Mozart children, because when they toured Nannerl was said to be more talented than Wolfgang; however, because she was a girl, she was not encouraged to perform and accompany Wolfgang after the age of eighteen.[1] Now the name of the "less-talented" boy has become synonymous with musical achievement, while the girl is an historical footnote.[2] In fact, although Mozart is known for having written symphonies by the age of twelve, most music critics argue that Wolfgang Mozart's juvenilia showed no obvious signs of greatness (save the fact that it was precocious) until he was 21.[3] In the Mozart family, all things being equal, superstar status is reserved for those who train, while inchoate talent is almost forgotten.

In the absence of "twins experiments," the only way to reliably demonstrate that learning music can increase intelligence, independent of the family's effects, would be to randomly divide a homogeneous group of children into two groups, and then teach only one group music and compare them with the children who did not study music. This is called a randomized prospective controlled study, and it is much more scientifically convincing of causality than comparing people after the fact (so-called cross-sectional studies). The problem with a prospective study is that it would have to start before any of the children had started studying music.

In 2004 Glenn Schellenberg used exactly this procedure with 132 six year olds.[4] His study began by advertising in a local newspaper, soliciting for parents interested in their six-year-old receiving free weekly "arts lessons." The children, who all had access to a keyboard at home for practice, were randomly allotted to one of four regimes:

---

1 Rieger E (2007). Mozart. *New Grove Dictionary of Music and Musicians*, online edition, Oxford: Oxford University Press.

2 In fact Mozart's sister Maria Anna (Nannerl) married well at the age of 33, and was by all accounts happy until her death at the age of 78. After her husband died, she supported herself by giving music lessons.

3 Robert Weisberg makes the point that Mozart's truly original composing did not start until the age of twenty-one, and that before that, his compositions were re-arrangements of works by other composers, a visible result of practice and rehearsal. See Weisberg RW (2006). *Creativity: understanding innovation in problem solving, science, invention and the arts.* Hoboken, New Jersey: John Wiley and Sons, pp. 215-217. See also Howe MJ, Davidson JW, and Sloboda JA (1998) Innate talents: Reality or myth? *Behavioural and Brain Sciences* 21: 330.

4 Schellenberg EG (2004). Music lessons enhance IQ. *Psychological Science* 15: 511-514.

keyboard lessons in groups of six, Kodály voice lessons,[1] drama lessons, or no lessons until after the study ended a year later. The classes were taught for thirty-six weeks at the Royal Conservatory of Music in Toronto, the oldest and most prestigious music conservatory in Canada. By the end of the year there were no changes in "intelligence" in the drama students or controls, but the IQ of the music students increased, as did a measure of their academic achievement. It was not simply "musical intelligence" that increased, but their scores for verbal comprehension, perceptual organization, freedom from distractibility, and processing speed. However, the research unexpectedly found that studying drama had a different developmental benefit, which the children studying music did not receive: better social skills. Schellenberg has joked that, personally, he would rather have a few more social skills than the extra points of IQ,[2] although in the longer term music students do seem to gain emotional intelligence (as opposed to university instructors).[3]

But not only does musical practice lead to a functional improvement in the brain, but it also *causes* a structural improvement. In a prospective experiment, Gottfried Schlaug and his colleagues did a before-and-after (longitudinal) study of 31 six-year-old children, who either received piano/violin lessons or did not.[4] Schlaug was interested in the size of the corpus callosum, which is the main connection between the higher centers of the left brain and the right brain, because learning these musical instruments will require developing coordination of the finger movements between the two hands. Amazingly, after twenty-nine months of practice Schlaug's study found a noticeably increased corpus callosum area.[5] At the beginning of the study there was no difference

---

1 Zoltán Kodály (1882-1967, pronounced Zol-tan Co-dye) was a Hungarian composer, ethnomusicologist and educator who promulgated principles in teaching music that included using hand signals to represent the different musical notes. His principles for musical education, which stress direct sensory experience rather than abstractions such as musical notation, have been particularly influential in the education of young people.

2 I heard Schellenberg make this joke this during a formal talk he gave in Leipzig in May 2005 at the "Neurosciences and Music II" conference, sponsored by the The Mariani Foundation.

3 Petrides KV, Niven L, Mouskounti T (2006). Trait emotional intelligence of ballet dancers and musicians. *Psicothema* 18(supplement): 101-107. Compare to Houser ML (2005). Are We Violating Their Expectations? Instructor Communication Expectations of Traditional and Nontraditional Students. *Communication Quarterly* 53(2): 213 –228.

4 Most (11) of the music learners took piano lessons, and the other seven children learned to play a string instrument, which included violin and other string instruments. The scientists were not measuring the total size of the corpus callosum but the size of individual regions of it; they focused on the middle third of the corpus callosum, which connects the prefrontal cortex, premotor, and supplementary motor areas. Schlaug G, Forgeard M, Zhu L, Norton A, Norton A, Winner E (2009). Training-induced Neuroplasticity in Young Children. *The Neurosciences and Music III: Disorders and Plasticity: Annals of the New York Academy of Sciences* 1169: 205–208.

5 Schlaug G, Forgeard M, Zhu L, Norton A, Norton A and Winner E (2009). The Neurosciences and Music III: Disorders and Plasticity; Training-induced Neuroplasticity in Young Children. *Annals of the New York Academy of Sciences* 1169: 205–208. The results of Schlaug's longitudinal study provide evidence that "early, intensive, and prolonged

in the corpora callosa (plural of corpus callosum) in the three groups of children (high practicing, low practicing, and no musical instrument), but after approximately 2 ½ years, those children who were practicing a lot (2–5 hours per week) developed an increase size in regions of their corpora callosa. To objectively test the improved manual abilities of the children, in addition to brain scanning, the children took a keyboard test of fine motor skills sequencing for both right and left hands, and the increase in corpus callosum size was related to the improvement in motor skills in their non-dominant (usually left) hand.

The developmental advantages for those who study music are plain to see — music lessons can make you a little bit smarter and make the relevant bits of the brain a little bit bigger. This raises the question whether music lessons should be a mandatory part of the curriculum. The studies on talent suggest that we all can achieve high levels of performance, and the evidence gathered by Schellenberg indicates that it is possible to make ourselves smarter just by learning to play music — so long as you practice. What makes Schellenberg's prospective study extraordinary is that it turns life itself into an experiment: the scientists influenced a major activity that the child did for nearly one year.

But Glenn Schellenberg is not going to come to your home and motivate you or your children to practice. Many children simply lack the necessary interest and motivation to master a musical instrument. In Schellenberg's study, which included only parents and children who during the screening interview had confirmed their willingness to participate, 8.3% of the children taking lessons discontinued before the end of the thirty-six weeks. Periods of low motivation for practice are common, especially amongst young musicians. In a sample of children selected to enter a specialist music school, all of the children remembered times when they would probably have given up practicing altogether, had their parents not made them practice.[1]

Of course, the effects of learning music on intelligence and academic achievement are meaningless for children who refuse to study — motivation, and thus encouragement, are essential to gain the benefits. The combination of social pressure (from the parents) and emotional attraction (from the music) creates an environment where continuing practice can occur. In other words, this environment for learning includes a sense of belonging and a feeling of being empowered, which fits within the definition of social territory in chapter two. Sometimes this territory for learning literally is a location, such as in the case of Joseph Haydn, whose parents sent him away to learn music at the home of a choirmaster at the age of six. He never lived with his parents again, but he shortly received the opportunity to move to Vienna as a chorister at St. Stephen's Cathedral. In Haydn's case the emotional territory for learning his musical genius was directly related to a physical place: it was Vienna and not a bump on his skull that made Haydn great.

skill learning leads to significant structural changes in the brain, changes that are associated with changes in related behavioral skill." (p.307).

1 Sloboda JA (1994). What makes a musician? *Guitar Journal* 5: 18-22.

CHAPTER 10. CAN MUSIC SURREPTITIOUSLY INFLUENCE WHAT WE DECIDE TO BUY IN SHOPS?

MUSIC IS NOT MIND CONTROL, BUT IT CAN INFLUENCE PEOPLE WHO ARE UNDECIDED.

> There are more love songs than anything else. If songs could make you do something, we'd all love one another.
>
> — Frank Zappa

Music can exert immense influence over people. As the young musician Alessandro Stradella discovered to his relief, music can even stop cold blooded murderers. Gaining his reputation as a fine singer and accomplished harpist in 17th century Venice, Stradella was hired as a music tutor to the mistress of an illustrious nobleman called Alvise Contarini.[1] However, his fortunes took a turn for the worse after Stradella illicitly stole her heart. The pair eloped and before long the enraged aristocrat issued an order for their deaths. Two assassins pursued the young couple to Rome, where they found Stradella preparing to perform a religious oratorio in the church of San Giovanni in Laterano, and they waited patiently for their time to strike. Yet upon hearing his angelic singing their hearts melted and they lost their will to kill. They forfeited their reward, conspiring instead to cover the tracks of the young lovers. Stradella's music literally reversed their cold-blooded intentions. If music creates territory, then Stradella's singing created the acme of them all — God's territory. But if music can impose God's territory upon hired assassins, could advertisers use music to foist Mammon's territory upon *us*? Retailers are also depending upon our being easily manipulated by music: does it really have charms to loosen our purse strings, or worse?

---

1 Hibberd S (2006). Murder in the cathedral? Stradella, musical power and performing the past in 1830s Paris. *Music & Letters* 87: 551-579.

The ability of Christmas music to get us into a festive mood is well known to retailers. To us, Christmas means giving presents to each other, and thus to retailers, it means cash. Every year as Christmas approaches, shops all across the country and, indeed the Christian world, undergo a remarkable transformation. Suddenly, Father Christmas is waving at us from inside the display window. Instead of Britney Spear's latest release or a succession of 80s tunes, *Jingle Bells* takes over the shop's loudspeakers. And sometimes even the very air we breathe is laden with the scent of apple and cinnamon, pine or vanilla. Shopkeepers believe that creating an atmosphere that puts us in a shopping mood (the *Christmas spirit*) will cause us to spend more money. Music is a very important part of this.[1] Indeed, when a 1979 study asked managers of 52 shops of various kinds about their beliefs regarding general background music in their stores, 76% of them were convinced that it would increase their sales, although they themselves had never read a single scientific study on the subject.[2] If music can elicit powerful feelings in the right context, then Christmas is the ultimate context.

On December 24, 1914, during the first year of World War I, Allied and German forces faced each other in their trenches along the front line running south of the fiercely contested Belgian town of Ypres. The German vision of a quick victory over France had turned out to be a false hope, and soldiers of both sides had fortified their positions, hoping for a successful offensive in the following year that would break the deadlock. Conditions in the trenches were dire — the coldness of the winter, the mud and rain only made the constant battle worse. But on that Christmas Eve, along much of the frontline, the guns fell silent[3]. Soldiers started to sing Christmas carols and the Germans started to put up little Christmas trees. Before long, after an exchange of songs, greetings and jokes, some soldiers even found the courage to leave their trenches and meet the people that had been their foes only a few hours earlier. The Christmas truce, as it is now known, became legendary. As the carols were sung and the trees were upraised, a field of death no longer separated Allied and German territory. Months of fear melted to the shared thoughts of softly ringing bells and popping chestnuts.

But just as music can be used to abate murder, it can be used to drive it forward. In the tale of the Pied Piper of Hamelin, children are subjugated or killed through the use of music. The facts of this historical incident in Germany (in which a disgruntled musician plays music that bewitches the city's children into willingly following the piper to death or exile) are disputed, and many academics currently favor the idea that those children lacking territory (i.e., illegitimate or not first born) were lured or sold into settling Eastern Europe, thus gaining their own territory.[4] The Grimm brothers' version with a rat catcher was able to capture the imagination of many artists and writers. The

---

1 Spangenberg ER, Grohmann B, Sprott DE (2005). It's beginning to smell (and sound) a lot like Christmas: the interactive effects of ambient scent and music in a retail setting. *Journal of Business Research* 58: 1583-1589.

2 Milliman RE (1986). The influence of background music on the behavior of restaurant patrons. *Journal of Consumer Research* 13: 286-289.

3 Galer G (2004). Myths of the western front. *Global Society* 18: 175-195.

4 See Harty S (1994). "Pied Piper Revisited." In Bridges D, Terence H, McLaughlin TH (eds.) *Education And The Market Place* Abingdon, UK: Routledge, p. 89. The nature of the historical incident remains disputed in many ways: the precise date (some time in the 13th century), whether the children were killed or exiled, whether the piper was real

poet Robert Browning (1812–1889) wrote a poem about the story set to music; in it, the children of the story are easily seduced by the music, whereupon they are led into a mountainside and never seen again. Browning was himself a keen amateur pianist who saw music as a way of mediating past a reflective or thoughtful side of one's character toward a passionate side;[1] in this way music does not make one act against one's will, but can allay the resistance to doing something one might otherwise wish to do — such as following an interesting and musical stranger.

It seems that whether one is an assassin seeking to murder a musical savant, or a parent considering the latest singing toy, music possesses the ability to drown out the voice of reason. This leaves us with a worrying question about whether music has a dark side: can music consistently and reliably control the behavior not just of an individual, but of the masses? If so, music might be hijacked, to be used as a tool for totalitarian states, or, more insidiously, as a covert form of mind control manipulated by advertisers and political spin doctors.

***

Some people willingly subject themselves to mind control to drown out the voice of reason. Take the example of marathon running: you can't take a break for hours on end and your legs are screaming in pain. Music may seem like a good way to deal with this, but Jennifer Goebel was disqualified from winning the 2009 Lakefront Marathon in Milwaukee because she was wearing an iPod.[2] It was not an act of random boredom, because she only wore the iPod while running from mile 19 to mile 21; she said, "I wasn't going to put the music on unless I thought I needed it." As with exercycling, music increases exercise tolerance for runners;[3] Goebel observed, "If you're bored, it pumps you up a little bit. Sometimes, on a long training run, I'll bring it along for the last half hour. When I run marathons sometimes I carry it and never put it on." In many cases, runners (or those leading an exercise class) choose songs where the exercise's actions can be matched to the song's tempo — known as entrainment.

---

or a metaphor for death, and whether it was children or adults who disappeared from Hameln; see also the website for the City of Hameln.

1 Robert Browning along with his father and son were keen amateur pianists. Browning was most influenced by Schumann (1810–1856, effectively his contemporary), and in his music collection (which is currently in the LL Bloomfield Collection in Brighton, UK) he held three separate copies of Schumann's Fantasiestücke (Op. 12). See Fowler R (1996). Browning's Music: The L.L. Bloomfield Collection. *The Review of English Studies* 47(185): 35-46. Fantasiestücke is made up of 8 short pieces in which the duality of Schumann's inner nature is given voice via his reflective/dreamy inner persona (Eusebius), which parlays with his passionate inner persona (Florestan).

2 Matyszczyk C (2009). Marathon winner disqualified for wearing iPod. *cNet News*, 11 October.

3 Thornby MA, Haas F, Axen K (1995). Effect of distractive auditory stimuli on exercise tolerance in patients with COPD. *Chest* 107(5): 1213-7. von Leupoldt A, Taube K, Schubert-Heukeshoven S, Magnussen H, Dahme B (2007). Distractive auditory stimuli reduce the unpleasantness of dyspnea during exercise in patients with COPD. *Chest* 132(5):1506-12. Szabo A, Small A, Leigh M (1999). The effects of slow- and fast-rhythm classical music on progressive cycling to voluntary physical exhaustion. *Journal of Sports Medicine and Physical Fitness* 39(3): 220-5.

In some cases, even if someone else chooses the music, people's actions are still entrained to the music's pulse.[1] This was highlighted in 1982 when an Associate Professor of Marketing devised an experiment to test whether changing the tempo of the background music would influence how people shopped in a supermarket.[2] Amazingly, the speed at which people moved around the store could be modulated by the tempo of the music played — music with a slower tempo was consistently associated with slower in-store traffic flow and a greater total sales volume than music with a faster tempo. Despite urging for a cautious interpretation of these results, the Professor of Marketing predicted that they might be generalizable to other commercial settings, including eating in restaurants. Sure enough, in 1986, he found that diners in a Texan restaurant could be made to eat more slowly or quickly by adjusting the tempo of the background music played — music with a fast tempo was associated with a faster turnover of tables, whereas slower music engendered slower eating and more spending at the bar.[3] Similar research has shown that background music can influence the customer's mood and their perception of time.[4]

In these examples people are being influenced outside their conscious awareness — the shoppers and diners are neither cognizant of the speed at which they are shopping and eating, nor the fact that the music is causing them to change their speed. In the commercial world there are many examples of music having a subliminal effect. A good example is the common perception that people will wait longer "on-hold" on the telephone if they are played pleasant music instead of a repeating spoken request to hold the line. A group of researchers put this to the test in a rather cheeky way: having put an advertisement in a local newspaper promising potential participants of their study £5 for filling in a "questionnaire on attitudes" over the phone, they had their unwitting victims "hold the line" for as long as possible.[5] Whilst one group listened to a continuous loop of excerpts from three songs by The Beatles (*Yesterday*, *Eleanor Rigby* and *Hey Jude*), and another group heard exactly the same songs played on a pan pipe, a third group had to endure the message, "I'm sorry, the line is busy. Please hold," every ten seconds. After five minutes, the scientists automatically terminated the calls of their most determined subjects.

It is not difficult to imagine the frustration that many of their participants must have felt, before they realized that had actually just taken part in the experiment itself. Immediately after the participants had hung up and their waiting time had been mea-

---

1   There is a growing scientific literature on how music therapy can use the process of entrainment to the beat to treat stroke victims. See Thaut MH (2005). The future of music in therapy and medicine. *Annals of the New York Academy of Sciences* 1060: 303-308.
2   Milliman RE (1982). Using background music to affect the behavior of supermarket shoppers. *Journal of Marketing* 46: 86-91.
3   Milliman RE (1986). The influence of background music on the behavior of restaurant patrons. *Journal of Consumer Research*, 13: 286-289.
4   Yalch RF, Spangenberg ER (2000). The effects of music in a retail setting on real and perceived shopping times. *Journal of Business Research* 49: 139-147. See also: Kellaris JJ, Kent RJ (1992). The influence of music on consumers' temporal perceptions: does time fly when you're having fun? *Journal of Consumer Psychology* 1: 365-376.
5   North AC, Hargreaves DJ, McKendrick J (1999). Music and on-hold waiting time. *British Journal of Psychology* 90: 161-164.

sured by the researchers, they were called back and finally asked to complete the promised questionnaire, asking them how much they liked what they had heard. Unsurprisingly, it turned out that people liked The Beatles and the pan pipe music more than the spoken message. It was also those people that had been listening to music, especially to the pan pipes, who had been holding the line for the longest time.

Scientists have tried to explain the psychology of why people stay on hold longer with music. One obvious possibility is the boredom factor — listening to music over your phone may simply entertain you a little bit more and thus make you wait a little bit longer than a spoken message. But the boredom factor does not explain why people listened longer to pan pipes than to the Beatles; surely the pan pipe cover version of Eleanor Rigby is less entertaining than the symphonic original. Which is precisely the point; it is possible to be *too* entertained — and too aroused — while waiting on hold.

For many situations the more aroused a person is, the better they perform — up to a point. The classic experiment demonstrating this occurred with athletes. It was first shown in 1908 that during a bicycle race, if the racers have an audience cheering them on, they will often perform better than they ever would when practicing on their own.[1] Among psychologists there is a famous graph depicting this (see figure 10.1, graph "A" on left); it is an "upside down U" shaped curve; it shows that for a given task there is an optimum amount of arousal (the peak of the curve). If a person starts too chilled out, they will perform better if they are more aroused. However, if they become too aroused, they will make mistakes.

Not all tasks have the same relationship between arousal and how well you perform: if you have a task that is straightforward, such as running or cycling, the optimum level of arousal is comparatively high (Figure 10.1, graph A), whereas if the task is complicated or difficult (for example, playing chess or public speaking) you very rapidly end up with diminishing returns — that is, increasing arousal by comparatively little will make you perform much worse (figure 10.1, graph B). As any teacher knows, there is an optimum level of arousal for classroom learning, and above that level the students may enjoy themselves but may not learn the relevant material.[2]

Just describing a person's emotions with a category (e.g., happy) is insufficient to predict whether they will buy. Some scientists looking at facial expressions believe that there are a limited number of universal emotions, including happy, sad, fear, anger, surprise and disgust (see chapter 2),[3] and other emotions (such as love) are thought to be constituted from a combination of the 6 basic emotions mixed with relevant objects and other people. Music is not easily squared with this six-category theory of emotions: in most cases the emotions provoked by music are not clearly one of the six universal emotions — much of music seems to result in tension and resolution; there seems to be a near-infinite range between these two feelings. Tension does not relate well to a cat-

---

1 This is the Yerkes-Dodson law, named after the initial paper: Yerkes RM, Dodson JD (1908). The relation of strength of stimulus to rapidity of habit-formation. *Journal of Comparative Neurology and Psychology* 18: 459-482.

2 See the example on teaching Thomas Becket in Cooper P & McIntyre D (1994). Teachers' and Pupils' Perceptions of Effective Classroom Learning: Conflicts and Commonalities. In Hughes M (ed.) *Perceptions of Teaching and Learning.* Clevedon, UK: Multilingual Matters, p. 66.

3 In many list of universal emotions, *contempt* is also listed as universal.

egorical description such as fear, and resolution is not really the same as happy. When looking at the fundamental auditory cues in music (e.g., tempo, volume, regularity of rhythm, major/minor), rather than having a tidy one-to-one correspondence between how the music sounds and which universal emotion people will typically feel, each emotion seems to require a mishmash of musical components.

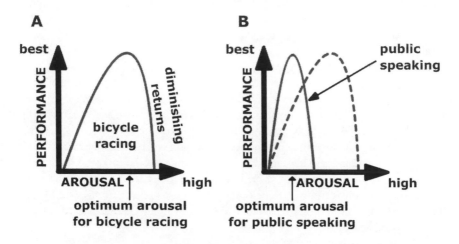

Figure 10.1 - Performance of a task (e.g., bicycle racing) can be improved by arousal (panel A). A more challenging task (e.g., public speaking, playing chess) may be very sensitive to arousal (panel B) and diminishing returns can occur at a much lower level of arousal than for bicycle riding; thus, a challenging task can have its performance deteriorate if arousal goes above a moderate level (e.g., when being watched by a crowd). For comparison, bicycle racing is shown in panel B as a dashed line.

The way music elicits feelings fits better with an alternative framework of looking at emotions (figure 10.2); it involves having a two-dimensional graph of where each emotion lies, such that each axis of the graph relates to a fundamental component of an emotional state. The classic example uses the Y-axis of the graph for emotions to range from positive to negative (valence), while on the X-axis emotions vary according to how much arousal they have.[1] Thus, the emotion *excited* would be highly aroused and slightly positive, *angry* would be both negative and aroused, *unhappy* would be quite negative and less aroused than normal, and *bored* would be very low arousal and mildly negative. Auditory cues from music fit well into such a dimensional system of emotions. For example, tempo could easily be thought of as corresponding to arousal, while major to

1 The original graph was proposed by Russell JA (1980). A circumplex model of affect. *Journal of personality and social psychology*, 39: 1161 - 1178. The version shown here is my own version of it.

minor would sweep along the valence axis going from positive to negative (see Figure 10.2 and compare to Figure 3.5 in chapter three).[1]

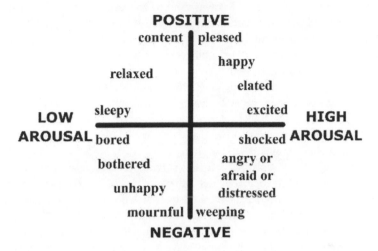

Figure 10.2 - A two dimensional model describing emotional states. This is also known as a circumplex model.[2]

Most music we deliberately pay attention to varies between all these ranges quite quickly, as if describing a narrative, but music to be used as the background for another activity (e.g., Muzak while shopping, film music, or dance music) varies much less and has much more consistent acoustic (and emotional) features. The dimensional Mehrabian-Russell Model of emotions has been proposed as an explanation for what makes us behave in an approving or disapproving way, which might unravel why people might spend money or leave the shop quickly. The combination of how an emotional state fits along each of these two axes (positive vs. negative, arousal vs. non-arousal) then determines what we do next in the environment — including whether we approve of it, whether we dislike it and whether we try to avoid it.[3] In particular, the two dimensional (circumplex) model suggests that music's influence arrives broadly via two pathways: via entrainment and via association. Entrainment controls arousal (e.g., in the case of marathon running), while mental associations controls valence (e.g., Christmas).

---

1 For a paper looking at this using psychophysiological measurements, see Gomez P, Danuser B (2007). Relationships between musical structure and psychophysiological measures of emotion. *Emotion* 7(2): 377-87.

2 One does not have to stop at two dimensions. When considering music, one could easily propose a wide variety of emotional dimensions corresponding to music, such that "breathy" vs. full sounds might extend from submissive to dominant, staccato to legato might sweep from light to serious, tempo might represent "activity," and consonant to dissonant might range from easy to challenging.

3 Foxall GR & Greenley GE (1999). Consumers' emotional responses to service environments. *Journal of Business Research* 46: 149-158.

In 2001, using the emotional response scale originally developed by Mehrabian and Russell in order to measure the level of arousal of their subjects, researchers confirmed that when music (along with scent) was used to increase the arousal of customers,[1] this was associated with increased subjective satisfaction, more approach to items on sale, and higher levels of impulse purchasing. Another study conducted in the same year interviewed patrons as they left a clothing store. Each individual was asked to complete a questionnaire that assessed an individual's attention to the background music, along with pleasure intensity of the music, attitude toward the servicescape, attitude toward the sales personnel, and store evaluation. A complex dependency was discovered, whereby enjoying the background music increased the customer evaluation of the servicescape, which combined with the attitude of the sales personnel, positively affected the individual's evaluation of the shop.[2]

However, bigger is not always better. It is true that greater arousal and pleasure often go hand in hand and elicit approach behaviors.[3] It has also been shown that once the decision to shop has been finalized, adjustments in one's emotional state can affect spontaneous purchases. Thus, if background music increases pleasure, it may cause you to spend more money[4]. However, there is an optimum level, above which there are diminishing returns; a high degree of arousal may also cause you to move faster and spend less time in a shop.

Using music's ability to elicit mental associations, scientists found that they could use different genres of music to change how much people were willing to spend.[5] They played either classical or top-forty chart music in a wine cellar while observing purchasing patterns. They found that although overall bottle sales were unaffected by the type of music played in the background, customers bought more expensive bottles when the classical music was playing. The associations of classical music subconsciously led the customers toward a "sophisticated" value system or pose — as if the classical music nudged their memories into a world of expensive restaurants and wine stewards, ushering them unconsciously toward the most costly vintages.

As these scientists pointed out, what may have been crucial in the example above is the relative *inexperience* of the shoppers. Having little knowledge of the product, they were more susceptible to outside influence and sought external cues as to the appropriate choice to make. Knowing only that wine appreciation is associated with sophistication, the presence of classical music with similar cultural associations would naturally persuade the shopper that the more they shell out, the higher the cultural cachet.

1 Mattila AS & Wirtz J (2001). Congruency of scent and music as a driver of in-store evaluations and behaviour. *Journal of Retailing* 77: 273-289.
2 Dubé L & Morin S (2001). Background music pleasure and store evaluation – Intensity effects and psychological mechanisms. *Journal of Business Research* 54: 107-113
3 Kenhove PV & Desrumaux P (1997). The relationship between emotional states and approach or avoidance responses in a retail environment. *The International Review of Retail, Distribution and Consumer Research* 7: 351-368
4 Sherman E, Mathur A & Smith RB (1997). Store environment and consumer purchase behaviour: mediating role of consumer emotions. *Psychology & Marketing* 14: 361-378.
5 Areni CS & Kim D (1993). The influence of background music on shopping behavior: classical versus top-forty music in a wine store. *Advances in Consumer Research* 20: 336-340.

All of which implies that we can mentally process and be influenced by cultural conventions, including subtleties such as snob appeal, without being consciously aware that we are even appraising the music. It is not as surprising that low level subconscious cues linked to arousal (such as the speed of background music) can exert a covert influence over the speed of our behavior. It is much more impressive that the brain can subconsciously process and make conclusions about quite complex representations of the music (e.g., snob appeal) and act upon these without the listener being aware of it.

In an exploration of wine buying in supermarkets, scientists at the University of Leicester found that they could consistently manipulate which wine people bought by simply aligning the national origin of the wine with the nationality of the music played in the background.[1] Imagine the scenario — you're in the drinks aisle faced with hundreds of bottles of wine, and then the sensual strains of an accordion melody drift subtly across the aisle. Without thinking you turn and notice little French flags forming a halo around a bottle boasting a suitably sophisticated label (naturally, also in French); you reach out for it with a feeling of accomplishment, closure and relief.

When they did this experiment, French folk music (on the accordion) successfully promoted French wine, while German Bierkeller band music (mostly brass) increased sales of German wine.[2] How is this possible? The shoppers were not consciously thinking about either country whilst they were in the shop. In exit interviews the customers were unaware of the music and seemed oblivious to the mental associations that finally led them to choose a bottle. The music went under the radar of the customers, and their ensuing thinking flashed through their minds below the level of conscious deliberation. In this way music marks the territory. When on that territory, your thinking is biased because the music is selecting which memories to recall: French music conjured up positive images of France while German music elicited thoughts of Germany and all things German.

***

November 9th, 1923. In the small Bavarian town of Uffing, an urgent knocking is heard at the door of the country residence of Ernst "Putzi" Hanfstaengl, German-American Art dealer and former Harvard acquaintance of Franklin Roosevelt. Waiting outside the door is a motley group led by a small man in an old raincoat, unshaven, his hair disordered and nursing a broken collarbone. Hanfstaengl's wife Helene is surprised by this out-of-the-blue visit, but the disheveled young man is well known to her — it is the young Adolf Hitler, upstart leader of the National Socialist Party to whom her husband had become a key supporter since hearing him speak less than a year before. Now, with his effort to seize power from Bavarian Government in disarray after the failed 'Beerhall Putsch', on the run from the Munich authorities, wounded and weary, the would-be dictator had turned to Hanfstaengl for refuge. In his darkest hour, it was re-assurance that Hitler needed, and re-assurance he got from Helene as the Munich police surrounded the house two days later; when Hitler threatened to end his life, she

---

1 North AC, Hargreaves DJ & McKendrick J (1999). The influence of in-store music on wine selections. *Journal of Applied Psychology* 84: 271-276.
2 In an initial pilot study, North et al. tested the music and found that the selections they chose were very recognizable as either French or German.

wrested the pistol from him and reminded him of his mission to save Germany. When Hitler was released from prison less than two years later, it was to Ernst Hanfstaengl's home that Hitler returned on Christmas Eve.

"What now, Hanfstaengl?" Hitler is said to have asked his host.

"You will go on. Your party still lives," came the steely reply.[1]

Hitler then asked Hanfstaengl to play for him at the piano. Wagner's *Tristan and Isolde*, which Hanfstaengl had first played for Hitler at his flat in 1922, was the immediate choice. "There is nothing like that to get me into tune before I have to face the public," Hitler said at the time.[2]

Figure 10.3 - Ernst Hanfstaengl (left) and friend.

Known as Putzi to his friends, Hanfstaengl (Figure 10.3) had something in his personality and style of playing that endeared him to the Führer more than any other musician. On one occasion a renowned Italian pianist was called in to play before Hitler. Asked if he would still like to hear Putzi's playing after hearing such a fine instrumentalist, Hitler replied, "I would rather hear Hanfstaengl play a hundred wrong notes than hear that man play one right one."[3] Hanfstaengl was able to rouse Hitler with his playing so that he would literally "yell with delight," or else chuckle with pleasure; but he could also calm Hitler, becoming a key source of relaxation during his rise to power when Hitler would work long into the night.[4] Louis P. Lochner, the Pulitzer prize-winning foreign correspondent for the Associated Press in Germany in the 1930s proposed that "Putzi was to Hitler what harp-playing was to Saul."[5]

Despite the closeness of the relationship between Hitler and Hanfstaengl in these crucial early years, their relationship suffered during the 1930s and Hitler eventually punished Hanfstaengl for upsetting comments he had allegedly made. In 1937 he had Goring fly Hanfstaengl over Spain on a supposed mission to help German journalists in the civil war, only to reveal (once the plane was airborne) that he was in fact to be parachuted behind Red enemy lines. Albert Speer in his memoirs insisted that this was all

1 Conradi P (2005). *Hitler's Piano Player*. London: Gerald Duckworth & Co, p.70.
2 Conradi P (2005). *Hitler's Piano Player*. London: Gerald Duckworth & Co, p.50.
3 Both the Martha Dodd quote and Hitler's retort are in Conradi, P (2005). *Hitler's Piano Player*. London: Gerald Duckworth & Co, p.131.
4 Conradi P (2005). *Hitler's Piano Player*. London: Gerald Duckworth & Co: 50-51.
5 Conradi P (2005). *Hitler's Piano Player*. London: Gerald Duckworth & Co, p.130.

an elaborate practical joke on Hitler's part — Putzi was no soldier and their intention was merely to terrify him — but the hapless victim insisted to the end of his life that it was a genuine assassination attempt, and after the plane landed (only ten minutes into the flight), Putzi fled to Britain.

In an extraordinary turn of events, Hanfstaengl was recruited by Franklin Roosevelt into what he called his "S-project" in 1942, a secret operation aimed at gathering information on the Nazi leadership. While a semi-captive in Washington in this role as an unofficial "consultant," Putzi was to analyze news from Berlin, read between the lines of Hitler's speeches and write reports on Hitler's character, including his musical interests. However, it was during a clever artifice in the form of a dinner party, that Putzi particularly assisted Roosevelt. All the details of the dinner party were predetermined, from Baked Alaska as the final course of supper to a communal agreement to forgo conversations of the war in lieu of culture and Harvard memories. Eventually, the talk turned to music and before long Putzi, needing little persuasion, drew the party into the drawing room where a Steinway grand awaited him on a white carpet.

From Debussy, Putzi slowly moved on to Hitler's favorites. *Tristan und Isolde*, the *Meistersinger* . . . slowly the previously light-hearted *bon-viveur*'s mood changed as his expression became fierce and violent: it seemed to a guest that Putzi was now playing for "Der Führer."[1] He then began addressing Hitler out loud as though he were there in the room, "mein Führer," emotionally imploring him to "stop the war, warning that the Allies were intent on destroying their beloved homeland."[2] No time was wasted in sending a secret recording of the incident to CBS, where it was pressed into thousands of phonograph records. Soon after, while this extraordinary recording was being broadcast by radio over enemy territory, thousands of addressed boxes containing the record were dropped by US aircraft over Germany. The mailing list read like a list of Washington's most-wanted: Ribbentrop, Goring, Himmler — and of course, Hitler.[3]

***

But two can play that game. In 1942, Hitler, hoping to provoke English surrender, authorized musical propaganda with messages of surrender packaged inside popular music, to act as a Trojan Horse. Josef Goebbels broadcast this propaganda abroad to Allied civilians and soldiers, transmogrifying jazz songs then popular in the United States and England, which the Germans re-recorded with defeatist lyrics.[4] At the time jazz music was deemed Judeo-Negroid by the Nazis, and they made it illegal, so finding German musicians who could play it convincingly should have been nearly impossible. Nevertheless, in 1940 Charlie Schwedler and his Orchestra released a version of the then-popular "Sheik of Araby," a song that was originally inspired by Rudolph Valen-

1 Conradi P (2005). *Hitler's Piano Player*. London: Gerald Duckworth & Co, p.303.
2 Conradi P (2005). *Hitler's Piano Player*. London: Gerald Duckworth & Co, p.303. See also Casey S (2000). Franklin D. Roosevelt, Ernst "Putzi" Hanfstaengl and the "S-Project," June 1942-June 1944. *Journal of Contemporary History* 35: 339-359.
3 Conradi P (2005). *Hitler's Piano Player*. London: Gerald Duckworth & Co, 303-304.
4 Morton BX (2003). Swing Time for Hitler *The Nation*, 15 Sept.

tino in *The Sheik*. After playing the first verse with the familiar words,[1] the next verse is introduced with, "Here is Mr. Churchill's latest song," after which Schwedler sings in English,

> I'm afraid of Germany
> her planes are beating me.
> At night, when I should sleep,
> into the Anderson I must creep.

> Although I'm England's leading man
> I'm led to the cellar by ten.
> A leader in the cellar each night
> that's the only damned way I can fight.

In retrospect, there was not a great clamor for surrender in England. It seems that words (or in this case lyrics) do not cause people to change their minds, even when accompanied by their favorite music.

Although both the Nazis and Roosevelt failed to actualize music as mind control, it has been suggested that heavy metal or rap lyrics could bewitch teenagers and young adults; they would be initially attracted by the energetic music and social atmosphere, and thereafter they would be overpowered by the violent or misogynistic lyrics.[2] It is possible that these fiery forms of music might have more luck than Hitler had with jazz because threatening musical genres tend to be more carefully listened to by their fans,[3] and young people have almost no ethical barriers as to how far they will follow their leaders. As mentioned previously, in one study 16% of high school students ranked *music* amongst the top three sources of moral guidance.[4] In comparison, it is hard to imagine a survey where fully grown adults would admit to consulting song lyrics for ethical counseling.

Youths and their morality may be particularly open — they are lacking in solid convictions and ripe for influence. Music *changes minds* by putting people in an emotional state where they might *naturally* make a different decision; this is why Hanfstaengl — who liked Hitler and Germany but not war — could easily be influenced to defeatist thoughts by a baked Alaska. By contrast, the reason why Hitler did not heed Putzi's message of surrender was his *determination*. He wanted to wage war and he wanted to win it — no one and nothing on this planet, not even his favorite and beloved music,

---

1 The lyrics to the original version by Ted Snyder, Harry B. Smith and Frances Wheeler being: I'm the Sheik of Araby,/Your love belongs to me./At night, when you're asleep/into your tent I'll creep./The stars that shine above/will light a way to love./You'll rule this land with me/the Sheik of Araby."

2 Barongan C & Hall GC (1995). The influence of misogynous rap music on sexual aggression against women. *Psychology of Women Quarterly* 19: 195-207.

3 Christenson PG & Roberts DF (1998). *It's not only rock & roll: Popular music in the lives of adolescents*. Cresskill, NJ: Hampton Press.

4 Rouner D (1990). Rock music use as a socializing function. *Popular Music and Society* 14: 97-107.

could have persuaded him otherwise. Hitler would have rather left Germany as a scorched piece of earth than even think of surrendering. Thus, Hanfstaengl's story embodies the answer to our second question: can music change our minds, even if we are determined? The answer, at least in Hitler's case, is a clear "no," even though he both liked the music and certainly felt aroused by it.

Likewise, Stradella's story, touching as it may be, is unfortunately just a legend disguising a sobering truth: the assassins did in fact try to kill him.[1] He was stabbed from behind while walking out of the convent where he had just signed his marriage contract. Stradella was lucky to have survived the assault. But why did the legend persist? Many people even today believe that music has the power to change our minds. Music may change our decisions, but indirectly by two other abilities: 1) it can change what memories pop into your head, and 2) it can change your mood, especially your level of arousal. There are many actions you might do if only you were in the right context; music does *not* change what you might do, but it *does* change your mood and the context as you perceive it. Your arousal is changed by entrainment, while the valence of the situation is changed by mental associations.

Hitler and Stradella may seem far-removed from the music that lures us into buying yet more stuff, but the underlying principles are the same. Music changes our behavior in shops only when we have no strong feelings or are uncertain ourselves. It does not tell us what to do. If you are determined to buy a bottle of wine because you know you need it for a dinner party in the evening, no music in the world will persuade you to buy beer instead. But unless you enter the shop knowing exactly which grape variety or winemaker you would prefer, you may be open to a suggestion from the shopkeeper — and equally open to a hint from the shop environment.

If the shop plays music you approve of, it might well provide you with a covert signal as to what sort of wine to buy, or which country of origin to single out. As a buyer, you will be aware of your decision to buy a particular wine. What you may not detect is that you are being nudged toward your final verdict by the shop manager's choice of background music. The difficulty for retailers in choosing the right music is the balance between the associations for selling a particular product inventory (do you want customers who are happy, greedy or needy) and the optimal level of arousal needed for shopping, which varies for different people. Shopping is a particularly unstructured activity, and for some people it is a form of leisure. Under those circumstances, your own uncertainty and indecisiveness make you susceptible to the triggering of a gimmicked mental association, while customers with a predetermined goal hear only music and do not feel the need to defend themselves as if advertised upon.

This why marketers — and advertisers, retailers and hypnotists — often use music to influence people — because in life people are often undecided. Not just about whims such as whether to get a drink now; even a deliberative act like writing a paragraph harbors a thousand small choices: from how long each sentence should be to whether to express hyperbole by saying *a thousand* or *a million*. Life is overflowing with small decisions that do not attract or deserve much notice. "What do I do next?" is not the most

---

1 Gianturco C (2001). Stradella, Alessandro. In Macy L (ed.), *Grove Music Online.*

momentous question in life, but it *is* the most pervasive. Music can provide an uncertain mind with the territorial context needed to fix calmly upon a final selection. As such, music is not a secret form of mind control, but if you are "looking for something" and don't know exactly what it is yet, you may find yourself following the pied piper.

CHAPTER 11. CAN MUSIC CURE?

MUSIC CAN SOOTHE AND AROUSE TO PROVIDE RELIEF.

"A person does not hear sound only through the ears; he hears sound through every pore of his body. It permeates the entire being, and according to its particular influence either slows or quickens the rhythm of the blood circulation; it either wakens or soothes the nervous system. It arouses a person to greater passions or it calms him by bringing him peace... In that way the physical body recuperates and becomes charged with new magnetism."

— Hazrat Inayat Khan, Mysticism of Sound

It was an eerily mild day in December 1801 when 15-year-old Nancy Hazard from Rhode Island was bitten on her hand by a large black spider with 'very shining black eyes'.[1] Earlier that day, Nancy and a friend had spontaneously decided to row to the island of Conanicut (now Jamestown) to gather dried straw for hats. It was the wrong season to gather straw, but the weather was deceptively good so the girls carried on oblivious to the creepy-crawlies lurking in the field. A large spider ran quickly across Nancy's hand and incited the girls to return home from fear. That afternoon, the girls noticed that Nancy's hand and arm had begun to twitch, becoming increasingly painful as the night drew on. The next day, young Nancy complained of a belly ache and launched into violent vomiting. And on the third day she developed hysterical fits. Neither bleeding nor medication prescribed by a local doctor had any effect upon the poor girl's spasms. But when music was played, the physician noted that the rhythmic drumming of Nancy's fingers upon her chest would follow the beat of the tune "in imitation of dancing." Her debilitated state led to an increased dosage of tonics, but her fits only

---

1 Carlson ET & Simpson MB (1971). Tarantism or hysteria? An American case of 1801. *Journal of the History of Medicine and Allied Sciences* 26: 293-302.

became more severe. When it became clear that only music produced any beneficial results, the medications were stopped and music became her therapy.

A young woman was summoned to sing softly by the afflicted girl's bedside. Nancy would follow the tune with her hands and her convulsive spasms diminished, but tension remained in her "conducting" fingers. The singing soon lost its impact, so an amateur violinist was called upon to play for Nancy. The violin had a much more profound effect and the young man spent many hours day and night trying to quell her spasms. At times she became calm when the young man held his violin close to her ear, but at other times she would respond only to a brisk melody. She then began to dance as part of her fits, sometimes for up to an hour and a half, keeping accurate time with the music. The physician noted that her fits resembled the *St. Vitus dance* in appearance.[1] Sometimes Nancy would dance wildly taking high leaps off the floor after which she would drop to the ground "like a log." When she was placed on her bed to rest, she would fall back into a stupor. The intensity of the dance was extreme, but she always seemed relieved afterwards and appeared to prefer it to simply listening to the music. Gradually, the periods between her fits grew longer and in August 1802 — eight months after her initial attack — she had a recurrence of pain in the bitten hand. A red spot, like a little pinprick, appeared where the bite had allegedly been and developed into what looked like a gangrenous lesion. When her hand became swollen, her fits transformed into whimpers. When the wound began to weep green ooze the fits stopped completely and never returned. The hand healed after some time, and Nancy eventually married, living a long and healthy life to the age of eighty-nine.

Nancy Hazard's case was not unique in music's long history of being a cure; traditionally music has been associated with medicine and science rather than mysticism. Scholars throughout history have proposed that music can be used to cure the sick. The ancient Greeks extolled the healing effects of music, and the list of its proponents is both long and legendary, including Homer, Plato, Pythagoras and Aristotle.[2] It is probably no coincidence that in Greek mythology Apollo, god of music, also fathered Asclepios, god of medicine. The genesis of music's curative role can be seen in the Bible, which tells of music that can cure afflictions. Over 3000 years ago, when King Saul, the first king of Israel, was tormented by "an evil spirit from the Lord," his wise attendants suggested he summon David, who was skilled in playing the lyre (1 Sam. 16:14). As David plucked and strummed, "Saul was refreshed, and was well, and the evil spirit departed from him" (1 Sam. 16:23). It has been suggested that the symptoms of King Saul's affliction suggest a diagnosis of bipolar disorder I — a mental illness cycling between manic and depressive behavior.[3]

Robert Burton, the depressed 17th century Oxford mathematician and scholar, presented a litany of mental conditions that music could treat, especially melancholia; he writes in his *Anatomy of Melancholy*:

---

1 Carlson ET & Simpson MB (1971). Tarantism or hysteria? An American case of 1801. *Journal of the History of Medicine and Allied Sciences* 26: p.293.

2 Chiu P & Kumar A (2003). Music therapy: loud noise or soothing notes? *International Pediatrics* 18: 204-208.

3 Ben-Noun L (2003). What was the mental disease that afflicted King Saul? *Clinical Case Studies* 2: 270-282.

Besides that excellent power it hath to expel many other diseases, it is a sovereign remedy against despair and melancholy, and will drive away the devil himself. Canus, a Rhodian fiddler, in Philostratus, when Apollonius was inquisitive to know what he could do with his pipe, told him, "That he would make a melancholy man merry, and him that was merry much merrier than before, a lover more enamoured, a religious man more devout."[1]

Even in the East, the Muslim scientist and scholar al-Farabi (c.870–950), who wrote 17 books on music, included advice in his treatise *Meanings of the Intellect* elaborating on the therapeutic effects of music on the soul.[2] As with all these quasi-medical examples, from Nancy Hazard's hysterical fits to bipolar disorder, melancholia, and restoring lonely sailors, "curing the soul" suggests that the historical uses of music were as a tonic or balm meant to soothe the mind, rather than being a specific medical treatment such as curing the kidney.

***

Nancy Hazard's recovery by music sounds too good to be true — almost like a miracle — but there are some features of her case that sound distinctly unmedical. The length of the cure, and the dancing that only appears when there is a young man playing music, make her treatment sound too erratic to be a direct cure for a spider toxin. Doubters amongst her group may have thought she was shirking, despite the fact that music had been suggested to cure spider bites in the medical literature for the past 650 years.[3] In the Apulia region of Italy's heel, especially the area surrounding the town of Taranto, the antidote to the deadly bite of a "tarantula" spider (actually a large wolf spider) was a frenetic dancing ritual accompanied by a particular form of music called the Tarantella.[4] First described during the middle of the 14th century, the Tarantella had become a widespread phenomenon by the 16th century, only to decline shortly thereafter.[5] The *tarantata* — as the victims of spider bites were called — were nearly always the women and the youths working in the field during the day. Once bitten, they would shake and dance with zeal to the music of mandolins and tambourines played by the villagers until the venom was sweated out of their pores and they were finally cured. At around the same time, frenetic dancing became something of an epidemic in Central Europe. In Utrecht the dancing was so vigorous that it caused the collapse of a bridge

1 Burton R (1638, updated 2004). *The Anatomy of Melancholy.* Accessed 15 April 2010; www.gutenberg.org/files/10800/10800-8.txt.

2 His complete name is Abu Nasr Mohammad Ibn Al-Farakh (Al-Farabi) and the English language source is in Amber Haque (2004). Psychology from Islamic Perspective: Contributions of Early Muslim Scholars and Challenges to Contemporary Muslim Psychologists. *Journal of Religion and Health* 43(4): 357-377. A short biography can be found in Wan Hazmy CH, Zainurashid Z, Hussaini R (2009). *Muslim Scholars and Scientists.* Islamic Medical Association of Malaysia.

3 In the medical writings of Dr Pietro Matthiole of Siena in 1370. See: Peck WB (1992). The tarantella. *Forum of the American Tarantula Society* I: 53-56.

4 Today the main use for tarantella music is to bring authentic Italian flavor to the soundtracks of films like *The Godfather.*

5 Peck WB (1992). The tarantella. *Forum of the American Tarantula Society* I: 53-56.

over the river Mosel.[1] While some claim Italian tarantism inspired this widespread dance mania, others blame an older disorder called the *St Vitus Dance*, which is strikingly similar in appearance to Italian tarantism. The *St. Vitus Dance* was a symptom of a "dance plague" in medieval Germany, and was so called because a visit to the saint's chapel was said to provide the cure. The famous alchemist and physician Paracelsus described *St. Vitus Dance* as a "lascivious dance," for "they that are taken from it can do nothing but dance till they be dead or cured."[2]

As remarkable as the tarantella rituals were, the wolf spider's venom is not dangerous enough to cause any severe effects, and far from being aggressive, these spiders actively avoid human contact.[3] Certainly the bite of a large wolf spider can be quite painful, making the skin on the affected area go black. The bite of the black widow spider even causes muscle aches, nausea and vomiting — the very symptoms that Nancy Hazard suffered from initially — but with both spiders the symptoms from toxins only last between one and four days. Even if Nancy and the Italian *tarantata* were mistaken about what species of spider had bitten them — if they had really been bitten at all — the duration of these ailments was suspiciously long. Could it be that tarantism was really just a clever ploy to evade religious proscriptions against dancing?

Tarantism occurred in an era and region of Europe in which sexual freedom was strictly prohibited. Yet the dancing *tarantata* never incurred problems for the sexual gestures characteristic of their dance. While pioneering Italian anatomist Giorgio Baglivi (1668–1707) believed the *tarantata* had been genuinely bitten, he suspected that the erotic dancing ritual was merely an excuse for women to dance and be merry. And not just women — Jesuit priests too. In 1687 the Bishop of Lecce attempted to reform the lax morals of the clergy (and especially the Jesuits) in the Apulia region where tarantism had its origins. He threatened a ten year imprisonment for racy clerics "who danced or were otherwise seized by the *morbo tarantae*."[4] It clearly worked. Soon Jesuit missionaries in Apulia were up in arms, "scandalized" by the fact that the dancers they witnessed of both sexes were in various states of nakedness.

Eminent medical practitioners of the 19th century have also succumbed to the curiosities of musical medicine. In 1803 in the region of Saxony-Anhalt in central Germany, Johann Christian Reil (1759–1813), Director of the Clinical Institute in Halle and chief physician to the city,[5] proposed "musical torture" — or shock therapy — for patients suffering the symptoms of what we would probably call today Attention-Deficit/Hyperactivity Disorder (ADHD). Inventing the term "Psychiaterie" almost half a century before the birth of Freud, the international leader in the treatment of mental illness had even attracted the attention of Goethe "who would travel some distance to seek

---

1 Peck WB (1992). The tarantella. *Forum of the American Tarantula Society* I: 53-56.
2 Gouk P (2000). Music, melancholy, and medical spirits in early modern thought. in: Horden P (ed.) *Music as Medicine – The History of Music Therapy Since Antiquity*. Aldershot: Ashgate, pp. 173-194.
3 Peck WB (1992). The tarantella. *Forum of the American Tarantula Society* I: 53-56.
4 Gentilcore D (2000). Ritualized illness in Music Therapy. In Horden P (2000). *Music as Medicine – The History of Music Therapy Since Antiquity*. Aldershot: Ashgate, pp. 261-267.
5 Richards RJ (1998). Rhapsodies on a cat-piano, or Johann Christian Reil and the foundations of romantic psychiatry. *Critical Inquiry* 24: 700-736.

his help."[1] To cure sufferers of ADHD, Reil conceived of the amazing "Katzenclavier," or Cat-Piano — a contraption constructed from "a series of cats selected by pitch and placed with their tails pointing backwards towards a keyboard of sharp nails" (see Figure 11.1).[2] By witnessing the cats wail a tune as their tails were struck by nails, Reil was sure that the patient would be cured of his difficulty in fixing his attention on external objects.

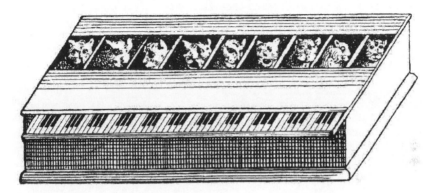

Figure 11.1 – Artist's representation of a Katzenclavier. From Gaspar Schott's book *Magia Naturalis* published in 1657.[3]

Weird music also played a role in the dubious therapies of Franz Anton Mesmer (1734–1815). Mesmer, whose name is the root for the word *mesmerize*, is now known more as a pioneering (if unwitting) hypnotist than as the medical doctor that he trained to be. He cured many people, but even before he was discredited in France, the scientific establishment described him as a conjuror.[4] He believed that he had discovered magnetic forces operating within the human body, that illness was caused by an obstruction of the flow of this *animal magnetism*, and that he personally could manipulate this force with his magnetic wands and thus restore the body to equilibrium. Latterly he came to believe that he could manipulate this magnetic effluvium with his fingertips alone.

Music, Mesmer believed, was a key ingredient to his treatment, claiming that "animal magnetism can be communicated, propagated, and reinforced by sound."[5] At his séances he played an instrument of spinning glass vessels filled with water, known as

---

1 Richards RJ (1998). Rhapsodies on a Cat-Piano, or Johann Christian Reil and the foundations of Romantic Psychiatry. *Critical Inquiry* 24: 706.
2 Kramer C (2000). Music as Cause and Cure of Illness in Nineteenth Century Europe. In: Horden P (ed.) *Music as Medicine – The History of Music Therapy Since Antiquity*. Aldershot: Ashgate, p. 401.
3 Source: Wikipedia. Gnu license allows publication.
4 Lopez CA (1993). Franklin and Mesmer: an encounter. *Yale Journal of Biology and Medicine* 66(4): 325–331.
5 Gallo DA, Finger S (2000). The power of a musical instrument: Franklin, the Mozarts, Mesmer, and the glass armonica. *History of Psychology* 3(4): 326-343.

a glass armonica.[1] When touched by a finger, the armonica vibrated with a ghostlike sound that permeated the otherworldly atmosphere of his rituals — Mesmer would walk around dressed like a wizard in a coat of lilac silk, checking on people and touching their afflicted body parts with his own magnetic wand.[2] In one instance Mesmer was aiding an army surgeon who was suffering from gout, and the haunting and uncanny power of the glass armonica nearly knocked the man to the floor:

> After several turns around the room, Mr. Mesmer unbuttoned the patient's shirt and, moving back somewhat, placed his finger against the part affected. My friend felt a tickling pain. Mr. Mesmer then moved his finger perpendicularly across his abdomen and chest, and the pain followed the finger exactly. He then asked the patient to extend his index finger and pointed his own finger toward it at a distance of three or four steps, whereupon my friend felt an electric tingling at the tip of his finger, which penetrated the whole finger toward the palm. Mr. Mesmer then seated him near the harmonica; he had hardly begun to play when my friend was affected emotionally, trembled, lost his breath, changed color, and felt pulled toward the floor.[3]

While modern science has shown that many events can elicit profound psychological reactions, the explanation for how Mesmer's hand-waving and music could cure so many had to be investigated by a royal commission of the French Academy of Sciences led by Benjamin Franklin. As the commissioners were able to replicate the convulsions and other effects of mesmerism when they wore a mesmerist's clothing, they concluded, with some fear and trepidation, that Mesmer was causing his patients to imitate each other by tapping into their imaginations. Mesmer could induce a medical mass hysteria.

This was the forerunner to the placebo effect — where one can heal oneself with the misguided belief that a powerful external force is doing the healing. The effect can also work in reverse, making believers more ill; in 1992 it was shown that irrespective of risk, women who felt that they were likely candidates for heart disease were four times more likely to die from the disease.[4] We now know that not only is the amount of healing modified by the patient's belief, but also the type of healing.

In an experiment involving one hundred medical students, each volunteer was given either a blue or pink placebo pill. Each student was informed that the pill was either a stimulant or a depressant.[5] 66% of those who ingested the blue pill felt less alert

---

1 By 1762, glass armonicas were being built commercially in London by Charles James and by Hughes and Co. at the Cockpit Glasshouse. See: Gallo DA, Finger S (2000). The power of a musical instrument: Franklin, the Mozarts, Mesmer, and the glass armonica. *History of Psychology* 3(4): 326-343.

2 Lopez CA (1993). Franklin and Mesmer: an encounter. *Yale Journal of Biology and Medicine* 66(4): 325-331.

3 Gallo DA, Finger S (2000). The power of a musical instrument: Franklin, the Mozarts, Mesmer, and the glass armonica. *History of Psychology* 3(4): 326-343.

4 The deleterious effect of a belief that one's health is deteriorating is known popularly as the "nocebo" effect. See Reid B (2002). The Nocebo Effect: Placebo's Evil Twin. *The Washington Post* newspaper (USA), 30 April.

5 de Craen AJM, Roos PJ, de Vries AL, Kleijnen J (1996). Effect of colour of drugs: systematic review of perceived effect of drugs and of their effectiveness. *Aspects of Drugs* 31: 1624-1626.

compared to 26% who imbibed the pink pill. The reverse was true for the perceived stimulant effect. 72% of those who took the pink pill felt more alert compared to 37% that were given the blue pill. Subconsciously the color of the pill helped define the belief of the pill's purpose, and therefore created the patient's response.[1] The placebo effect would not be described in its modern usage for another 150 years, so Mesmer's uncanny cures — supported by testimonials and dramatic physical effects — were difficult to discredit with the public.[2]

The public's brief infatuation with mesmerism was immortalized in Mozart's opera *Così fan Tutte* (1790), which has a plot where all is deception and trickery:[3]

Questo è il pezzo di calamita,	This is the magnet,
Pietra mesmerica	That mesmeric stone,
ch' ebbe origine nell Alemagna	Which originated in Germany
che poi si celèbre là in Francia fu.	And then became so famous in France.

Then the convulsions of the patients are mocked:

How they writhe about, twisting and turning,

They're almost banging their heads on the floor.

As a young boy Mozart had met Mesmer. The young Mozart had even been commissioned by Mesmer to write a musical piece. While Mozart was not convinced by Mesmer, many others were. In a case of guilt by association, years later it would seem that music as a cure had allied itself with quackery fuelled by the patient's belief. Music is not the only therapy to be tarnished by this kind of fiasco.

***

It's confusing. The history of music as a cure is replete with both success stories and mirages. The broad acceptance of any controversial cure depends on a combination of two kinds of scientific evidence: 1) examples of the cure's success, often statistically validated, and 2) an explanation of how it works.[4] If there were an adequately scientific-

---

1 The implications of color, however, are culturally manufactured. For instance a study by anthropologist Daniel Moerman noted that while Italian women perceived blue pills as a sedative, males did not because the Italian national football team's color is blue: see Reid B (2002). The Nocebo Effect: Placebo's Evil Twin. *The Washington Post* newspaper (USA), 30 April.

2 Beecher HK (1955). The powerful placebo. *Journal of the American Medical Association* 159(17): 1602-6.

3 The libretto for *Cosi fan tutti* was written by Lorenzo Da Ponte, as were those of *Le nozze di Figaro* and *Don Giovanni*.

4 When scientists go to the trouble of explaining what the burden of proof should be, they invariably use a combination of statistics (to show that the link occurs) and a mechanism. The historical example is Koch's postulates (for proof of causality and pathogenicity), but more recently Evans' postulates function in a similar (although both more technically accurate *and* longer-winded) way. See Evans AS (1976). Causation and disease: the Henle-Koch postulates revisited. *Yale Journal of Biology and Medicine* 49(2): 175–95.

sounding mechanism for how music cured, there would be far more enthusiasm for its implementation.[1]

Music is not alone. Many researchers remain skeptical of the mumbo jumbo surrounding *all* psychotherapies as a group. In 1936 it was first noted that many different kinds of psychotherapy produced very similar, hardly distinguishable results.[2] It was proposed that the only active aspects of most psychotherapeutic treatments were those of therapy in general. Maybe the only benefit of attending a therapy session was independent of the precise process and only depended on having the attention of a plausible therapist. This reductionist distillation remains a tantalizing, universal explanation for the profusion of different therapies, as if all therapy worked the same way as faith healing. Are the profound cures attributed to music little more than a heady brew of belief and laying on of hands: a *faith healing effect*?[3]

Medical science acknowledges that a person's belief in the medical treatment drastically affects the usefulness of the treatment;[4] less than a century ago it was not uncommon for physicians to prescribe sugar placebo tablets for their patients who complained of ailments that were not recognizable or accessible to medicine of the day.[5] Does this mean the faith healing effect demonstrated through psychotherapy can be reduced to the placebo effect?

All talking therapies start with your belief in them and then share three processes: 1) talking about your problem, 2) being listened to by someone you trust, and 3) achieving insight into the issue. Talking with a trusted individual is a curative technique that appears naturally appreciated. How often do you seek out a close confidant when you have a bad day? While trust is important, a desire for someone to be willing to help is just as pertinent. Not only does a therapist provide trust and a helpful disposition, but he also helps eliminate the tendency to feel sociologically isolated. All talking therapies provide more than what a placebo pill provides.

---

1 It is no coincidence that the official music therapy literature has focused on the word *entrainment*; I have no opinions about the success of entrainment, but merely point out that linguistically the word is exactly what the field needs to be taken seriously.
2 In the literature the question of whether all therapies work via the same mechanism (i.e. the process of being looked after by a therapist) is known as The Dodo Bird Verdict. Luborsky L., Rosenthal R., Diguer L., Andrusyna TP, Berman JS, Levitt JT, Seligman DA, Krause ED (2002). The dodo bird verdict is alive and well. *Clinical Psychology – Science and Practice* 9: 2-12. Rosenzweig S (1936). Some implicit common factors in diverse methods of psychotherapy. *American Journal of Orthopsychiatry* 6: 412–415.
3 Hillecke T, Nickel A & Bolay HV (2005). Scientific perspectives on music therapy. *Annals of the New York Academy of Sciences* 1060: 271-282.
4 At least with subjective effects such as pain relief. For a refutation of the placebo effect, see Hróbjartsson A, Gøtzsche PC (2001). Is the placebo powerless? An analysis of clinical trials comparing placebo with no treatment. *New England Journal of Medicine* 344(21): 1594–1602. Hróbjartsson A, Gøtzsche PC (2004). Placebo interventions for all clinical conditions. *Cochrane Database Systematic Reviews* (3): CD003974.
5 Hróbjartsson A, Norup M. (2003) The use of placebo interventions in medical practice--a national questionnaire survey of Danish clinicians. *Evaluation and the Health Professions* 26(2):153-65. Hróbjartsson A, Gøtzsche PC (2001). Is the placebo powerless? An analysis of clinical trials comparing placebo with no treatment. *New England Journal of Medicine* 344(21): 1594–1602.

Interestingly, faith healing also includes the same three processes as therapy, so long as you acknowledge that "accepting religion into your heart" is a kind of insight. Thus, faith healing is a lot like generic therapy. Could it be that the doctor-patient relationship, based on trust and support, determines the effectiveness of therapy treatment?[1] This would mean that all therapy methods are equally good, exposing the specific methods (which have typically been propounded by charismatic healers) as irrelevant. If this were true, then music therapy is successful not because it uses music, but only because of generic social forces.

An interesting characterization of the faith healing effect is that it is limited in its pathological phylum. While depression tends to be equally cured despite the specific therapeutic methodology, obsessive-compulsive disorder (OCD) does not.[2] Certain maladies require specific therapeutic intervention. The question is: when music therapy cures the patient, which is the active ingredient — the music or the therapy?

* * *

The way music remedies ADHD distinguishes music from faith healing. The lead singer of the rock band Nirvana, Kurt Cobain, who was diagnosed with ADHD in 1974,[3] for all intents and purposes used music as his therapy. As a child Cobain would frequently be seen running around the neighborhood banging on a marching drum while yelling at the top of his lungs. Another presumed ADHD sufferer, George Gershwin, reflected upon himself in a 1924 interview: "*Studying the piano made a good boy out of a bad one. It took the piano to tone me down ... I was a changed person after I took it up.*"[4]

The power of music to attract and focus one's attention explains this phenomenon and holds true even in extreme instances. One such documented case involved a destructive boy, Robbie, who suffered severely from the disorder.[5] Robbie had never been able to stay at school and could neither read nor write owing to his disruptive behavior. Alongside weekly visits to the psychiatrist, his caretakers involved him in after-school occupational therapy such as pottery, woodworking, and various sports in an attempt to cure Robbie's hyperactivity and temper-tantrums. Nothing worked. Having suffered through twelve foster homes and two treatment centers, he described himself as "The Boy That Nobody Wanted." When he was nine, the staff of the psychiatric hospital

---

1 Ahn H & Wampold BE (2001). Where oh where are the specific ingredients? A meta-analysis of component studies in counselling and psychotherapy. *Journal of Counselling Psychology* 48: 251-257.

2 Chambless, DL (2002). Beware the Dodo Bird: The Dangers of Overgeneralization. *Clinical Psychology: Science and Practice* 9: 13-16.

3 Cross CR (2001). *Heavier Than Heaven — A Biography of Kurt Cobain.* New York: Hyperion, p.400.

4 Peyser J (1998) *The Memory of All That — The Life of George Gershwin.* New York: Watson-Guptill Publications, p. 319. Gershwin is often described medically as having symptoms of ADHD, although these were never diagnosed. See the description by psychiatrist Dr. Richard Kogan in Worth SA (2009). Pianist-psychiatrist explores the healing power of music. *University of South Florida Health News*, 24 September.

5 Herman F (1996). The boy that nobody wanted: creative experiences for a boy with severe emotional problems. In Bruscia KE (ed.), *Case Studies in Music Therapy.* Gilsum, NH, USA: Barcelona Publishers, p. 638.

decided to test music therapy "*as a last resort*."[1] Surprisingly, Robbie responded very well to the new therapy and eventually learned to play the autoharp. Over the course of the treatment, Robbie's improvement in verbal communication increased his self-esteem. After 120 sessions he was no longer depressed, his attention span returned to normal, and he learned to cope better with anger and frustration. Two years later he was happily adopted.

ADHD is not the only adversity which music helps to relieve. Music works wonders even at a pre-reflective capacity. Premature babies born before 34 weeks cannot suck and need to be fed by tube. In order to feed by mouth, the baby has to suck, swallow the fluid, and breathe before the next suck. This takes neurological coordination that is not present before the 34th week. Encouraging sucking is important because babies who can suck a portion of their daily dose of fluid tend to gain more weight than those who are fed solely by tube. In a controlled study of 40 premature infants matched for age, sex and birth-weight, 20 of them had lullabies sung to them once or twice a week.[2] The music group gained weight, shortening their hospital stay by an average of 6.25 days compared to the control group, showing that music can help in neonatal development.[3]

In light of these results, in 2000, Dr Jayne Standley, developed a Pacifier-Induced Lullaby system (PAL) to induce the sucking reflex. When the baby sucks, the PAL plays a lullaby, but when the infant fails to suck the device shuts off.[4] After 3 or 4 minutes the infant learns to keep the music playing. The desire to continue listening to the lullaby actively teaches the baby to suck fluids for longer, thereby gaining weight.

By calling forth emotions, music has the ability to induce positive behaviors where verbal communication cannot. Music can elicit responses from otherwise unresponsive people. Since many psychiatric disorders can be seen as emotional disturbances, music's ability to deliberately modulate emotions greatly assists in the treatment of depression and other mental illnesses. One famous example of such a treatment was given by the Austro-Hungarian composer Franz Liszt. As a young man, Liszt used to visit hospitals and insane asylums.[5] A newspaper cutting entitled "L'idiote mélomane" from 1831–32 reports how he played before a sixty-year-old woman who had been a patient in one of the Parisian asylums since childhood. Whilst the woman could not understand language, speak, or even dress herself, she would respond immediately to music. When Liszt played the piano, "she appeared to enter a highly charged state, and she vibrated to every chord struck by the young musician. The passage he played produced a visible effect on her similar to that of an electrical discharge."

---

1 Herman F (1996). The boy that nobody wanted: creative experiences for a boy with severe emotional problems. In Bruscia KE (ed.), *Case Studies in Music Therapy*. Gilsum, NH, USA: Barcelona Publishers, p. 638.

2 Marwick C (2000). Music Hath Charms for Care of Preemies. *Journal of American Medical Association* 283: 468-469.

3 Music was not the only form of treatment; the experimental neonates also received massage.

4 Standley JM (2003). The effect of music-reinforced nonnutritive sucking on feeding rate of premature infants. *Journal of Pediatric Nursing* 18(3): 169-173.

5 Walker A (1983). *Franz Liszt*, vol. 1: *The Virtuoso Years 1811–1847*. New York: Cornell University Press. Quoted in: Horden P (ed.) (2000) *Music as Medicine — The History of Music Therapy Since Antiquity*. Aldershot: Ashgate Publishing, p. 401.

The famous neurologist Oliver Sacks noted the healing power of music on Frances D., an intelligent and personable woman who suffered from post-encephalitic Parkinson's disease. "One minute would see Miss D. compressed, clenched, and blocked, or jerking, ticking, and jabbering — like a sort of human bomb."[1] Yet, whenever music was played to her, these symptoms would vanish and Miss D., with a "blissful ease," would smilingly "conduct" the music with her fingers or dance to it. Frances D.'s example shows the power of music to evoke movement without the necessity of conscious will.

Music appears to touch something primordial, bypassing the complications of higher cognitive functioning. Research has shown that listening to music can dramatically reduce some symptoms of Alzheimer's disease.[2] As the disease progresses, a disturbing consequence is a gradual loss of the ability to understand verbal communication. This leads to confusion, which induces stress and, in severe cases, can lead to agitation. One way to reduce confusion is to help Alzheimer's patients reconnect with their largely intact, positive memories, which are not only more coherent but also reassuringly familiar. Studies show that music is more effective at triggering these past memories than verbal communication. In fact, the ability to understand and produce music typically remains long after the ability to understand language is gone.[3] In 1999 the Veterans Administration Center at the University of Arkansas conducted a study on the effects of music upon Alzheimer's patients.[4] It was shown that familiar songs were much more effective at reducing the patients' disruptive and agitated behavior than either silence or a generic selection of the happy-sounding classical music of Grieg, Beethoven or Schubert.

One subject in this study was a 75-year-old widow residing in a special care unit. Although English was her mother-tongue, she also spoke German and had previously lived in a German ethnic neighborhood. The caretakers had been informed by the patient's daughter that she enjoyed listening to German polka music; her favorite songs being "Do Do Liest Mier Inhansen" and the catchy tune "Tante Anna." One day, she became extremely agitated, asking for her parents and siblings. She even became verbally abusive towards her roommate, repeatedly telling her to "shut up!" Breaking down into tears, she prayed to God to call her to Heaven. When her caretakers switched on her favorite polka music she quickly calmed down, smiled and murmured, "My, isn't this nice music we are blessed with ... It's so beautiful ... I could listen to this all day and night." By tapping into a familiar territory, the music lowered her level of arousal from agitated to contented. Heaven could wait.

Whether you're a boy that nobody wants or someone whom everyone wants a piece of, music has shown its rehabilitative nature repeatedly. Its therapeutic ability can even

1 Sacks O (1973). *Awakenings*. New York: Harper Collins.
2 Svansdottir HB and Snaedal J (2006). Music therapy in moderate and severe dementia of Alzheimer's type: a case–control study. *International Psychogeriatrics* 18(4): 613-621.
3 Schlaug G, Marchina S, Norton A (2008). From Singing to Speaking: Why singing may lead to recovery of expressive language function in patients with Broca's Aphasia. *Music Perception* 25(4): 315-319. See also Wilson S, Parsons K, Reutens D (2006). Preserved singing in Aphasia: A Case Study of the Efficacy of Melodic Intonation Therapy. *Music Perception* 24(1): 23-36.
4 Gerdner LA (2000). Effects of individualized versus classical "relaxation" music on the frequency of agitation in elderly persons with Alzheimer's disease and related disorders. *International Psychogeriatrics* 12: 49-65

transcend verbal communication. By contrast, the Faith Healing Effect postulates that the reason "you've seen one therapy, you've seen them all" is because all therapies share three things: a therapist who listens, a discussion of the problem, and a patient who gains insight into the problem. There is something special about music — and it is plainly not just faith healing — because none of those three things are needed. One does not have to formulate one's problem, let alone discuss it or achieve insight into it. As George Gershwin's example shows, even the therapist is unnecessary. Instead of attempting to intellectualize emotional pain, music can transport us instantaneously to a healthier place: our own territory.

From that territory we can find soothing from daily annoyances or from the dark crevices that medical science has yet to shine its light upon. When words cannot be found, or are forever lost, music bridges the painful gap between what we feel and where we want to be. But how?

***

Medical science is rife with conflicting evidence, and as stated above the formula for convincing the academic establishment that a treatment is valid rests on demonstrating two things: 1) that there is a statistical association between the remedy and health, and 2) that there is an intelligible biological explanation for why it would work. Until the mid-1990s, research on the therapeutic benefits of music was mostly relegated to alternative health practitioners because finding a biological mechanism for music therapy was seen as impossible: it was *all in the mind*. Measuring the effect of music upon the brain was deemed too difficult to warrant serious study in allopathic medicine. Today, advances in cognitive neuroscience and the development of new brain scanning tools such as fMRI, which tracks the brain's blood flow in relation to mental activities, means that physicians and researchers can see with their own eyes — in vivid, computer-colored images — that music has a definite effect upon the brain. While music therapists would claim that many clinical situations could be ameliorated by music, doctors are not fond of panaceas. They not only want evidence, but they want to know specifically when music would be a valid therapy — and when it wouldn't.

At 2:20 on the morning of April 15th 1912, the little that was left of the passenger liner RMS Titanic — the greatest ship of her time — sank to the bottom of the ocean, bringing death to 1522 passengers and a halt to the most glorious, most luxurious, and most deadly maiden voyage across the Atlantic.[1] On the moonless night of the 14th, with no wind disturbing the sea's surface, the Titanic's lookouts in the crow's nest failed to spot the dark side of an iceberg that was facing the ship.[2] At 11.40 pm disaster struck: the ship — unable to turn away in time — rammed the iceberg, tearing a series of holes into its starboard side. Soon it became clear that the "practicably unsinkable" ship was in fact sinking. The frightened passengers swarmed the promenade while the ship's crew squirmed about the shortage of lifeboats. People were desperate, and panic was imminent; but Wallace Hartley, the leader of the ship's musicians was not about to let it take over his spirit. Together with the rest of the Titanic's musicians he played his

---

1 Titanic. (2007). In *Encyclopaedia Britannica*. Encyclopaedia Britannica Online.
2 Bingham JC (Lord Mersey) (1912). British Wreck Commissioner's Inquiry. Report on the loss of the "Titanic" (s.s.). In: Titanic Inquiry Project.

violin to keep the passengers calm until the bitter end. Witnesses report to have heard them play the hymn *Nearer, my God, to Thee.*[1] None of the band members survived but their bravery became legendary. A plaque at Liverpool's Philharmonic hall honors Hartley's sense of duty: *They bravely continued playing to soothe the anguish of their fellow passengers until the ship sank in the deep.*[2]

In 2003, a scientific team from Montreal and Marseille decided to gather hard scientific evidence that music really does have this calming effect, which Wallace Hartley had selflessly put to use. Imagine the following experiment: you are taken to a room in a laboratory — let's call it Room A — where a lab technician inserts an indwelling catheter in your cheek to take samples of your saliva at regular intervals over the next hour and a half. 30 minutes later you are escorted into a second room (Room B) in which you find three people already sitting at a table, and a video camera and tape recorder are installed. One of the three investigators now asks you to assume the role of a job applicant who has been invited to a personal interview with the company's staff managers. You are told that after a preparation period you should speak to the managers in free, uninterrupted speech for five minutes to convince them you are the ideal candidate for the job. You are told that the managers are specially trained to monitor non-verbal behavior. You are also informed that your talk will be tape-recorded, and a voice frequency analysis will be performed on the recording. In addition, they will also make a video analysis of your performance, looking at all non-verbal behaviors. You are now escorted back to Room A, where you are given a pen and paper and 10 minutes to prepare your talk, but you will not be allowed to consult your notes during the interview. After 10 minutes you are guided back to Room B where you are asked to begin your speech. You are urged to continue if your speech finishes before the 5 minutes are up. You are now asked to perform a numerical task — counting backwards from a large prime number (2083, for example) in increments of 13 as quickly and accurately as possible, but if you make a mistake you must restart from the beginning. The stress-inducing task is now complete, and you are escorted back to Room A where you are debriefed about the goal of the study and reassured that neither voice pattern nor video analysis will actually be performed. While you rest, a lab technician takes samples of your saliva to measure levels of the stress hormone cortisol.[3]

This is exactly the experiment that the Montreal and Marseille team conducted. The volunteers, who were university students, were made to perform this stress task, known as the Trier Social Stress Test (TSST).[4] After the task, the students were asked

1 Bevil JM (1999). And the band played on: hypotheses concerning what music was performed near the climax of the *Titanic* disaster. Paper presented at the October 1999 meeting of the Southwest Regional Chapter of the American Musicological Society, Rice University, Houston.

2 Titanic's Band or Orchestra (2010). Accessed 13 May 2010; http://www.titanic-titanic.com/titanic_band.shtml

3 Kirschbaum C, Pirke KM & Hellhammer DH (1993). The Trier Social Stress Test—a tool for investigating psychobiological stress responses in a laboratory setting. *Neuropsychobiology*, 28: 76-81.

4 Khalfa S, Bella SD, Roy M, Peretz I & Lupien SJ (2003). Effects of relaxing music on salivary cortisol level after psychological stress. *Annals of the New York Academy of Sciences* 999: 374-376. A similar study comparing major to minor music on salivary cortisol

to wind down and relax over a period of 45 minutes. While half of the students spent their relaxation time in silence, the other half listened to relaxing music by Enya, Vangelis and Yanni. During all this time, saliva samples were taken at regular intervals to measure the presence of the amount of the stress hormone cortisol. As expected, in the students that spent their time in silence, cortisol levels rose quickly during the task itself and continued to increase for a period of 30 minutes after the task had ended. By contrast, the group that was allowed to listen to relaxing music showed a decrease in the amount of salivary cortisol immediately after the end of the TSST.[1] The results suggested that listening to relaxing music after a psychologically stressful ordeal can measurably reduce stress.

This psychological effect, to soothe people by lowering their arousal, is one of the well-springs behind music's ability to heal the sick. For example, music can lower one's level of arousal so much that it can lull one to sleep. With its wide usage for preventing fatigue, it is ironic that music can also be used to help one drift off to the land of nod. Lullabies have been a constant in societies, many being passed down for generations. An experiment consisting of college students who all suffered moderate sleep problems shed light on this aspect of music's healing ability.[2] The individuals were assigned to one of three groups, which had to go to sleep every night with either music, an audio book, or in silence. After three weeks the sleep quality of the music group had drastically increased, far surpassing that of the audio book group. The music group even displayed significantly fewer depressive symptoms. Since lack of sleep quality is known to lead to depressive symptoms, music is able to relax the body so that it can normalize to a healthier equilibrium. Thus, music indirectly helped cure several pathological symptoms by eliminating the root cause: being too aroused

But increasing arousal can be useful in other situations, and music can do this as well. On long car trips in the evening it is a struggle to combat fatigue. A frequent response to sleepiness is caffeine, and fuel stations around the world make their profits by recognizing the link between driving and caffeinated beverages. The connection makes sense psychobiologically, as caffeine has been shown to decrease fatigue and depression.[3] But cars don't only come with cup holders; many car buyers think having music in their car is essential.[4] In a study involving professional truck drivers, music was used to measure the effects of fatigue while driving.[5] Each driver was permitted to bring his

is Suda M, Morimoto K, Obata A, Koizumi H, Maki A (2008). Emotional responses to music: towards scientific perspectives on music therapy. *Neuroreport* 19(1): 75-8.

1 Kirschbaum C, Pirke KM & Hellhammer DH (1993). The Trier Social Stress Test--a tool for investigating psychobiological stress responses in a laboratory setting. *Neuropsychobiology*, 28: 76-81.

2 Harma L, Takács J, and Bódizs R (2008). Music improves sleep quality in students. *Journal of Advanced Nursing* 62(3): 327-335.

3 Arciero PJ, Ormsbee MJ (2009). Relationship of blood pressure, behavioral mood state, and physical activity following caffeine ingestion in younger and older women. *Applied Physiology Nutrition and Metabolism* 34: 754-762.

4 In one unpublished experiment my team has done for Honda UK, we found that 1–2% of everything the customers said in the dealer's showroom was about playing music in the car.

5 Oron-Gilad T, Ronen A, Shinar D (2008). Alertness maintaining tasks (AMTs) while driving. *Accident Analysis & Prevention* 40: 851-860.

favorite music into a driving simulator and this was compared against driving in silence and to driving while playing a trivia game. In each forty-five minute simulation there was no attention deterioration while listening to music. This was not the case without music. In fact, none of the other methods tested outperformed music's ability to keep fatigue in check. So, music can help people by keeping them awake as well as by helping them sleep. Either up or down, music can change arousal back toward what is situationally appropriate. This can be done by entrainment, and as shown in chapter ten, there are optimum levels of arousal for different activities, so what is the "best" music varies depending on the situation.

Because so much of health is a "state of mind," music can make people feel physically better. Not only does music calm a person during an emergency such as on the Titanic, but it also provides an anesthetic when trauma actually occurs. Research has shown that patients recovering from intestinal surgery felt 16-40% less pain when listening to relaxing music of their choice (classical orchestral, piano, slow jazz, synthesizer or harp) than patients recovering in silence.[1] While reductions in subjective measures of pain are promising, they are not as objective — or as clinically-relevant — as measurements showing that the treatment can reduce the drug dosage needed. For example, after routine hernia surgery patients listening to music needed less morphine.[2] Likewise, listening to certain types of music can even lower blood pressure in patients with high blood pressure.[3]

With all these different types of experiments, there are two scientific conundrums facing the medical community[4]: what medical conditions music can actually treat, and what quality of evidence is needed to prove it. Dr Mark Tramo, Director of Harvard Medical School's Institute of Music and Brain Science is both optimistic and realistic about using music in medicine; while music has been shown to alleviate some of the fear, anxiety, and fatigue in chemotherapy patients,[5] he cautions that one must not conflate the "healing" powers of music with the curative results of medication: "It's not going to be that music shrinks your tumor."[6] The mechanism for music's healing mechanism remains shrouded in mystery,[7] and the randomized, multi-center, large-population,

---

1 Good M, Anderson GC, Ahn S, Cong X & Stanton-Hicks M (2005). Relaxation and music reduce pain following intestinal surgery. *Research in Nursing and Health* 28: 240-251.

2 Nilsson U, Unosson M, Rawal N (2005) Stress reduction and analgesia in patients exposed to calming music postoperatively: a randomized controlled trial. *European Journal of Anaesthesiology* 22(2): 96-102.

3 Teng XF, Wong MY, Zhang YT (2007). The effect of music on hypertensive patients. *Conference Proceedings IEEE Engineering in Medicine and Biology Society 2007* 46: 49-51.

4 This overlooks the issue of cost as well, but there is always money for new drugs.

5 Ferrer AJ (2007). The effect of live music on decreasing anxiety in patients undergoing chemotherapy treatment. *Journal of Music Therapy* 44: 242-255.

6 Ostrom CM (2005). Music as medicine. *The Seattle Times* newspaper (USA), 25 May.

7 Music therapists and some neurobiologists have even speculated that the physiological mechanism behind music therapy is based on its rhythm. Rhythmic stimulation through music may "entrain" timing processes in the brain which can be used to help stroke patients regain their gait or treat the movement disorders of people suffering from Parkinson's Disease. See: Thaut, MH (2005). The future of music in therapy and medicine. *Annals of the New York Academy of Sciences* 1060: 303-308

statistically-sound clinical trials to investigate it are still lacking.[1] All the results from smaller experiments that added music to the treatment of coronary heart disease were put together in 2009 into one giant, statistical meta-analysis, which concluded that music can lower blood pressure, heart rate, breathing rate, pain, and anxiety; however, the quality of the evidence was deemed as *not strong* and the clinical significance as unclear.[2] It is uncertain how medicine will be able to resolve the conflict between the need for a biological mechanism and the overwhelming evidence that music does *something* to the body.

The answer may come from spinning classes.[3] Music has effects on how much exercise can be tolerated, and what it feels like, although there remains a question as to how. In medical studies, music is often claimed to act as merely an auditory distraction, although no evidence is given. For example, when lung patients with breathing difficulties (e.g., wheezing) were asked to pedal an exercise bicycle for as long as possible, not only was their subjective exertion measured, but also the objective total physical work done.[4] Music resulted in a higher exercise tolerance compared to silence, as well as less subjective unpleasantness; however, when patients were asked to do the same exercise with a non-musical auditory distraction (grey noise), grey noise *did* decrease the subjective unpleasantness, but did not increase the amount of exercise done. The implication is that although distraction may decrease your discomfort, it will not make you stronger — music has qualitatively different effects from pure distraction.

Not only is music different from grey noise, but music differs in its effects depending on whether it is fast or slow.[5] Healthy university students achieved higher exercycling workloads when they listened to classical music that started slow and became faster compared to music with other tempos. This implies that for music to achieve these effects, it cannot be any old noise; it cannot even be any old music. In the pieces chosen, there is something special about the music *per se*.

In almost all of the experiments mentioned, the music was the sort of music the patient or volunteer would like or want; in some cases the experimental participant

---

1 This quote is from Mark Tramo: Ostrom CM (2005). Music as medicine. *The Seattle Times* newspaper (USA), 25 May.

2 Bradt J, Dileo C (2009). Music for stress and anxiety reduction in coronary heart disease patients. *Cochrane Database Systematic Review* 15(2): CD006577.

3 Spinning is the name of a structured, indoor exercise class based on pedalling a stationary exercycle. See Ellin A (2007). Indoor Cycling Finds Its Way Back With Proper Training. *The New York Times* newspaper (USA), 24 May.

4 These patients suffer from COPD (chronic obstructive pulmonary disease), who have difficulty exercising because they find breathing difficult (dyspnea). See: Thornby MA, Haas F, Axen K. (1995). Effect of distractive auditory stimuli on exercise tolerance in patients with COPD. *Chest* 107 (5): 1213-7. von Leupoldt A, Taube K, Schubert-Heukeshoven S, Magnussen H, Dahme B (2007). Distractive auditory stimuli reduce the unpleasantness of dyspnea during exercise in patients with COPD. *Chest* 132(5): 1506-12.

5 The other tempos tested were "fast to slow," constantly fast, and constantly slow. Participants subjectively preferred constantly fast and "slow to fast" tempos. Szabo A, Small A, Leigh M (1999). The effects of slow- and fast-rhythm classical music on progressive cycling to voluntary physical exhaustion. *Journal of Sports Medicine and Physical Fitness* 39(3): 220-5.

personally selected the music. If the experiment did not explicitly allow one to choose one's own music, the choice was made based on appropriateness; the culture, the activity and the situation were all considered, so that the music would not be rejected. In other words, the person performed the experiment on his own territory. This fits with the concurrent ability of music to increase and focus arousal (as when getting premature infants to suck) or to soothingly decrease arousal (as in ADHD and pain relief).

Music is more than a diversion away from pain; it is a beacon toward empowerment. Music's effects on the mind are real effects, not just faith healing or the placebo effect. In the examples of shopping, music guided people who were undecided due to a lack of knowledge or preference, but with maladies music can determine the tipping point in the "indecision"; when the "choice" is territorial feelings versus an unwanted behavior or feeling, music can move the mind toward unity. And where the mind leads, the body will follow. Music transports us to our territory, and once there, the power of territory works its magic. On our own territory we can endure the stresses of the day, and the stresses of the body. We are ready for what is to come, and we can handle what has come to pass. We are capable. We are confident. We are secure. We are strong. When music from our own territory envelops us, it serves to fine tune our levels of both mental and physical arousal, which empowers the music to put our body in a state that can allay our afflictions.

AFTERWORD: THE POWER OF MUSIC

"These are days you'll remember." If you recall nothing else from your graduation ceremony, remember you heard the New Jersey Governor quote from 10,000 Maniacs."

— Christine Todd (b. 1946), New Jersey Governor, at the Wheaton College Graduation, 1995

If you have read this far, you have probably already decided you believe music can make a positive difference to the world. But then, nobody thinks that music as a whole is a bad thing. As Samuel Johnson put it, "Music is the only sensual pleasure without vice." It is not immoral, illicit or fattening. No one wants to make music in its entirety illegal, or to spare us from its baneful consequences. Despite its potentially manipulative effects, such as when keeping people on hold or when marketing, even a skeptical scientist like me will agree with you that music is, generally speaking, a pretty good thing.

But it does seem like I am preaching to the converted. The real reason we all want to know more about the power of music is not to determine whether music is good or bad, but because it appears to be a missed opportunity. It seems that we could take music much further, so that we as individuals and as society collectively could benefit in ways we have yet to imagine. We know how: entrainment changes arousal, associations change valence — and we know who: people who are undecided or driven in conflicting directions.

Scientists have been on the look out for these opportunities, and two promising ones are worth mentioning, both concerning learning and memory in children. First, music improves the communication ability of autistic children. Although autistic children have communication disabilities that include failure to recognize vocal and facial expressions of emotions, they are able to recognize emotions in music.[1] When autistic

---

1 Capps L, Yirmiya N & Sigman M (1992). Understanding of simple and complex emotions in nonretarded children with autism. *Journal of Child Psychology and Psychiatry* 33: 1169–1182. Heaton P, Hermelin B & Pring L (1999). Can children with autistic spec-

children were taught language by being asked to imitate the teacher, they performed better when the words were sung rather than spoken.[1] In another study, ten weeks of music therapy sessions improved the autistic children's ability to express themselves.[2] Overall, a meta-analysis (synthesizing data from multiple studies) showed that music therapy improved to a statistically significant level verbal and gestural communication skills of autistic children.[3]

Simply listening to pleasant music can also improve the short-term memory of healthy children. In one study 10–12 year-olds were asked to memorize ten sentences in which they had to remember a target adjective from a sentence with men performing an action, such as "The *ugly* men bought some plastic"; having been told to remember 10 such sentences, the children were cued with the same sentences missing the adjective ("the ... men bought some plastic") and asked to recall the correct adjective.[4] Compared to when there was no music, the children performed significantly better when there was pleasant calming music in the background, and significantly worse when listening to unpleasant aggressive music.

This relationship between music and memory is extraordinary. Music differs from other sounds such as speech because music taps into powerful memories even when the memories have not been memorized, the learning was subconscious and the sounds have changed from the original. Not just with songs like *Twinkle Twinkle Little Star*, which was contrived to be unforgettable, but even when adolescents do not know the words to their favorite song, music can be a hook for memories because the territorial memory of music is based on recognition, not recall. To tap into your own territory, you only need to know a few elements of the song to identify it, as shown in chapter four. A song remains recognizable when it is transposed to a different key, played on a kazoo, or sped up to the point where the emotional tone is completely changed (such as when the Benny Hill television show accompanied chase scenes with a zippy 4/4 version of Beethoven's *Für Elise*). Territory can be recognized from mere elements of the music, as in the case of Snowball the sulfur-crested cockatoo (whom we met in chapter four), who actually had a favorite song ("Everybody" by the Backstreet Boys) that he learned to dance to with his owners; furthermore, he could keep time to fast tempo and slow tempo versions of that same song. Snowball shows us that 1) music can be changed and you can nonetheless recognize and respond to it, and 2) even cockatoos can adopt

---

trum disorders perceive affect in music? An experimental investigation. *Psychological Medicine* 29: 1405-410.

1 Buday EM (1995). The effects of signed and spoken words taught with music on sign and speech imitation by children with autism, *Journal of Music Therapy* 32(3): 189-202.

2 Edgerton CL (1994). The effect of improvisational music therapy on the communicative behaviours of autistic children, *Journal of Music Therapy* 31(1): 31-62.

3 However, it did not lessen their behavior problems. Gold C, Wigram T, Elefant C (2006). Music therapy for autistic spectrum disorder. *Cochrane Database of Systematic Reviews* Issue 2. Art. No.: CD004381.

4 Hallam S & Katsarou G (1998). The effects of listening to background music on children's altruistic behaviour and success in memorising text. Paper presented at the conference of the British Educational Research Association, August 27th-30th 1998, Belfast.

music from their "peers," thereafter behaving as though the music was in their own territory.

The fact is that a small subset of elements of the music is sufficient to recognize a tune. Here is an experiment to try at home: ask a friend to play with you "name that tune"; you will play them a tune, and then they have to guess as fast as possible what song it is. Then "play" the tune by rapping your knuckles on a table, so that there are no pitches, only rhythm. If you are playing with someone familiar with Western music, start off with *Jingle Bells*. Most people can guess this in less than ten seconds — from the thousands of songs they must know, using nothing but rhythmic cues.

This means that we have an incredible implicit memory for rhythm that we never even consider. While having only the rhythm of a song is probably not sufficient to elicit the feelings of territory, the most stripped down version of the musical pitches *can* elicit those emotions: whistling. The fact that you only need a tiny bit of song to tap into the empowering feelings of territory means that you can etch a song into your memory just by half-hearing it in the background, without getting bored of the canonical version. Thus, when listening to music within your territory, you can hear it (and learn it) without listening.[1] While a child might not sit down and actively devote themselves to memorizing the music, the ear takes it in, like a familiar scent. Because music can be passively absorbed, it can be repeatedly enjoyed without eliciting boredom. While one might only rarely read a novel twice, let alone three times, a good song can be appreciated hundreds of times over. This repetition makes our memory for music astonishingly enduring, with childhood melodies still remembered and found reassuring into old age (and even among Alzheimer's patients, as seen in chapter eleven).[2]

This detailed way our minds remember music is not to be taken for granted. In experiments on eye-witness testimony, people's recollections have been shown to be highly flawed and open to suggestion.[3] In one study participants were shown a 30 second video of two cars colliding, and were then asked several questions about the collision. One group was asked, "How fast were the cars going when they *hit*?" For other participants the word *hit* was substituted with *smashed*, *collided*, or *contacted*. Not only were the recollections of the speed of the car faster for *smashed* (40 miles per hour) than *contacted* (31 miles per hour), but the "smashed" volunteers were twice as likely to later recall seeing broken glass. The truth about our memory of the world is that it is made up of small, precariously balanced signposts, like cairns, of what we actually experienced, and the

---

1 The concept of "hearing without listening" is the opposite of what happens in an argument when people "listen without hearing." In the example of an argument, the listener nods their head, but they will neither agree nor remember in the future, which is listening without hearing. With music in the background, you may be doing other tasks and remain unaware of attending to it, but if you hear it a few times (even without "listening") years later you will remember the melody and possibly even the words.

2 Gerdner LA (2000). Effects of individualized versus classical "relaxation" music on the frequency of agitation in elderly persons with Alzheimer's disease and related disorders. *International Psychogeriatrics* 12: 49-65.

3 Loftus EF, Palmer JC (1974). Reconstruction of an automobile destruction: an example of the interaction between language and memory. *Journal of Verbal Learning and Verbal Behaviour* 13: 585-589.

rest is recreated (or even confabulated) when it is needed for recall.[1] Not so with music, which is often remembered exactly.

Because identity itself is at stake. Music forms one of the central pillars of how people define themselves. When two people meet for the first time, it is not long before they need to know, "What kind of music do you listen to?" In fact, the ability of music to delineate groups and where they belong may outlast the places they are supposed to be attached to. No longer constrained by the small communities of our ancestors, the global society threatens to homogenize identity. Some academics propose that music will be crucial in retaining our disparate identities in an increasingly fragmented world. It seems that music can mediate the memory of social territory. As one leader in music education put it:

> Music ... can also be a powerful means of maintaining the continuity and stability of societies through folk music and songs which give accounts of myths and legends and record important events. In our increasingly global society, folk music is likely to become an important means of preserving the identity of minority cultures.[2]

Because music is so effective as a mnemonic aid, it contributes to the construction and constancy of both individual and social identity. Music is one way we remember who we are.

***

The evidence presented in the preceding eleven chapters leads to one undeniable conclusion: over the past twenty years scientists have devised ingenious ways of interrogating how music affects us. The scientists have amassed astounding evidence for many notions that were previously intuited, while turning some old ideas on their heads. What has remained unanswered is the following question: what does music do to humans, and does that explain why it evolved?

The archaeological record shows that primitive humans were making music with flutes carved from bone from at least thirty thousand years ago.[3] Surrounded by the sounds of a camp fire and crickets, would the hairs on the backs of their necks have stood up on end when the flute's sweet, melodic timbre cut through the night air and called forth whatever god they believed would guard them through the hours of darkness? How strange and inexplicable the sounds must have seemed to the animals nearby. And if in the distance another man from a tribe without such flutes had heard this

---

1   The ideas of reconstructive memory based on schemas that "make sense" are fundamental psychological concepts promulgated by Frederic Bartlett (1886-1969); the suggestibility of eyewitness testimony was work pioneered by Elizabeth Loftus. More recently certain kinds of memories have been shown to be relatively stable over the course of a year, so there is a bit of controversy. For a text book explanation see Gross R (2005). *Psychology: the Science of Mind and Behaviour*, Fifth Edition. London, Hodder Arnold, pp. 358-360.

2   Hallam S (2001). *The power of music: the strength of music's influence on our lives.* London: Performing Musical Rights Society, p. 13-14.

3   The exact date is disputed, so I have selected the lowest date for this Slovenian find. Huron D (2001). Is music an evolutionary adaptation? *Annals of the New York Academy of Sciences* 930: 43-61.

harmonious song that no bird would ever make, would he have felt curiously pulled toward it or cautiously urged away? The wonder and amazement seems so foreign to our modern world, yet we are surrounded by this power of music without even recognizing it.

In Southampton on the south coast of England there is a nightclub for students which cannot be named here due to legal reasons, but all the University of Southampton students know its name, if for no other reason than it would often sell pints of beer at a price of 50 pence, whereas in a normal pub beer would cost five times as much. The toilets are filthy, the floor is covered in swill, and the students drink until they are ill under the table. Shocking to outsiders, the Southampton University athletes and regulars love it, affectionately calling it "The Palace of Dreams."

The dance floor there is tiny, and the music is cheesy, but it taps into something that gives the students the strength to flaunt whatever rules the adult world foists upon them. Whenever the Baywatch theme tune "I'll be ready" is played,[1] the dancers — both male and female — immediately start taking off their clothes, singing and dancing to it in various states of nakedness. Then, once the song ends, they put their clothing back on and act as if nothing strange had happened.[2] This not only explains the popularity of the club with rugby players and the ladies hockey team, but also clarifies the comments of one aficionado who explained that the club "is like a horror movie: most of the time you are uncomfortable and want to leave, yet the experience is so thrilling that you want to go back for more."[3] Another blogger described the club's territorial benefits even more succinctly [italics mine]: "It may be a dirty AIDS infested dump, but it's *our* amazing AIDS infested dump!"[4] Plainly the club elicits intense loyalty from its patrons, and the dancing and disrobing to "I'll be ready" is one of the central territorial displays within the club.

This Southampton nightclub may finally show us the missing ingredient in the explanation for how music leads to social territory. Up to this point territorial displays have been illustrated as unchanging and standalone: a certain uniform, a particular song, something you choose and find attractive in others. The Baywatch theme tune is different. This is not their favorite song — they think it is cheesy; if anything, the students who party here have to *learn to like* this song. Nor is nudity the uniform of choice for

---

1 It is not the original version of the song, but a cover version by the band Sunblock. The original version sung by Jimi Jamison of Survivor is often referred to as "I'm Always Here."

2 This ritual shows that there is definitely something *funny* about this place.

3 This is the diary entry for 17 March 2009, which was accessed on 2 April 2010; http://mysouthampton.blogspot.com. A similar statement was made by Thomas Bird, the webmaster from the University of Southampton Physics Society, which is: "the so called palace of dreams. Some hate it, most love it, no words can do it justice. A word of advice, don't wear white or new shoes (seriously)." Accessed 3 April 2010; http://physoc.org.uk/maps/Portswood_by_Night.

4 Note that these are the words of the blogger and are not condoned by the author of this book. In addition, neither the author of this book, nor probably the blogger, believes that the club or its patrons are suffering from AIDS — the statement seems to be hyperbole in an attempt at juvenile humor. Furthermore, this book does not condone humor at the expense of those who suffer from AIDS, which is a very serious condition. Accessed on 8 April 2010; http://www.bebo.com/Profile.jsp?MemberId=14899549.

---

rugby players, even if they often have to shower together. Finally, singing along with a music recording can be considered weird and socially worrisome. Each aspect of this territorial display would be strange out of context. It is the *social construction of the place* that authorizes the display; specifically it is the group's mental associations to the place and not the space *per se* that is important. These elements of the display go together to make a socially constructed territory. There is a tacit agreement between the DJ (who plays these songs), the club management (which tolerates nudity) and some of the patrons (who join in and thus make it their own territory). This territory is a social construction in the literal sense of the words. At this nightclub the social territory says three things: we belong here, we are happy, and we know how to have a good time. But who does it say this to?

To each other and themselves.

So, having started with David Hasselhoff souvenir-hunting at the Berlin Wall, we finish bare-breasted with the Baywatch theme tune. This is the final example to show that *music establishes territory, for individuals and for their social groups.* The ramifications of being in one's own territory go far beyond aggression and war; they permeate the hidden meaning and unspoken emotions of everyday life. Territory is a genuine human need. Human beings need it no less than the song bird or the humpback whale does, and any thought that music is "auditory cheesecake" is myopic. The scientific evidence and the narratives presented here have demonstrated time and again that music has a role in shaping our intelligence, our happiness, and our connection to our fellow human beings. In short, music constitutes who we are.

BIBLIOGRAPHY

Ahn H & Wampold BE. (2001). Where oh where are the specific ingredients? A meta-analysis of component studies in counselling and psychotherapy. *Journal of Counselling Psychology*, 48: 251-257.

Albritton C (2009). The Official Cynthia Plaster Caster Website. Accessed 15 March 2010; http://www.cynthiaplastercaster.com/flash/home.html.

American Academy of Pediatrics: Committee on Communication (2001). Impact of Music, Lyrics and Music Videos on Children and Youth. *Pediatrics*, 108: 1222-1226.

American Psychiatric Association (2000). *Diagnostic and Statistical Manual Edition IV-TR*, Arlington, Virginia: American Psychiatric Association.

Anderson CA, Carnagey NL & Eubanks J (2003). Exposure to violent media: the effects of songs with violent lyrics on aggressive thoughts and feelings. *Journal of Personality and Social Psychology*, 84: 960-971.

Ankney CD (1992). Sex Differences in Relative Brain Size: The Mismeasure of Woman, Too? *Intelligence*, 16: 329-336.

Arciero PJ, Ormsbee MJ (2009). Relationship of blood pressure, behavioral mood state, and physical activity following caffeine ingestion in younger and older women. *Applied Physiology Nutrition and Metabolism*, 34: 754-762.

Areni CS & Kim D (1993). The influence of background music on shopping behavior: classical versus top-forty music in a wine store. *Advances in Consumer Research*, 20: 336-340.

Arnett J (1991). Adolescence and heavy metal music: from the mouths of metalheads. *Youth and Society*, 23: 76-98.

Associated Press (1989). Upheaval in the East: Berlin; Near the Wall, Bernstein Leads an Ode to Freedom. *The New York Times*, December 26.

Azevedo P (2006). Doom Metal: The Gentle Art of Making Misery. *Chronicles of Chaos* webzine. Accessed on 22 March 2010; www.chroniclesofchaos.com

Badisches Landesmsueum (State Museum of Baden) (2003), Online Museum: *Karlsruher Tuerkenbeute. Die Musik der Osmanen.* Accessed 31 March 2010; http://www.tuerken-beute.de/kun/kun_han/ OsmanischeMusik_de.php

Bahr W (2000). *Tote auf Reisen.* NP Buchverlag: St. Pölten

Ball P (2010). *The Music Instinct: How Music Works and Why We can't Do Without It.* London: The Bodley Head.

Ballard M, Dodson A & Bazzini D (1999). Genre of music and lyrical content: expectation effects. *Journal of Genetic Psychology,* 160: 476-487.

Bangert M & Schlaug G (2006). Specialization of the specialized in features of external human brain morphology. *European Journal of Neuroscience,* 24: 1832-1834.

Barenbaum NB, Winter DG (2008). History of Modern Personality Theory and Research. In (Eds.) John OP, Robins RW, Pervin LA, *Handbook of Personality: Theory and Research.* New York: The Guilford Press, pp. 3-28.

Barnes M (2009). Come on, feel the noise. *The Guardian* newspaper (London), 09 January.

Barongan C & Hall GC (1995). The influence of misogynous rap music on sexual aggression against women. *Psychology of Women Quarterly,* 19: 195-207.

Barrett L, Dunbar R & Lycett J (2002). *Human evolutionary psychology.* London: Palgrave.

BBC News (1999). Bing keeps troublemakers at bay. *BBC News Online,* 8 July.

BBC News (2003). Sesame Street breaks resistance of Iraqi POWs. *BBC News online,* 20 May.

BBC News (2004). Did David Hasselhoff really help end the Cold War? *BBC News Online,* 6 Feb.

BBC News (2005). Timeline: Blur v Oasis after Britpop. *BBC News online,* 16 August.

BBC News (2006). Singer Blunt 'irritates public'. *BBC News,* 31 July.

BBC News (2006). Blunt Words of a Sensitive Soldier, *BBC news online,* 16 February.

BBC News (2006). Manilow to drive out 'hooligans'. *BBC News Online,* 17 July.

BBC Northern Ireland Learning Online edition (2007). William III: Bigot or Hero? Billy Boy's Smash Hit. BBC online. Accessed 31 March 2010; http://www.bbc.co.uk/north-ernireland/learning/william/ backpage.shtml.

BBC World Service (2005). What is the BBC World Service signature tune? *BBC World Service,* 10 August. Accessed 31 March 2010; http://www.bbc.co.uk/worldservice/faq/news/story/2005/08/ 050810_wssigtune.shtml

Beecher HK (1955). The powerful placebo. *Journal of the American Medical Association,* 159(17): 1602-6.

Ben-Noun L (2003). What was the mental disease that afflicted King Saul? *Clinical Case Studies,* 2: 270-282.

Berezin M (2003). Territory, emotion and identity: spatial recalibration in a new Europe. In Berezin M & Schain M (eds.) *Europe with Borders: Remapping Territory, Citizenship and Identity in a Transnational Age.* London: The Johns Hopkins University Press.

Berlioz H (2002). *The Memoirs of Hector Berlioz.* Cairns D (editor & translator). London: Everyman's Library Classics.

Berson M (2010). 'Fiddle and the Drum' presents a new facet of songsmith Joni Mitchell. *The Seattle Times* newspaper, 20 February.

Bevil JM (1999). And the band played on: hypotheses concerning what music was performed near the climax of the *Titanic* disaster. Presented at the October, 1999 meeting of the Southwest Regional Chapter of the American Musicological Society, Rice University, Houston. Accessed 15 April 2010; http://home.earthlink.net/-llywarch/tnc02.html.htm

Bichat FX (1827). *Physiological Researches on Life and Death*, trans. F. Gold. London: Longmans, 62: 252.

Biles JA (1994). GenJam: A genetic algorithm for generating jazz solos. In *Proceedings of the 1994 International Computer Music Conference.* San Francisco: International Computer Music Association: 131-137.

Bingham JC (Lord Mersey) (1912). British Wreck Commissioner's Inquiry. Report on the loss of the "Titanic"(s.s.). In: Titanic Inquiry Project.

Bistori A (1976). Anglers To Hunt Sharks; Shark fishing off the jersey coast Shark Fishing To Begin Soon. *New York Times*, 23 May.

Blood AJ, Zatorre RJ (2001). Intensely pleasurable responses to music correlate with activity in brain regions implicated in reward and emotion. *Proceedings of the National Academy of Sciences, USA*, 98: 11818–11823.

Blood AJ, Zatorre RJ, Bermudez P, Evans AC (1999). Emotional responses to pleasant and unpleasant music correlate with activity in paralimbic brain regions. *Nature Neuroscience*, 2(4): 382-7.

Börger L, Dalziel BD and Fryxell JM (2008). Are there general mechanisms of animal home range behaviour? A review and prospects for future research. *Ecology Letters*, 11: 637–650.

Börsenkurier, Nov 1912. Quoted in Reich W (1971). *Schoenberg: A Critical Biography*, trans. Leo Black. London: Longman Group Ltd., p. 78.

Boulez P (1991). "Possibly..." (1952). In *Stocktakings from an Apprenticeship*, collected and presented by Paule Thévenin, translated by Stephen Walsh, with an introduction by Robert Piencikowski. Oxford: Clarendon Press, p. 111–40.

Bourdieu P (1984). *Distinction: A Social Critique of the Judgement of Taste*. Translated by Nice R. London: Routledge.

Bouwsma OK (1965). The Expression Theory of Art. In *Philosophical Essays*. University of Nebraska Press.

Bradt J, Dileo C (2009). Music for stress and anxiety reduction in coronary heart disease patients. *Cochrane Database Systematic Review*, 15(2): CD006577.

Breiter HC, Gollub RL, Weisskoff RM, Kennedy DN et al. (1997). Acute effects of cocaine on human brain activity and emotion. *Neuron*, 19: 591-611.

Breuer J & Freud S (1895, translated 1955). *Studies in hysteria*, Vol. 2, Brill AA, (Trans.). London: Hogarth.

Brockner J, Tyler T, & Cooper-Schneider R (1992). The influence of prior commitment to an institution on reactions to perceived injustice: The higher they are, the harder they fall. *Administrative Science Quarterly*, 37 : 241-261.

Buday EM (1995). The effects of signed and spoken words taught with music on sign and speech imitation by children with autism, *Journal of Music Therapy*, 32(3): 189-202.

Buechner HK (1961). Territorial behavior in Uganda Kob. *Science* 133: 698-9.

Burnham D, Kitamura C, Vollmer-Conna U (2002). What's new, pussycat? On talking to babies and animals. *Science*, 296(5572): 1435-1435.

Burrell B (2005). *Postcards from the Brain Museum*. Chapter 14. New York: Broadway (Random House).

Burton R (1638, updated 2004). *The Anatomy of Melancholy*. Accessed 15 April 2010; www.gutenberg.org/files/10800/10800-8.txt.

Bushman BJ (2002). Does venting anger feed or extinguish the flame? Catharsis, rumination, distraction, anger, and aggressive responding. *Personality and Social Psychology Bulletin*, 28: 724–731.

Byron GG (1857). *Don Juan* (canto XV, st. 5). Edited by Widger D, Project Gutenberg EBook #21700.

Cain AJ & Provine WB (1991). Genes and ecology in history. In Berry RJ et al. (eds) *Genes in Ecology*: the 33rd Symposium of the British Ecological Society. Oxford: Blackwell, p. 9.

Caleon IS & Subramaniam R (2007). From Pythagoras to Sauveur: tracing the history of ideas about the nature of sound. *Physics Education*, 42: 173-179.

Campbell D (2001). *The Mozart Effect: Tapping the Power of Music to Heal the Body, Strengthen the Mind, and Unlock the Creative Spirit*. Harper Collins: New York.

Capps L, Yirmiya N & Sigman M (1992). Understanding of simple and complex emotions in nonretarded children with autism. *Journal of Child Psychology and Psychiatry*, 33: 1169–1182.

Carlson ET & Simpson MB (1971). Tarantism or hysteria? An American case of 1801. *Journal of the History of Medicine and Allied Sciences* 26: 293-302.

Carlson S, Rämä P, Artchakov D & Linnankoski I (1997). Effects of music and white noise on working memory performance in monkeys. *NeuroReport*, 8: 2853–2856.

Carner M (1958). *Puccini, A Critical Biography*. London: Gerald Duckworth & Co Ltd.

Carron AV, Loughhead TM & Bray SR (2005). The home advantage in sport competitions: Courneya and Carron's (1992) conceptual framework a decade later. *Journal of Sports Sciences*, 23(4): 395 – 407.

Casey S (2000). Franklin D. Roosevelt, Ernst 'Putzi' Hanfstaengl and the 'S-Project', June 1942-June 1944. *Journal of Contemporary History*, 35: 339-359.

Catchpole CK (1983). Variation in the song of the great reed warbler Acrocephalus arudinaceus in relation to mate attraction and territorial defence. *Animal Behavior*, 31, 1217-1225.

Cazden N (1962). Sensory theories of musical consonance. *The Journal of Aesthetics and Art Criticism*, 20: 301-319.

Ceci SJ, & Williams WM (1997). Schooling, intelligence and income. *American Psychologist*, 52: 1051–1058.

Chabris CF (1999). Prelude or requiem for the 'Mozart effect'? *Nature*, 400: 826–828.

Chaleff I (2003). *The courageous follower*. 2nd ed. San Francisco: Berrett-Koehler.

Chambless, DL (2002). Beware the Dodo Bird: The Dangers of Overgeneralization. *Clinical Psychology: Science and Practice*, 9: 13-16.

Chang L (2002). Letter to the Editor: Leonard Bernstein; Phantasy? Phooey. *The New York Times*, 16 June.

Chase AR (2001). Music discriminations by carp (Cyprinus carpio). *Animal Learning & Behavior*, 29(4): 336–353.

Chiu P & Kumar A (2003). Music therapy: loud noise or soothing notes? *International Pediatrics*, 18: 204-208.

Christenson PG & Roberts DF (1998). *It's not only rock & roll: Popular music in the lives of adolescents*. Cresskill, NJ: Hampton Press.

City of Hameln (2010). The Pied Piper. Accessed 5 April 2010; http://www.hameln.com/tourism/piedpiper/rf_sage_gb.htm

Clark JK (2004). 'Wharton, Thomas, first marquess of Wharton, first marquess of Malmesbury, and first marquess of Catherlough (1648-1715)', *Oxford Dictionary of National Biography*, Oxford: Oxford University Press. Clark RW (1971). *Einstein: the life and times*. New York: Thomas Crowell.

Clarke SR, Norman JM (1995). Home ground advantage of individual clubs in English soccer. *The Statistician*, 44(4): 509-521.

Cloonan M, Johnson B (2002). Killing me softly with his song: an initial investigation into the use of popular music as a tool of oppression. *Popular Music*, 21(1): 27–39.

Collinson D (2006). Rethinking followership: A post-structuralist analysis of follower identities. *The Leadership Quarterly*, 17: 179– 189.

Colombo JA, Reisin HD, Miguel-Hidalgo JJ, Rajkowska G. (2006). Cerebral cortex astroglia and the brain of a genius: a propos of A. Einstein's. *Brain Research Reviews*, 52(2): 257-63.

Cone CD Jr, Cone CM (1976). Induction of mitosis in mature neurons in central nervous system by sustained depolarization. *Science*, 192(4235):155-8.

Cooper P & McIntyre D (1994). Teachers' and Pupils' Perceptions of Effective Classroom Learning: Conflicts and Commonalities. In Hughes M (ed.) *Perceptions of Teaching and Learning*. Clevedon, UK: Multilingual Matters, p. 66.

Courneya KS & Carron AV (1992). The Home Advantage in Sport Competitions: A Literature Review. *Journal of Sport and Exercise Psychology*, 14(1): 13-27.

Coursey RD, Buchsbaum MS, Murphy DL (1979). Platelet MAO activity and evoked potentials in the identification of subjects biologically at risk for psychiatric disorders. *British Journal of Psychiatry*, 134: 372-381

Cox TJ (2008), Scraping sounds and disgusting noises. *Applied Acoustics*, 69(12): 1195-1204.

Crammond DJ (1997). Motor imagery: never in your wildest dreams. *Trends in Neuroscience*, 20: 54–57.

Crick A (2009). Passion partners parade privates. *The Sun* newspaper (UK), 30 April.

Cross CR (2001). *Heavier Than Heaven – A Biography of Kurt Cobain*. New York: Hyperion.

Cross CR (2005). *Room full of mirrors: a biography of Jimi Hendrix*. London: Hodder & Stoughton.

Cusick SG (2006). Music as torture / Music as weapon. *TRANS Revista transcultural de Música*. Number 10. (Barcelona: Sociedad de Etnomusicología).

Dalley J (2010). Two shows that further our love for India. *The Financial Times* newspaper (UK), 12 March.

Darke S, Zador D (1996). Fatal heroin 'overdose': a review. *Addiction*. 91: 1765-1772.

Darwin C (1871). *The descent of man, and selection in relation to sex*, Volume II, Chapter 19, London: John Murray. http://darwin-online.org.uk/content/frameset?viewtype=text&itemID=F937.2&pageseq=1

Darwin C (1958). *The Autobiography of Charles Darwin, 1809-1882*. New York: Harcourt, Brace, World.

de Craen AJM, Roos PJ, de Vries AL, Kleijnen J (1996). Effect of colour of drugs: systematic review of perceived effect of drugs and of their effectiveness. *Aspects of Drugs*, 31: 1624-1626.

Deleuze G, Guattari F (1987). *A Thousand Plateaus: Capitalism and Schizophrenia*, trans. Minneapolis: University of Minnesota Press, p. 311.

DeNora T (2002). The Role of Music in Intimate Culture. *Feminism and Psychology*. 12: 176-178.

Deutsch OE (1947). *The Schubert Reader*, (trans. Eric Blom). New York: Norton.

Diamond MC, Scheibel AB, Murphy GM Jr, Harvey T (1985). On the brain of a scientist: Albert Einstein. *Experimental Neurology*, 88(1): 198-204.

Dickinson JL (1998). Birds in the Bushes: A Story about Margaret Morse Nice. *The Condor* 100(3): 583.

Diener E & Diener C (1996). Most people are happy. *Psychological Science*, 7: 181-185.

Draganski B, Gaser C, Busch V, Schuierer G, Bogdahn U, May A (2004). Neuroplasticity: changes in grey matter induced by training. *Nature*, 427(6972): 311-2.

Draganski B, May A (2008). Training-induced structural changes in the adult human brain. *Behavioural Brain Research*, 192: 137–142.

Dubé L & Morin S (2001). Background music pleasure and store evaluation – Intensity effects and psychological mechanisms. *Journal of Business Research*, 54: 107-113.

Edgerton CL (1994). The effect of improvisational music therapy on the communicative behaviours of autistic children, *Journal of Music Therapy*, 31(1): 31-62.

Eibl-Eibesfeldt I (1973). The expressive behavior of the deaf-and-blind born. In von Cranach M & Vine I (Eds.), *Social communication and movement*. London: Academic Press, 163-194.

Ekman P & Friesen WV (1971). Constants across cultures in the face and emotion. *Journal of Personality and Social Psychology*, 17: 124-129.

Ellin A (2007). Indoor Cycling Finds Its Way Back With Proper Training. *The New York Times* newspaper (USA), 24 May.

Ericsson KA, Krampe RT & Tesch-Römer C (1993). The role of deliberate practice in the acquisition of expert performance. *Psychological Review*, 100, 363-406

Evans AS (1976). Causation and disease: the Henle-Koch postulates revisited. *Yale Journal of Biology and Medicine*, 49(2): 175–195.

Everitt M (2005). Noel Gallagher "I'm Voting Labour". *XFM* (London). 12 April.

Farmer HG (1949). Crusading martial music. *Music and Letters* XXX(3):243-249.

Fénelon F, Routier M (1980). *Playing for Time*. Landry J (English translation) *Sursis pour l'Orchestre*. London: Sphere Books.

Fernald A & Kuhl P (1987). Acoustic Determinants of Infant Preference for Motherese Speech. *Infant Behavior and Development*, 10: 279-293.

Fernald A (1993). Approval and disapproval - infant responsiveness to vocal affect in familiar and unfamiliar languages. *Child Development*, 64(3): 657-674.

Fernald A, Taeshner T, Dunn J, Papousek M, de Boysson-Bardies B & Fukui I (1989) A Cross Language Study of Prosodic Modifications and Mothers' and Fathers' Speech to Preverbal Infants. *The Journal of Child Language*, 16: 477-501.

Ferrer AJ (2007). The effect of live music on decreasing anxiety in patients undergoing chemotherapy treatment. *Journal of Music Therapy*, 44: 242-255.

Feuer A (2009). "At a sex club, the outré meet the ordinary." *The New York Times*, 25 February.

Finger S (2004). Pioneers in Neurology: Paul Broca (1824-1880). *Journal of Neurology*, 251: 769-770.

Firnhaber JC (1932). A Correction, Contributing to Musical History. Der Freimüthige, December 3rd, 1825, in Unger M, 'The First Performance of Haydn's 'Surprise' Symphony' *The Musical Times*, 73(1071): p. 413. London: Musical Times Publications Ltd.

Fishman YI, Volkov IO, Noh MD et al. (2001). Consonance and dissonance of musical chords: neural correlates in auditory cortex of monkeys and humans. *Journal of Neurophysiology*, 86: 2761-2788.

Forgas JP & Moylan SJ (1987). After the movies: Transient mood and social judgment. *Personality and Social Psychology Bulletin*, 13: 467-477.

Forman M (2002). *The 'hood comes first: race, space, and place in rap and hip-hop*. Middletown, Connecticut: Wesleyan University Press.

Forstmeier W & Balsby TJS (2002). Why mated dusky warblers sing so much: territory guarding and male quality announcement. *Behaviour*, 139: 89–111.

Fowler R (1996). Browning's Music: The L.L. Bloomfield Collection. *The Review of English Studies* 47(185): 35-46.

Foxall GR & Greenley GE (1999). Consumers' emotional responses to service environments. *Journal of Business Research*, 46: 149-158.

Friedenberg J, Silverman G (2006). Mind as a Black Box: The Behaviorist Approach, In *Cognitive Science: An Introduction to the Study of Mind*, London: Sage Publications, pp 85-88.

Fritz T, Jentschke S, Gosselin N, Sammler D, Peretz I, Turner R, Friederici A & Koelsch S (2009). Universal Recognition of Three Basic Emotions in Music. *Current Biology*, 19(7): 573-576.

Fulker DW, Eysenck SBG, & Zuckerman M (1980). A genetic and environmental analysis of sensation seeking. *Journal of Research in Personality*, 14: 261-281.

Galer G (2004). Myths of the western front. *Global Society*, 18: 175-195.

Gallagher M (2009). Personal Blog: About Me. Accessed on 8 April 2010; http://www.bebo.com/Profile.jsp?MemberId=14899549.

Gallo DA, Finger S (2000). The power of a musical instrument: Franklin, the Mozarts, Mesmer, and the glass armonica. *History of Psychology*, 3(4): 326-343.

Gaser C & Schlaug G (2003). Brain structures differ between musicians and non-musicians. *The Journal of Neuroscience*, 23: 9240-9245.

Geissman T (2000). Gibbon songs and human music from an evolutionary perspective. In Wallin NL, Merker B, Brown S (eds.). *The origins of music*. (Cambridge, Mass.: MIT Press) pp. 103-123.

Gentilcore D (2000). Ritualized illness in Music Therapy. In Horden P (2000). *Music as Medicine – The History of Music Therapy Since Antiquity*. Aldershot: Ashgate, pp. 261-267.

Georgiadis JR, Kortekaas R, Kuipers R, Nieuwenburg A, Pruim J, Reinders AA, Holstege G (2006). Regional cerebral blood flow changes associated with clitorally induced orgasm in healthy women. *European Journal of Neuroscience*, 24(11): 3305-16.

Gerdner LA (2000). Effects of individualized versus classical "relaxation" music on the frequency of agitation in elderly persons with Alzheimer's disease and related disorders. *International Psychogeriatrics*, 12: 49-65

Gerevich J, Bácskai E, Farkas L and Danics Z (2005). A case report: Pavlovian conditioning as a risk factor of heroin 'overdose' death. *Harm Reduction Journal*. 2: 11.

Gianturco C (2001). Stradella, Alessandro., In L. Macy (ed.), *Grove Music Online*.

Gibbs CH (2000). *The Life of Schubert*. Cambridge UK: Cambridge University Press. pp. 95-97.

Gill SP (2007). Entrainment and musicality in the human system interface. *AI & Society* 21(4): 567-605.

Gold C, Wigram T, Elefant C (2006). Music therapy for autistic spectrum disorder. *Cochrane Database of Systematic Reviews*, Issue 2. Art. No.: CD004381.

Goleman D (1995). *Emotional Intelligence*. New York: Bantam Books.

Gomez P, Danuser B (2007). Relationships between musical structure and psychophysiological measures of emotion. *Emotion,* 7(2): 377-87.

Good M, Anderson GC, Ahn S, Cong X & Stanton-Hicks M (2005). Relaxation and music reduce pain following intestinal surgery. *Research in Nursing and Health*, 28: 240-251.

Gordon T, Hakanen E & Wells A (1992). Music preferences and the use of music to manage emotional states: correlates with self-concept among adolescents. Paper presented at the *Annual Meeting of the International Communication Association*, Miami, FL.

Gouk P (2000). Music, melancholy, and medical spirits in early modern thought. in: Horden P (ed.) *Music as Medicine – The History of Music Therapy Since Antiquity*. Aldershot: Ashgate, pp. 173-194.

Gould SJ (1981). *The Mismeasure of Man.* New York: W.W. Norton & Co.

Gowensmith WN & Bloom LJ (1997). The effects of heavy metal music on arousal and anger, *Journal of Music Therapy*, 1: 33-45.

Grabb WC, Hodge GP, Dingman RO, Oneal RM (1968). The Habsburg Jaw. *Plastic and Reconstructive Surgery*, 42(5): 442-445.

Greenfield PM, Bruzzone L & Koyamatsu K et al (1987). What is rock music doing to the minds of our youth? A first experimental look at the effects of rock music lyrics and music videos. *Journal of Early Adolescence*, 7: 315-329.

Greeson LE & Williams RA (1986). Social implications of music video for youth. *Youth and Society*, 18: 177-189.

Gregory AH (1998). Tracking the emotional response to operatic arias. In Yi SW (ed.), *Proceedings of the Fifth International Conference of Music Perception and Cognition*. Seoul, Korea: Western Music Research Institute, College of Music, Seoul National University.

Gross R (2005). *Psychology: the Science of Mind and Behaviour*, Fifth Edition. London, Hodder Arnold, pp. 358-360.

Gunderson R (1985). *An investigation of the effects of rock music videos on the values and self-perceptions of adolescents.* Doctoral dissertation, Ann Arbor, MI: United States International University.

Gutiérrez-Cebollada J, de la Torre R, Ortuño J, Garcés JM, Camí J (1994). Psychotropic drug consumption and other factors associated with heroin overdose. *Drug and Alcohol Dependence.* 35: 169–174.

Guy G, Horvath B, Vonwiller J, Daisley E, and Rogers I (1986). An intonation change in progress in Australian English. *Language in Society*, 15: 23–52.

Haier RJ, Jung RE, Yeo RA, Head K, and Alkire MT (2004). Structural brain variation and general intelligence *NeuroImage*, 23(1): 425-433.

Hajnal J (1965). European marriage patterns in perspective. In Glass DV & Eversley DEC (eds), *Population in History.* Chicago: Aldine Publishing.

Hallam S & Katsarou G (1998). The effects of listening to background music on children's altruistic behaviour and success in memorising text. Paper presented at the conference of the British Educational Research Association, August 27th-30th 1998, Belfast.

Hallam S (2001). *The power of music: the strength of music's influence on our lives.* London: Performing Musical Rights Society.

Halpern L, Blake R & Hillenbrand J (1986). Psychoacoustics of a chilling sound. *Perception and Psychophysics.* 39(2): 77–80.

Hansen CH & Hansen RD (1990). Rock music videos and antisocial behaviour. *Basic and Applied Social Psychology*, 11(4): 357-369.

Haque A (2004). Psychology from Islamic Perspective: Contributions of Early Muslim Scholars and Challenges to Contemporary Muslim Psychologists. *Journal of Religion and Health*, 43(4): 357-377.

Hardy P (2006). Me and My Motors, the *Times Online*, 12th February.

Harma L, Takács J, and Bódizs R (2008). Music improves sleep quality in students. *Journal of Advanced Nursing*, 62(3): 327-335.

Harris C and Wiederhorn J (2007). Metal File: Manowar, A Life Once Lost, Origin & More News That Rules. *MTV News*, 09 Feb. www.mtv.com/news/articles/1552016/20070208/manowar.jhtml

Harris J (2004). *The last party: Britpop, Blair and the demise of English rock.* London: Harper Perennial.

Harty S (1994). Pied Piper Revisited. In: Bridges D, Terence H, McLaughlin TH (eds.) *Education And The Market Place*, Abingdon, UK: Routledge, p. 89.

Heaton P, Hermelin B & Pring L (1999). Can children with autistic spectrum disorders perceive affect in music? An experimental investigation. *Psychological Medicine*, 29: 1405-410.

Henrich J & Gil-White F (2001). The evolution of prestige: Freely conferred deference as a mechanism for enhancing the benefits of cultural transmission. *Evolution and Human Behavior*, 22: 165-196.

Henry WA & Pappa E (1990). Did The Music Say Do It? *Time* Magazine (USA), July 30.

Hepper PG (1991). An examination of foetal learning before and after birth, *The Irish Journal of Psychology*, 12: 95-107.

Herman F (1996). The boy that nobody wanted: creative experiences for a boy with severe emotional problems. In Bruscia KE (ed.), *Case Studies in Music Therapy*. Gilsum, NH, USA: Barcelona Publishers, p. 638.

Hernandez S, Vander Wal JS, Spring B (2003). A Negative Mood Induction Procedure With Efficacy Across Repeated Administrations in Women. *Journal of Psychopathology and Behavioral Assessment*, 25(1): 49-55.

Hevner K (1936). Experimental studies of the elements of expression in music. *American Journal of Psychology*, 48: 246-268.

Hibberd S (2006). Murder in the cathedral? Stradella, musical power and performing the past in 1830s Paris. *Music & Letters*, 87: 551-579.

Higgins C (2006). Big demand for classical downloads is music to ears of record industry. *The Guardian* newspaper (London, UK), 28th March.

Hillecke T, Nickel A & Bolay HV (2005). Scientific perspectives on music therapy. *Annals of the New York Academy of Sciences*, 1060: 271-282.

Hillman R (2003). Cultural memory on film soundtracks. *Journal of European Studies*, 33: 323-332.

Hogue MJ (1950). Brain cells from human fetuses and infants, cultured in vitro after death of the individuals. *The Anatomical Record*, 108: 457-475.

Hogue MJ (1953). A study of adult human brain cells grown in tissue cultures. *American Journal of Anatomy*, 93: 397-427.

Holstege G, Georgiadis JR, Paans AM, Meiners LC, van der Graaf FH, Reinders AA (2003). Brain activation during human male ejaculation. *Journal of Neuroscience*, 23: 9185-9193.

Horden P (ed.) (2000) *Music as Medicine – The History of Music Therapy Since Antiquity*. Aldershot: Ashgate Publishing.

Houser ML (2005). Are We Violating Their Expectations? Instructor Communication Expectations of Traditional and Nontraditional Students. *Communication Quarterly*, 53(2): 213 – 228.

Houston Chronicle (1999), November 28, p. Zest-23.

Howard L (2007). The popular reception of Samuel Barber's 'Adagio for Strings'. *American Music*, 25: 50-80.

Howe MJ, Davidson JW, and Sloboda JA (1998) Innate talents: Reality or myth? *Behavioural and Brain Sciences*, 21: 399–442.

Hróbjartsson A, Gøtzsche PC (2001). Is the placebo powerless? An analysis of clinical trials comparing placebo with no treatment. *New England Journal of Medicine*, 344(21): 1594–1602.

Hróbjartsson A, Gøtzsche PC (2004). Placebo interventions for all clinical conditions. *Cochrane Database Systematic Reviews*, (3): CD003974.

Hróbjartsson A, Norup M. (2003). The use of placebo interventions in medical practice--a national questionnaire survey of Danish clinicians. *Evaluation and the Health Professions*, 26(2): 153-65.

Huber FJ (1942). ed., Propagandisten-Fibel. Herausgegeben vom Gaupropagandaamt Oberdonau der NSDAP. Wels: Leitner & Co.

Hulse SH, Bernard DJ & Braaten RF (1995). Auditory discrimination of chord-based spectral structures by European starlings (*Sturnus vulgaris*). *Journal of Experimental Psychology: General*, 124: 409-423.

Huron D (2001). Is music an evolutionary adaptation? *Annals of the New York Academy of Sciences*, 930: 43-61.

Huron D (2006). *Sweet anticipation: music and the psychology of expectation*. Cambridge, Mass: The MIT Press, p. 344.

Hurst JL and Beynon RL (2004). Scent wars: the chemobiology of chemical signalling in mice. *BioEssays*, 26: 1288-1298.

Husain G, Thompson WF & Schellenberg EG (2002). Effects of musical tempo and mode on arousal, mood, and spatial abilities. *Music Perception*, 20: 151-171.

Internet Movie Data Base (1975). Trivia for Jaws. IMDB.com.

Isen AM, Daubmann KA & Nowicki GP (1987). Positive affect facilitates creative problem solving. *Journal of Personality and Social Psychology*, 52: 1122–1131.

Isen AM, Shalker T, Clark M & Karp L (1978). Affect, accessibility of material in memory and behavior: A cognitive loop? *Journal of Personality and Social Psychology*, 36: 1-12.

Izumi A (2000). Japanese monkeys perceive sensory consonance of chords. *Journal of the Acoustical Society of America*, 108: 3073-3078.

Jacob BL (1996). Algorithmic composition as a model of creativity. *Organised Sound*, 1(3): 157-165.

Jaret C (1993). Characteristics of successful and unsuccessful country music songs. In Lewis GH (ed.), *All that glitters: Country music in America*, Bowling Green, USA: Bowling Green State University Popular Press.

Jensen AR (1998). *The g factor: The science of mental ability*. Westport, CT: Praeger.

Johnson JD, Jackson LA & Gatto L (1995). Violent attitudes and deferred academic aspirations: deleterious effects of the exposure to rap music. *Basic and Applied Social Psychology*, 16: 27-41.

Johnston VS, Hagel R, Franklin M, Fink B, Grammer K (2001). Male facial attractiveness: evidence for hormone-mediated adaptive design. *Evolution and Human Behavior*, 22(4): 251-267.

Juslin P (2001). Communicating emotion in musical performance: a review and theoretical framework. In Juslin PN & Sloboda JN (eds). *Music and Emotion: theory and research*. Oxford: Oxford University Press, 309-337.

Juslin PN & Laukka P (2003). Communication of Emotions in Vocal Expression and Music Performance: Different Channels, Same Code? *Psychological Bulletin*, 129(5): 770–814.

Juslin PN (2000). Cue Utilization in Communication of Emotion in Music Performance: Relating Performance to Perception. *Journal of Experimental Psychology*, 26(6): 1797-1813.

Kahn-Harris K (2002). "I hate this fucking country": Dealing with the global and the local in the Israeli extreme metal scene. In Young R (ed.) *Music, Popular Culture, Identities*. Amsterdam: Rodopi BV, pp. 133-152.

Kale J (2005). *Sex Between the Beats: The Ultimate Guide to Sex Music*. Venice, California: Blush Books.

Kazi RA & Peter RE (2004). Christian Albert Theodor Billroth – master of surgery. *Journal of Postgraduate Medicine*, 50: 82-83

Keegan J (1993). *A History of Warfare.* London: Pimlico.

Kellaris JJ, Kent RJ (1992). The influence of music on consumers' temporal perceptions: does time fly when you're having fun? *Journal of Consumer Psychology* 1: 365-376.

Kenhove PV & Desrumaux P (1997). The relationship between emotional states and approach or avoidance responses in a retail environment. *The International Review of Retail, Distribution and Consumer Research*, 7: 351-368.

Khalfa S, Dalla Bella S, Roy M, Peretz I & Lupien SJ (2003). Effects of relaxing music on salivary cortisol level after psychological stress. *Annuals of the New York Academy of Sciences*, 999: 374-376.

Kirby T (2006). "If you're happy and you know it, listen to Lily. If not, it's the Verve." *The Independent* newspaper (London), 11 December.

Kirschbaum C, Pirke KM & Hellhammer DH (1993). The Trier Social Stress Test--a tool for investigating psychobiological stress responses in a laboratory setting. *Neuropsychobiology*, 28: 76-81.

Kivy P (2002). *Introduction to a Philosophy of Music.* Oxford: Oxford University Press.

Knobloch-Westerwick S, Musto P & Shaw K (2008). Rebellion in the top music charts: Defiant messages in rap/hip-hop and rock music 1993 and 2003. *Journal of Media Psychology: Theories, Methods, and Applications.* 20(1): 15-23.

Knoll F and Schwarz-Wings D (2009). Paléoneuroanatomie de Brachiosaurus (Palaeoneuroanatomy of Brachiosaurus). *Annales de Paléontologie*, 95: 165–175.

Kogan R (2009). Pianist-psychiatrist explores the healing power of music. *University of South Florida Health News*, 24 September.

Kraemer U (1976). 'Wer hat Mozart verhungern lassen?', *Musica* 30(3): 203-11. From United Press International (1977). Mozart a Big Gambler. 9 February.

Kramer C (2000). Music as Cause and Cure of Illness in Nineteenth Century Europe. In: Horden P (ed.) *Music as Medicine – The History of Music Therapy Since Antiquity.* Aldershot: Ashgate, p. 401.

Krumhansl C, Sandell G, and Sergeant D (1987). The Perception of Tone Hierarchies and Mirror Forms in Twelve-Tone Serial Music. *Music Perception*, 5: 153–184.

Krumhansl CL (1997). An Exploratory Study of Musical Emotions and Psychophysiology. *Canadian Journal of Experimental Psychology* 51(4): 336-353.

Kunst-Wilson WR & Zajonc RB (1980). Affective discrimination of stimuli that cannot be recognized. *Science*, 207: 557-558.

Kurth P (1993). In The House of Grimaldi. *Cosmopolitan* magazine, July.

Kuwahara Y (1992). Power to the people y'all: rap music, resistance and black college students. *Humanity and Society*, 16: 54-73.

Lack D (1939). The behaviour of the Robin. Part I. The life-history, with special reference to aggressive behaviour, sexual behaviour, and territory. Part II. A partial analysis of aggressive and recognition behaviour. *Proceedings of the Zoological Society of London A* 109: 169–219.

Lack D (1947). *Darwin's Finches.* Cambridge: Cambridge University Press (reissued in 1961 by New York: Harper).

Lack D (1957). *Evolutionary theory and Christian belief: the unresolved conflict.* London: Methuen.

Lack D (1971). *The Life of the Robin.* London: Collins.

Lakoff G (1987). *Women, Fire, and Dangerous Things: What Categories Reveal About the Mind.* Chicago: University of Chicago Press.

Lang PH (1958). *Musical Quarterly*, 44(4): 507-8.

Lax R & Smith F (1989). *The Great Song Thesaurus*, 2nd edition, New York: Oxford University Press, p. 243.

Lazaro-Perea C, Snowdon CT & de Fátima Aruda M. (1999). Scent-marking behaviour in wild groups of common marmosets (*Callithrix jacchus*). *Behavioural Ecology and Sociobiology*, 46: 313-324.

LeBlanc A (1979). Generic Style Music Preferences of Fifth-Grade Students. *Journal of Research in Music Education*, 27: 255-270.

LeBlanc A, Cote R (1983). Effects of Tempo and Performing Medium on Children's Music Preference. *Journal of Research in Music Education*, 31: 57-66.

Lebrecht N (2001). Why We're Still Afraid of Schoenberg. *La Scena Musicale*, 8 July.

Lebrecht N (2003). Arnold Schoenberg's Second String Quartet. *La Scena Musicale*, 9(4): p. 46.

Leslie KR, Johnson-Frey SH & Grafton ST (2004). Functional imaging of face and hand imitation: towards a motor theory of empathy. *Neuroimage* 21: 601-7.

Levitin D (2006). *This is your brain on music: The science of a human obsession.* New York: Dutton.

Lewin K, Lippitt R & White R (1939). Patterns of aggressive behaviour in experimentally created social climates. *Journal of Social Psychology*, 10: 271-299.

Ley D, Cybriwsky R (1974). Urban graffiti as territorial markers. *Annals of the Association of American Geographers*, 64(4): 491-505.

Lindblad P (2004). Live Forever: Best of Britpop (Film review). *LAS Magazine*, May 27.

Lindsey DG, Kearns RA (2008). The Writing's on The Wall: Graffiti, Territory and Urban Space in Auckland. *New Zealand Geographer*, 50(2): 7 – 13.

Litle P & Zuckerman M. (1986). Sensation seeking and music preferences. *Personality and Individual Differences.* 7: 575-577.

Livianos-Aldana L, Rojo-Moreno L, Sierra-Sanmiguel P (2007). F.J. Gall and the phrenological movement. *American Journal of Psychiatry*, 164(3): 414.

Locke KD, Horowitz LM (1990). Satisfaction in Interpersonal Interactions as a Function of Similarity in Level of Dysphoria. *Journal of Personality and Social Psychology*, 58(5): 823-831.

Loftus EF, Palmer JC (1974). Reconstruction of an automobile destruction: an example of the interaction between language and memory. *Journal of Verbal Learning and Verbal Behavior*, 13: 585-589.

Lopez CA (1993). Franklin and Mesmer: an encounter. *Yale Journal of Biology and Medicine*, 66(4): 325–331.

LRAD Corporation (2010). Homepage for Long Range Acoustic Devices (formerly American Technology corporation (ATC)). Accessed 19 May 2010; http://www.lradx.com/site/.

Luborsky L, Rosenthal R, Diguer L, Andrusyna TP, Berman JS, Levitt JT, Seligman DA, Krause ED (2002). The dodo bird verdict is alive and well. *Clinical Psychology – Science and Practice* 9: 2-12.

Lumsden CE (1959). In Russell DS, Rubenstein LT, Lumsden CE (Eds.), *The Pathology of Tumours of the Nervous System*, London: Arnold, pp. 272-309.

Lundqvist LO, Carlsson F, Hilmersson P and Juslin PN (2009). Emotional responses to music: experience, expression, and physiology. *Psychology of Music*, 37(1): 61-90.

Lusk, J (2000). The Real Keith Moon. Accessed: Feb 8th, 2010. http://www.channel4.com/history/microsites/R/real_lives/moon.html

Lynch MP, Eiler RE, Oller KD, Urbano RC & Wilson P (1991). Influences of acculturation and musical sophistication on perception of musical interval patterns. *Journal of Experimental Psychology: Human Perception and Performance*, 17: 967-975.

Lynn R, Wilson RG & Gault A (1989). Simple musical tests as measures of Spearman's *g*. *Personality and Individual Differences*, 10: 25–28.

Lynne. *A sound match.* Accessed on 03 December 2010; http://asoundmatch.com/how-asmworks.php

MacDonald M (2008). *Schoenberg* 2nd edition. New York: Oxford University Press USA: 6-8.

Maddern E (1988). 'We have survived': Aboriginal music today. *The Musical Times*, 129: 595-597.

Maguire ER, Snipes JB (1994). Reassessing the Link between Country Music and Suicide. *Social Forces*, 72: 1239-1243.

Manowar concert (2006). Secrets of Steel part 2. Accessed 19 Jan 2010; http://www.youtube.com/watch?v=5uQY_GzP2GM

Manowar concert (2007). Athens, 4 April. Accessed 19 Jan 2010; http://www.youtube.com/watch?v=y9STO5p8Qj0.

Manowar concert (2007). Athens, 4 April. Accessed 19 Jan 2010; http://www.youtube.com/watch?v=VhEmYtljTkU&feature=related

Manowar concert (2009). Finland. Accessed 19 Jan 2010; http://www.youtube.com/watch?v=Mxtm8_jgb08&feature=related.

Manowar interview (2002). TV Total with Stefan Raab, April. Accessed 28 April 2010; http://www.youtube.com/watch?v=Fb-hQoGHKpQ

Mark Tramo, Ostrom CM (2005). Music as medicine. *The Seattle Times* newspaper (USA), 25 May.

Martin G, Clarke P & Pearce C (1993). Adolescent suicide: music preference as an indicator of vulnerability. *Journal of the American Academy of Child Adolescent Psychology*, 32: 530-535.

Marwick C (2000). Music Hath Charms for Care of Preemies. *Journal of American Medical Association*, 283: 468-469.

Masataka N (2006). Preference for consonance over dissonance by hearing newborns of deaf parents and of hearing parents. *Developmental Science*, 9: 46-50.

Matsumoto J (2002). Why do people listen to sad music: effects of music on sad mood. *Japanese Journal of Educational Psychology*, 50: 23-32.

Mattila AS & Wirtz J (2001). Congruency of scent and music as a driver of in-store evaluations and behaviour. *Journal of Retailing*, 77: 273-289.

Matyszczyk C (2009). Marathon winner disqualified for wearing iPod. *cNet News*, 11 October. Accessed 28 Mar 2010; http://news.cnet.com/8301-17852_3-10372586-71.html

Mauk GW, Taylor MJ, White KR and Allen TS (1994). Comments on Stack and Gundlach's "The Effect of Country Music on Suicide:" An "Achy Breaky Heart" May Not Kill You. *Social Forces*, 72(4): 1249-1255.

McCarthy C (2009). ComScore: In U.S., MySpace-Facebook race goes on. *Cnet news*, 13 Jan.

McDaniel MA (2005) Big-brained people are smarter: A meta-analysis of the relationship between in vivo brain volume and intelligence. *Intelligence* 33(4): 337-346.

McDermott J & Hauser M (2004). Are consonant intervals music to their ears? Spontaneous acoustic preferences in a nonhuman primate. *Cognition*, 94: B11–B21.

McSmith A (2008) Sublime - or ridiculous? The art of noise. *The Telegraph* newspaper (London), 3 January.

Menon V, Levitin DJ (2005). The rewards of music listening: response and physiological connectivity of the mesolimbic system. *Neuroimage*. 28(1):175-84.

Merriam AP (1964). *The Anthropology of Music*. Evanston, Illinois: Northwestern University Press.

Miller G. 2000. Evolution of human music through sexual selection. In Wallin NL, Merker B & Brown S (Eds) *The Origins of Music*. Cambridge, MA: MIT Press, 329–360.

Milliman RE (1982). Using background music to affect the behavior of supermarket shoppers. *Journal of Marketing*, 46: 86-91.

Milliman RE (1986). The influence of background music on the behavior of restaurant patrons. *Journal of Consumer Research*, 13: 286-289.

Mitani JC (1987). Territoriality and monogamy among agile gibbons (Hylobates agilis). *Behavioral Ecology and Sociobiology*, 20: 265-269.

Mitchell D (1993). *The Language of Modern Music*. London: Faber and Faber.

Mithen SJ (2005) *The Singing Neanderthals: the Origins of Music, Language, Mind and Body*. London: Weidenfeld & Nicolson.

Monger JC (2005) James Blunt. Accessed 31 March 2010; http://www.mp3.com/albums/658343/summary.html

Montgomery J (2009). Eminem Is The Best-Selling Artist Of The Decade: Sales numbers from Nielsen SoundScan reveal Em beat the Beatles in the '00s. *MTV News*, 12 August.

Moore D (1960 estimated). Dudley Moore's Beethoven Sonata Parody from Beyond the Fringe. Accessed 26 March 2010; http://www.youtube.com/watch?v=GazlqD4mLvw

Moore JC & Brylinsky JA (1993). Spectator effect on team performance in college basketball. *Journal of Sport Behavior*, 16: 77–84.

Morris JS, Frith CD, Perrett DI, et al (1996). A differential neural response in the human amygdala to fearful and happy facial expressions. *Nature*, 383:812-5.

Morton BX (2003). Swing Time for Hitler. *The Nation*, 15 Sept.

Murphy DL, Belmaker RH, Buchsbaum MS, Martin NF, Ciaranello R & Wyatt RJ. Biogenic amine related enzymes and personality variations in normals. *Psychological Medicine*. 7: 149-157.

My Southampton pseudonym (2009). Diary entry for 17 March 2009. Accessed on 2 April 2010; http://mysouthampton.blogspot.com.

Myers DG & Diener E (1995). Who is happy? *Psychological Science*, 6: 10-19.

Mykytowycz, R, Hesterman, ER, Gambale, S & Dudzinski (1976). A comparison of the effectiveness of the odors of rabbits *Oryctolagus cuniculus*, in enhancing territorial confidence. *Journal of Chemical Ecology*, 2: 13-24

Näätänen R, Paavilainen P, Rinne T, & Alho K (2007). The mismatch negativity (MMN) in basic research of central auditory processing: A review. *Clinical Neurophysiology*, 118: 2544-2590.

Nakai J and Okamoto M (1963). Identification of neuroglial ceils in tissue culture. In Nakai J (Ed.) *Morphology of Neuroglia*. Tokyo: Igaku Shoin, p. 65.

Nantais KM & Schellenberg EG (1999). The Mozart effect: An artifact of preference. *Psychological Science*, 10: 370–373.

National Safety and Transportation Board (1991). NTSB Identification: MIA92FA051. Aircraft registration: N47506. Stored on microfiche 46312.

Nercessian A (2007). *Defining music: an ethnomusicological and philosophical approach.* Lewiston, NY: Edwin Mellen Press.

Neumayr A (1994). *Music and Medicine*, Volume 1, translated by Clarke BC. Bloomington, Illinois: Medi-Ed Press.

New York Times (1975). Impact of 'Jaws' Has Anglers and Bathers on Lookout, *New York Times*, 11 July.

Newbould B (1997). *Schubert: The Music and the Man.* Berkeley, California: University of California Press.

Nice MM (1941). The role of territory in bird life. *The American Midland Naturalist* 26(3): 441-487.

Nilsson U, Unosson M, Rawal N (2005) Stress reduction and analgesia in patients exposed to calming music postoperatively: a randomized controlled trial. *European Journal of Anaesthesiology*, 22(2): 96-102.

Noble GK (1939). The role of dominance in the life of birds. Auk, 56: 263-273.

North A (2003). US psy-ops play it loud. *BBC News Online*, 17 March.

North AC, Hargreaves DJ, McKendrick J (1999). The influence of in-store music on wine selections. *Journal of Applied Psychology*, 84: 271-276.

North AC, Hargreaves DJ (2007). Lifestyle correlates of musical preference: 1. Relationships, living arrangements, beliefs, and crime. *Psychology of Music*, 35(1): 58-87.

North AC, Hargreaves DJ, McKendrick J (1999). Music and on-hold waiting time. *British Journal of Psychology*, 90: 161-164.

Online Dictionary of Cockney Rhyming Slang. Accessed March 31 2010; http://www.cockneyrhymingslang.co.uk/slang/J /

Oron-Gilad T, Ronen A, Shinar D (2008). Alertness maintaining tasks (AMTs) while driving. *Accident Analysis & Prevention* 40: 851-860.

Ostrom CM (2005). Music as medicine. *The Seattle Times* newspaper (USA), 25 May.

Parker SG (1996). Tiny Music Critics. Right Now, *Harvard Magazine*, November-December.

Parrott WG, Gleitman H (1989). Infants' Expectations in Play: The Joy of Peek-a-boo. *Cognition and Emotion*, 3(4): 291-311.

Patel AD, Iversen JR, Bregman MR, Schulz I (2009). Experimental Evidence for Synchronization to a Musical Beat in a Nonhuman Animal. *Current Biology*, 19(10): 827-830.

Patterson AH (1978). Territorial behaviour and fear of crime in the elderly. *Environmental Psychology and Nonverbal Behaviour*, 2: 131-144.

Peck WB (1992). The tarantella. *Forum of the American Tarantula Society* I: 53-56.

Peterson DL & Pfost KS (1989). Influence of rock videos on attitudes of violence against women. *Psychological Reports*, 64: 319-322.

Petrides KV, Niven L, Mouskounti T (2006). Trait emotional intelligence of ballet dancers and musicians. *Psicothema* 18(supplement): 101-107.

Peyser J (1998) *The Memory of All That - The Life of George Gershwin*. New York: Watson-Guptill Publications, p. 319.

Pinker S (2003). *The Language Instinct*. London: Penguin Science.

Plailly J, Tillmann B & Royet JP (2007). The feeling of familiarity of music and odors: the same neural signature? *Cerebral Cortex*, 17(11): 2650-8.

Plettenbacher, EO (1990). Die Odyssee des Haydn-Schädels – Eine Criminal-Geschichte. *Mitteilungen der Gustinus Ambrosi-Gesellschaft* 7: 23-50.

Potter EH, Rosenbach WE, & Pittman, TS (2001). Followers for the times: Engaging employees in a winning partnership. In WE Rosenbach, & RL Taylor (Eds.), Contemporary issues in leadership 5th ed. Boulder, Colorado: Westview Press.

PR Newswire (2007). Internet Entrepreneur & MySpace Founder Brad Greenspan Leads Investment Group Seeking to Take Non-Controlling Stake in Dow Jones Corp. Accessed 20 May 2010; http://www.examiner.com/p-3057-Internet_Entrepreneur__MySpace_Founder_Brad_Greenspan_Leads_Investment_Group_Seeking_to_Take_Non_Controlling_Stake_in_Dow_Jones_Corp_.html

Pratkanis AR (1992). The Cargo-Cult Science of Subliminal Persuasion. *Skeptical Inquirer* (Amherst, New York: Committee for Skeptical Inquiry): 16.3.

Proctor D (1992). *Music of the sea*. London: HMSO, p. 55.

Prod'homme J-G & Martens FH (1922). Camille Saint-Saëns. *The Musical Quarterly*, 8: 469-486

Pyatt J (2009). Who's giving one one on one's lawn. *The Sun* newspaper (UK), 30 April.

Rachlow JL, Kie JG & Berger J (1999). Territoriality and spatial patterns of white rhinoceros in Matobo National Park, Zimbabwe. *African Journal of Ecology*, 37: 295-304.

Rapoport A & Guyer MJ (1976). *The 2 x 2 game*. Ann Arbor, MI: University of Michigan Press.

Rauscher FH (2006). The Mozart Effect: Music Listening is Not Music Instruction. *Educational Psychologist*, 41(4): 233-238.

Rauscher FH, Shaw GL, Ky KN (1993). Music and spatial task performance. *Nature*, 365: 611.

Rauscher FH, Shaw GL, Ky KN (1995). Listening to Mozart enhances spatial-temporal reasoning: Towards a neurophysiological basis. *Neuroscience Letters*, 185: 44–47.

Redmond DE, Murphy DL, Baulu J (1979). Platelet monoamine oxidase activity correlates with social affiliative and agonistic behaviors in normal rhesus monkeys. *Psychosomatic Medicine, 41,* 87-100.

Reed JD, Stratte-McClure J, Bentley L (1990). Another tragedy for Monaco. *People* magazine 34(15): 86-87. October 15.

Reich W (1971). *Schoenberg: A Critical Biography,* trans. Leo Black, London: Longman Group Ltd.

Reid B (2002). The Nocebo Effect: Placebo's Evil Twin. *The Washington Post* newspaper (USA), 30 April.

Richards RJ (1998). Rhapsodies on a cat-piano, or Johann Christian Reil and the foundations of romantic psychiatry. *Critical Inquiry,* 24: 700-736.

Richert M (2008). The internet grows up. *The Guardian* (London) online, 23 October.

Rieger E (2007). Mozart. *New Grove Dictionary of Music and Musicians,* online edition, Oxford: Oxford University Press.

Roberts DF, Christenson PG & Gentile DA (2003). The effects of violent music on children and adolescents. In Gentile DA (Ed.). *Media Violence and Children.* Westport, CT: Praeger.

Rogers C (1959). A theory of therapy, personality and interpersonal relationships as developed in the client-centered framework. In Koch S (Ed.). *Psychology: A study of a science.* Vol. 3: Formulations of the person and the social context. New York: McGraw Hill.

Root-Bernstein RS (2001). Music, creativity and scientific thinking. *Leonardo,* 34: 63-68

Rosenzweig S (1936). Some implicit common factors in diverse methods of psychotherapy. *American Journal of Orthopsychiatry,* 6: 412–415.

Rosselli J (1998). *The Life of Mozart.* Cambridge: Cambridge University Press.

Rouner D (1990). Rock music use as a socializing function. *Popular Music and Society.* 14: 97-107.

Rushton JP & Ankney CD (2009). Whole Brain Size and General Mental Ability: A Review. *International Journal of Neuroscience,* 119: 691–731.

Russell JA (1980). A circumplex model of affect. *Journal of Personality and Social Psychology,* 39: 1161 - 1178.

Russo MF, Stokes GS, Lahey BB, Christ MAG, McBurnett K, Loeber R, Stouthamer-Loeber M, & Green SM (1993). A sensation seeking scale in children: Further refinement and psychometric development. *Journal of Psychopathology and Behavioral Assessment,* 15: 69-86.

Sacks O (1973). *Awakenings.* New York: Harper Collins.

Savage J (2008). *Teenage: The Creation of Youth - 1875-1945.* London: Pimlico.

Schachner A., Brady TF, Pepperberg IM, and Hauser MD (2009). Spontaneous motor entrainment to music in multiple vocal mimicking species. *Current Biology,* 19(10): 831–836.

Schauffler RH (1949). *Franz Schubert: the Ariel of Music.* New York: Putnam's, p. 202.

Schellenberg EG & Hallam S (2005). Music listening and cognitive abilities in 10- and 11-year-olds: The Blur Effect. In Avanzini G, Lopez L, Koelsch S, Manjo M (eds.) *The Neurosciences and Music II: From perception to performance. Annals of the New York Academy of Sciences.* 1060: 202-209.

Schellenberg EG (2001). Music and Nonmusical Abilities. *The Annals of the New York Academy of Sciences*, 930: 355-71.

Schellenberg EG (2004). Music lessons enhance IQ. *Psychological Science*, 15: 511-514.

Schellenberg EG and Trehub SE (1999). Culture-General and Culture-Specific Factors in the Discrimination of Melodies. *Journal of Experimental Child Psychology*, 74: 107–127.

Scherer KR & Zentner MR (2001). Emotional effects of music: production rules. In: Juslin PN and Sloboda J (eds.) *Music and Emotion: Theory and Research*, Oxford: Oxford University Press.

Schlaug G, Forgeard M, Zhu L, Norton A, Norton A, Winner E (2009). Training-induced Neuroplasticity in Young Children. *The Neurosciences and Music III: Disorders and Plasticity: Annals New York Academy of Sciences*, 1169: 205–208.

Schlaug G, Marchina S, Norton A (2008). From Singing to Speaking: Why singing may lead to recovery of expressive language function in patients with Broca's Aphasia. *Music Perception* 25(4): 315-319.

Schoenberg A (1958). *Arnold Schoenberg Letters*, edited by Stein E. London: Faber and Faber.

Schoenberg A (1975) *Style and Idea: Selected Writings* , edited by Stein L, London: Belmont.

Schooler C, Zahn TP, Murphy DL & Green SB. (1978). Psychological correlates of monoamine oxidase activity in normals. *Journal of Nervous and mental Disease*. 166: 177-186.

Schweitzer, A. 2007. In *Encyclopædia Britannica online*. Retrieved 2 August 2007; http://www.britannica.com/eb/article-9066272

Sell LA, Morris J, Bearn J, Frackowiak RS, Friston KJ, Dolan RJ (1999). Activation of reward circuitry in human opiate addicts. *European Journal of Neuroscience*, 11: 1042-1048.

Semmelweis K (1954). Die abenteuerliche Wanderfahrt des Craniums Joseph Haydns, *Volk und Heimat*, 10: 8-10.

Semmelweis K (1954). Eisenstadt erhält den Haydn-Schädel, *Wiener Zeitung* 58, 11th October.

Seteroff SS (2003). *Beyond leadership to followership*. Victoria, B.C.: Trafford.

Sethares W (1992). Relating Tuning and Timbre. *Experimental Musical Instruments* IX (2).

Shelley PB (1820). To a Skylark. Accessed 10 April 2010; http://classiclit.about.com/library/bl-etexts/pshelley/bl-pshel-sky.htm.

Shepherd J (1990). *Music as a social text*, Cambridge, UK: Polity Press.

Sherman E, Mathur A & Smith RB (1997). Store environment and consumer purchase behaviour: mediating role of consumer emotions. *Psychology & Marketing*, 14: 361-378.

Shirer WL (1941). *Berlin Diary - The Journal of a Foreign Correspondent 1934-1941*. New York: Alfred A. Knopf.

Siegel S (1984). Pavlovian conditioning and heroin overdose: Reports from overdose victims. *Bulletin of the Psychonomic Society*. 22: 428–430.

Simms BR (2003). "My dear Hagerl": self-representation in Schoenberg's String Quartet No. 2. *19-th Century Music*, 26: 258-277.

Simpson M (2003). Return of the lone stranger. *The Guardian* newspaper (London, UK), 31 May.

Sinclair T (1938). The Nazi party rally at Nuremberg. *The Public Opinion Quarterly*, 2: 570-583.

Sloboda JA (1991). Musical structure and emotional response: Some empirical findings. *Psychology of Music*, 19: 110-120

Sloboda JA (1994). What makes a musician? *Guitar Journal*, 5: 18-22.

Sloboda JA and O'Neill SA (2001). Emotions in everyday listening to music. *Music and Emotion: Theory and Research*. Oxford University Press: Oxford, pp. 415-430.

Sloboda JA, Davidson JW, Howe MJA, Moore DG. (1996). The role of practice in the development of performing musicians. *British Journal of Psychology*, 87: 287-309.

Snipes JB, Maguire ER (1995). Country Music, Suicide, and Spuriousness. *Social Forces*, 74(1): 327-329.

Sober E & Wilson DS (1998). *Unto others: The evolution and psychology of unselfish behaviour.* Cambridge, MA: Harvard University Press.

Spangenberg ER, Grohmann B, Sprott DE (2005). It's beginning to smell (and sound) a lot like Christmas: the interactive effects of ambient scent and music in a retail setting. *Journal of Business Research*, 58: 1583-1589.

Speck WA (2006). Book reviews: Harris, T. (2005) *Restoration: Charles II and his Kingdoms, 1660-1885*; Harris, T. (2006) Revolution: The great Crisis of the British Monarchy 1685-1720. *The English Historical Review* 494, 1463-1467.

Stack S and Gundlach J (1992). The effect of country music on suicide. *Social Forces*, 71(1): 211-218.

Stack S, Gundlach J (1995). Country Music and Suicide - Individual, Indirect, and Interaction Effects: A Reply to Snipes and Maguire. *Social Forces*, 74(1): 331-335.

Stack S, Krysinskad K, Lester D (2007). Gloomy Sunday: did the "Hungarian suicide song" really create a suicide epidemic? *Omega*, 56(4): 349-358.

Standley JM (2003). The effect of music-reinforced nonnutritive sucking on feeding rate of premature infants. *Journal of Pediatric Nursing*, 18(3): 169-173.

Stewart K (1993). Engendering narratives of lament in country music. In Lewis GH (ed.), *All that glitters: Country music in America.* Bowling Green, USA: Bowling Green State University Popular Press.

Stokes M (1994). Introduction. In Stokes, M. (ed.) *Ethnicity, Identity and Music: The Musical construction of Place.* Oxford: Berg Publishers.

Storr A (1992). *Music and the Mind.* London: Harper Collins.

Stradling S, Meadows M, Beatty S (2004). Characteristics and crash involvement of speeding, violating and thrill-seeking drivers. In Rothengatter T, Huguenin RD (eds.) *Traffic and transport psychology: theory and application.* Oxford: Elsevier, pp. 177-194.

Strasburger V & Wilson B (2002). *Children, adolescents and the media.* London: Sage Press.

Stratton V and Zalanowski A (1991). The Effects of Music and Cognition on Mood. *Psychology of Music*, 19:121-127.

Stuckenschmidt HH (1977). *Schoenberg: His Life, World and Work.* Translated by Humphrey Searle. New York: Schirmer Books.

Suda M, Morimoto K, Obata A, Koizumi H, Maki A (2008). Emotional responses to music: towards scientific perspectives on music therapy. *Neuroreport* 19(1): 75-8.

Süzükei V (2006). Listening The Tuvan Way. In Levin T (ed.), *Where Rivers and Mountains Sing: Sound, Music and Nomadism in Tuva and Beyond.* Bloomington: Indiana University Press.

Svansdottir HB and Snaedal J (2006). Music therapy in moderate and severe dementia of Alzheimer's type: a case–control study. *International Psychogeriatrics* 18(4): 613-621.

Szabo A, Small A, Leigh M (1999). The effects of slow- and fast-rhythm classical music on progressive cycling to voluntary physical exhaustion. *Journal of Sports Medicine and Physical Fitness,* 39(3): 220-5.

Szulc T (1998). *Chopin in Paris: the Life and Times of the Romantic Composer.* New York: Scribner.

Tajfel H, Turner J (1979). An Integrative Theory of Intergroup Conflict. In Austin WG, Worchel S (Eds) The Social Psychology of Intergroup Relations. Monterey, CA: Brooks-Cole, pp. 94–109.

Tandler J (1909). Über den Schädel Haydns, *Mitteilungen der Anthropologischen Gesellschaft,* 39: 260-279.

Teng XF, Wong MY, Zhang YT (2007). The effect of music on hypertensive patients. *Conference Proceedings IEEE Engineering in Medicine and Biology Society 2007* 46: 49-51.

Terry PC, Walrond N, Carron AV (1998). The influence of game location on athletes' psychological states. *Journal of Science and Medicine in Sport,* 1(1): 29-37.

Thaut MH (2005). The future of music in therapy and medicine. *Annals of the New York Academy of Sciences* 1060: 303-308.

The Sisters of Two Great Composers (1901) *The Musical Times and Singing Class Circular,* 42 (696): 82-85.

The Sun (2005). James Blunt Becomes Top Wedding Song. *The Sun* (London) newspaper, 5 November.

The Sun online (2008). Posh Blunt's topless babes. *The Sun* newspaper, 22 July.

Thompson WF, Schellenberg EG, & Husain G (2001). Arousal, mood, and the Mozart effect. *Psychological Science,* 12: 248–251.

Thornby MA, Haas F, Axen K (1995). Effect of distractive auditory stimuli on exercise tolerance in patients with COPD. *Chest,* 107(5): 1213-7.

Tijs A (2006). Manilow To Challenge Rockdale Yobbos, 6th June. http://www.undercover.com.au/news/2006/jun06/20060606_barrymanilow.html

Time Magazine (1936). Letters, April 13.

Times Online (2007). Morrissey complains that immigration has led to the loss of Britain's identity. *Times Online* (London, UK), 29 November.

Titanic. (2007). In *Encyclopaedia Britannica.* Encyclopaedia Britannica Online.

Titanic's Band or Orchestra (2010). Accessed 13 May 2010; http://www.titanic-titanic.com/titanic_band.shtml

Tomatis A (1991). *Pourquoi Mozart.* Paris: Fixot.

Trautman MB (1977). In Memoriam: Margaret Morse Nice. *Auk,* 94: 430-441.

Trehub (2001). Musical predispositions in infancy. *Annals of the New York Academy of Sciences,* 930:1-15.

Turner S (1998). *Trouble Man: The Life and Death of Marvin Gaye.* London: Michael Joseph.

United Press International (1977). Mozart a Big Gambler. 9 February.

Van Every, D (2009). "Rock Drum Greats – Keith Moon of The Who" Jan. 16th. Accessed. 8th Feb, 2010; http://biographiesmemoirs.suite101.com/article.cfm/rock_drum_greats_keith_moon_of_the_who

Van Vugt M (2006). Evolutionary Origins of Leadership and Followership. *Personality and Social Psychology Review*, 10(4): 354-371.

Van Vugt M, Jepson SF, Hart CM & De Cremer D (2004). Autocratic leadership in social dilemmas: A threat to group stability. *Journal of Experimental Social Psychology*, 40: 1-13.

Vaughn K (2000). Music and Mathematics: Modest Support for the Oft-Claimed Relationship. *Journal of Aesthetic Education*, 34 (3/4): 149-166.

von Leupoldt A, Taube K, Schubert-Heukeshoven S, Magnussen H, Dahme B (2007). Distractive auditory stimuli reduce the unpleasantness of dyspnea during exercise in patients with COPD. *Chest* 132(5): 1506-12.

Von Wyhe J (2002). The authority of human nature: the Schädellehre of Franz Joseph Gall. *The British Journal for the History of Science*, 35: 17-42.

Waite BM, Hillbrand M & Foster HG (1992). Reduction of aggressive behavior after removal of Music Television. *Hospital and Community Psychiatry*, 43: 173–175.

Walker A (1983). *Franz Liszt*, vol. 1: *The Virtuoso Years 1811-1847*. New York: Cornell University Press.

Wallechinsky D, Wallace A (2005). *The New Book of Lists: The Original Compendium of Curious Information*. Edinburgh: Canongate Books.

Wan Hazmy CH, Zainurashid Z, Hussaini R (2009). *Muslim Scholars and Scientists*. Islamic Medical Association of Malaysia.

Wass H, Miller DM & Reditt CA (1991). Adolescent and Destructive Themes in Rock Music: A Follow Up. *OMEGA: Journal of Death and Dying*, 23: 199-206.

Webmaster University of Southampton Physics Society (2007). Portswood by Night. University of Southampton Physics Society. Accessed 3 April 2010; http://physoc.org.uk/maps/Portswood_by_Night.

Weisberg RW (2006). *Creativity: understanding innovation in problem solving, science, invention and the arts*. Hoboken, New Jersey: John Wiley and Sons, pp. 215-217.

Weisskirch RS, Murphy LC. (2004). Friends, porn, and punk: sensation seeking in personal relationships, internet activities, and music preference among college students. *Adolescence*, 39(154): 189-201.

Werner D (1984). Amazon Journey: An Anthropologist's Year Among Brazil's Mekranoti Indians. New York: Simon and Schuster.

Wertenbaker L (1967). *The World of Picasso*. Time–Life Library of Art. Alexandria, Virginia: Time-Life Books, p. 11.

Wilson S, Parsons K, Reutens D (2006). Preserved singing in Aphasia: A Case Study of the Efficacy of Melodic Intonation Therapy. *Music Perception*, 24(1): 23-36.

Winkler I, Háden GP, Ladinig O, Sziller I, Honing H (2009). Newborn infants detect the beat in music. *Proceedings of the National Academy of Sciences USA*, 106 (7): 2468-71.

Winternitz E (1958). 'Gnagflow Trazom': An Essay on Mozart's Script, Pastimes, and Nonsense Letters. *Journal of the American Musicological Society*, 11: 200-216.

Wise JM (2000). Home: Territory and Identity. *Cultural Studies* 14(2): 295–310.

Witelson SF, Beresh H, Kigar DL. (2006). Intelligence and brain size in 100 postmortem brains: sex, lateralization and age factors. *Brain*, 129(Pt 2): 386-98.

Witelson SF, Kigar DL, Harvey T (1999). The exceptional brain of Albert Einstein. *The Lancet* 353(9170): 2149-53. Erratum in: *The Lancet* 354(9174): 258.

Woodford P (1978). *Schubert*. London: Omnibus Press.

Woods E (1997). *Training a Tiger*. London: Harper Collins, p. 11.

Worchel, Stephen. The Social Psychology of Intergroup relations. Monterey, CA. Brooks-Cole, pp. 94-109

Wright AA, Rivera JJ, Hulse SH, Shyan M & Neiworth JJ (2000). Music perception and octave generalisation in rhesus monkeys. *Journal of Experimental Psychology: General*, 129: 291-307

Yahoo music news (2006). English radio station bans James Blunt songs. *Yahoo music news*, 29 May.

Yalch RF, Spangenberg ER (2000). The effects of music in a retail setting on real and perceived shopping times. *Journal of Business Research*, 49: 139-147.

Yerkes RM, Dodson JD (1908). The relation of strength of stimulus to rapidity of habit-formation. *Journal of Comparative Neurology and Psychology*, 18: 459-482.

Young RM (1968). The functions of the brain: Gall to Ferrier. *Isis*, 59: 261–268.

Zentner MR, Kagan J (1998). Infant's perception of consonance and dissonance in music. *Infant Behavior & Development*, 21: 483-492.

Zentner MR, Kagan J (1996). Perception of music by infants. *Nature*, 383(6595): 29.

Zentner MR quoted from Parker SG. (1996). Tiny Music Critics. Right Now, *Harvard Magazine*, Nov-Dec.

Zuckerman M (1994). *Behavioral Expressions and Biosocial Bases of Sensation Seeking*. Cambridge: Cambridge University Press, pp.291-301.

Zuckerman M, Eysenck SBG, Eysenck HJ (1978). Sensation seeking in England and America: Cross-cultural, age, and sex comparisons. *Journal of Consulting and Clinical Psychology*, 46: 139-149.

INDEX

I

J

K

L

M

N